AN ILLUSTRATED HISTORY OF ROCK & ROLL MOVIES

Rockin' Reels

AN ILLUSTRATED HISTORY OF ROCK & ROLL MOVIES

Rockin' Reels

JAN STACY &
RYDER SYVERTSEN

Contemporary Books, Inc.
Chicago

Library of Congress Cataloging in Publication Data

Stacy, Jan.
    Rockin' reels.

    Includes indexes.
    1. Moving-pictures, Musical—United States—
History and criticism.   I. Syvertsen, Ryder.
II. Title.
PN1995.9.M86S73   1984   791.43′7   84-14233
    ISBN 0-8092-5421-2

This book was produced by
The Photographic Book Company
in conjunction with Contemporary
Books, Inc.

Published by Contemporary Books, Inc.
180 North Michigan Avenue
Chicago, Illinois 60601

Manufactured in the United States of America

Library of Congress Catalog Card Number: 84-14233

International Standard Book Number:
0-8092-5421-2

Published simultaneously in Canada by
Beaverbooks, Ltd.
195 Allstate Parkway, Valleywood Business Park
Markham, Ontario L3R 4T8 Canada

Table of Contents

The Big Beat • Blackboard Jungle • Gidget • The Girl Can't Help It • Girl's Town • Go, Johnny, Go! • High School Caesar • High School Confidential • Hound-Dog Man • Jailhouse Rock • King Creole • Let's Rock • Love Me Tender • Mardi Gras • A Private's Affair • Rock Around the Clock • Rock, Pretty Baby

2 the Sixties

THE EXPLOSION 36

Alice's Restaurant • Beach Ball • Beach Blanket Bingo • Beach Girls and the Monster • Beach Party • Because They're Young • The Big T.N.T. Show • Bikini Beach • Blowup • Blue Hawaii • Blues for Lovers • Bye Bye Birdie • Candy • Changes • Clambake • Don't Knock the Twist • Don't Look Back • Dr. Goldfoot and the Bikini Machine • Double Trouble • Easy Rider • Ferry Cross the Mersey • Festival • Flaming Star • Follow that Dream • Get Yourself a College Girl • Ghost in the Invisible Bikini • G.I. Blues • Gidget Goes Hawaiian • Gidget Goes to Rome • Go Go Mania • Good Times • The Graduate • A Hard Day's Night • Having a Wild Weekend • Head • The Hellcats • Help! • Hold On • How to Stuff a Wild Bikini • I Love You Alice B. Toklas • Just for Fun • Let's Twist • The Lively Set • Magical Mystery Tour • Midnight Cowboy • Monterey Pop • Mrs. Brown, You've Got A Lovely Daughter • Muscle Beach Party • Pajama Party • Palm Springs Weekend • Paradise, Hawaiian Style • Petulia • Privilege • Psych-Out • Revolution • Ride the Wild Surf • Roustabout • Ski Party • Spinout • State Fair • The T.A.M.I. Show • Tammy and the Doctor • Tammy Tell Me True • To Sir With Love • The Trip • Twist All Night • Twist Around the Clock • Valley of the Dolls • Village of the Giants • What's New, Pussycat? • What's Up, Tiger Lily? • When the Boys Meet the Girls • Where the Boys Are • The Wild Angels • Wild in the Streets • Wild Wild Winter • Yellow Submarine • You're a Big Boy Now • You Are What You Eat • Young Animals

3

the Seventies

DANCE AND DARKNESS 134

Been Down So Long It Looks Like Up to Me • Billy Jack •
The Blank Generation • The Buddy Holly Story • A Bullet
for Pretty Boy • C.C. and Company • Celebration at Big Sur •
A Clockwork Orange • Cocksucker Blues • Coming Home •
Concert for Bangladesh • Cotton Comes to Harlem •
Eraserhead • Fillmore • Friends • G-AS-S-S or It May Become
Necessary to Destroy the World In Order To Save It • Getting
Straight • Gimme Shelter • Grease • Groupies • Hair • The
Harder They Come • Imagine • Jesus Christ Superstar • Jimi
Plays Berkeley • Keep On Rockin' • The Kids Are Alright •
Ladies and Gentlemen, The Rolling Stones • Lady Sings the
Blues • The Last Waltz • Let It Be • Mad Dogs and
Englishmen • The Magic Christian • The Man Who Fell to
Earth • Medicine Ball Caravan • Nashville • O Lucky Man •
Pat Garrett and Billy the Kid • Performance • Quadrophenia •
Radio On • Rock 'n' Roll High School • Rockers • The Rocky
Horror Picture Show • Saturday Night Fever • Sgt. Pepper's
Lonely Hearts Club Band • Shaft • Shampoo • Slumber Party
'57 • Soul to Soul • The Strawberry Statement • Superfly • To
Russia . . . With Elton • Tommy • Two Hundred Motels •
What's Happening? • The Wiz • Woodstock • WUSA

4

the Eighties

THE NEW WAVE 210

American Pop • Atomic Cafe • The Big Chill • The Blues Brothers • Cat People • Caveman • Class of '84 • Coal Miner's Daughter • Cruising • Diner • Eddie and the Cruisers • Fame • Flashdance • Footloose • Get Crazy • Grease II • Honey - suckle Rose • No Nukes • Pink Floyd The Wall • Porky's • Private Lessons • Reggae Sunsplash • Roadie • Rude Boy • Rumblefish • Staying Alive • Xanadu

10

Introduction

For thirty years rock and roll has been the soundtrack of the Atomic Generation syncopating everything in existence from hairstyles to lifestyles. The silver screen has been no exception to this influence. In fact, next to hot wax itself, no medium offers a better chronicle of the history of rock than celluloid. This book looks at the films that made rock and roll history — and the films that made rock and roll.

The movie cameras of the fifties took a hot craze, a teenage fad, and crystallized it for millions of fans into a cultural fact. It was life imitating art imitating art. Movies *Blackboard Jungle* (1955) and *Love Me Tender* (1956) sent rock tunes to the top of the charts and Elvis look-alikes to the theaters in droves. The films of the 1950s created a new culture hero — the rebel teenager — completely equipped with his own sound and his own moves. In New York City or Omaha, Nebraska, the alienated outsider sporting a black leather jacket still lived only as far away as the local movie house. With a string of low-budget rock vehicles, often contrived by that ace B-grade artist Sam Katzman, rock turned its grasp on teens into a stranglehold.

Moviemakers quickly caught onto the fact that rock and roll made money, and no one made money like Elvis Presley, the King. *Love Me Tender* and *Jailhouse Rock* (1957) were box-office smashes. Hollywood — and teenagers around the world — groaned in dismay when Elvis was inducted into the Army; when he came out, he was put right back to work.

Hollywood rode Elvis's wave of popularity for all it was worth, but these films were stale compared to what hit the screen in 1964. *A Hard Day's Night* catapulted the rock movie into maturity, with style and sophistication. Featuring songs composed especially for the film and using the Beatles' own irreverent humor and down-to-earth intelligence, A Hard Day's Night delighted both teenagers and more mature audiences and critics. If Elvis and Bill Haley and the Comets started the first rock explosion with 20 tons of TNT, the Beatles capped it with a nuclear bomb. The Beatles threw the moviemakers, like everyone and everything else they touched, into a tailspin. Out of the wreckage of the tired rock movie scene emerged a spawn of British and American imitators and imitations — some better than others. A slew of other Beatles movies followed, each one not only making box-office history but also receiving critical acclaim. Even "serious" movies began to appear with rock soundtracks; rock had finally achieved legitimacy on the screen.

As the world moved into the youth culture phenomenon of the late sixties and early seventies, rock movies spread its spectacle everywhere. *Woodstock* (1970) gave its name to an entire generation, becoming synonymous with youthful expressions of peace, brotherhood, love. But the other great rockumentary of the early 1970s, *Gimme Shelter* (1971), showed that generation's darker side. Suddenly, nostalgia for the halcyon days of the 1950s became very lucrative. *American Graffiti* (1973) was the beginning of this trend. The blockbuster *Saturday Night Fever* (1977) was a 1950s rock movie set to a disco beat. Retro-fit fifties flicks like *Grease* (1978), *Rock 'n' Roll High School* (1979), and *Sgt. Pepper's Lonely Hearts Club Band* (1978) followed. The trend, like the beat, goes on and on. In the eighties there have been feature-length rock films like *Flashdance* (1983), animated histories of rock like *American Pop* (1981), and good, old-fashioned, rebel-outsider-romps-through-rock-and-roll features like *Footloose* (1984). If it's sad that we're back where we started, at least it means rock and roll movies are here to stay.

the Fifties

Rockin' Reels

The Beginning (1955-1959)

The 1950s saw the birth of rock and roll on film with the movie *Blackboard Jungle* (1955). From the very beginning, rock and roll had a certain unsavory quality: it was blatantly sexy (for the period in which it originated), undeniably "tough," and perhaps worst of all, undeniably "negro" in its origins. Teenagers, of course, embraced it like a long-lost friend; rock was both a reaction to the increasingly bland pop music of the early post-war years and a genuinely new musical medium in its own right, forged from the pleasures and pains of modern teen life. Parents, religious leaders and politicians were appalled. *Blackboard Jungle* did little to dispel conservative fears: the heroes were juvenile delinquents, they carried switchblades, and they acted "tough" and "cool."

At least on the surface, the image of the clean-cut, all-American hero was out. His replacement was a hood with greasy, slicked-back hair and a black leather jacket who talked tough and didn't have much in common with the high school football star. But of course, like most of the teenagers who emulated him, he was badly misunderstood. He was a lonely rebel, alienated from society and even from his peers, but ready to finally open up to the right girl, the one who could see beyond the surface. Needless to say, this good-bad boy was also almost always the most courageous and intelligent teen in the film. Thus the loner, the outcast as hero, made his first appearance in film and, ultimately, in the consciousness of Western civilization.

By today's standards, all these misunderstood teenage rebels appear insufferably tame. What's a DA haircut and motorcycle boots compared to a punk rocker with spiky vermilion hair and self-inflicted razor cuts who dances on broken glass? The answer, of course, is that everything is relative. Rock and roll in film has always been sexy, tough, and intentionally challenging to the status quo. These are merely the qualities that teenagers are most drawn to; only the outward manifestations change.

Although *Blackboard Jungle* was the first "official" rock film, it was not a musical; it featured rock only in its theme song. The first real rocker was *Rock Around the Clock* (1956), which was made as soon as producer Sam Katzman saw the reaction to *Blackboard Jungle*. It featured Bill Haley and His Comets, the Platters, and the biggest radio disc jockey of the day — Alan Freed, the self-proclaimed King of Rock and Roll. The plot was nothing to write home about, but then, the majority of rock flicks have depended more on the music and the charisma of their performers to carry the action along. The plot, such as it is, concerns a band (Haley's) with an innovative new sound called rock and roll. Because of the conservatism of promoters and record people, they can't reach the public on a large scale, although their small teenage audiences go wild with excitement wherever they appear. Finally they get their proverbial "big break" and make it, much to the delight of screaming, mesmerized teenaged movie audiences. Songs included such rock immortals as "Only You," "The Great Pretender," "See You Later Alligator," "Mambo Rock," and perhaps the greatest rock song of them all, the title tune "Rock Around the Clock" (which, 30 years later, can still make you move your feet).

The film was one of the smash hits of 1956, largely due to the fact that it stirred up trouble everywhere. It was banned in several cities both in the United States and England, and where it was shown, teenagers allegedly rioted in some of the theaters. As every rock promoter from Sam Katzman to Brian Epstein to Malcolm McLaren has realized, the surest way to success for a rock band or film is through controversy —

fainting girls, fights, attacks from the conservative Establishment. If the teen audiences were too tame, the promoters hired *agents provocateurs*. Brian Epstein did it for the early Beatles' concerts, and the rest is history.

Katzman quickly followed up his first rock success with a series of similar films, named for one of the songs featured in the movie. *Go, Johnny, Go!* (1958) and other early rock films were little more than an express train of acts, but they gave teenagers a chance to see their favorite recording artists strut their stuff. Appearing in these films were such rock immortals as Little Richard, Fats Domino, Joe Turner, Chuck Berry, the Moonglows, Clyde McPhatter, Frankie Lymon and the Teenagers, Brook Benton, Ritchie Valens, Jackie Wilson, Eddie Cochran, the Cadillacs, and the Flamingos. For the first time, the teen audience was recognized as a viable and lucrative market with its own subculture and its special tastes and needs. Rock and roll was the cement that bound the teen subculture together and separated it from the adult world; it was the teenagers' "own thing," secret, mysterious and inaccessible to their elders.

The first big-budget rock film was *The Girl Can't Help It* (1956), produced by Frank Tashlin for 20th Century-Fox and starring Jayne Mansfield, the archetypal big-busted dreamgirl of the 1950s. Also starring Little Richard and Gene Vincent, the film featured truly imaginative musical numbers. It was humorous, satirical, and showed the superior production values made possible by the backing of a major studio.

Encouraged by this success, 20th Century-Fox decided, with a certain amount of trepidation, to go all the way and introduce Elvis Presley to the moviegoing public. This apprehension was well founded; Elvis the Pelvis (who, ironically, spent the later days of his career delighting blue-haired grandmothers in Las Vegas nightclubs) was the most controversial entertainer since Little Egypt. With his thrusting hips and black-influenced rhythm and blues musical style, Elvis was considered by many to be the greatest threat to Western civilization since Attila the Hun. Understandably torn between the desire to protect their reputation and the lure of a big money-maker, 20th Century-Fox designed Elvis's first film, *Love Me Tender* (1956), to downplay the more outrageous elements of the singer's style. The relatively bland movie, set during the Civil War, was not exactly a critical success, but it offended no one and the public flocked to see it in droves. In two weeks the studio earned back all it had spent in the production. Once 20th Century realized that the world wouldn't come to an end if Elvis swiveled his pelvis on the silver screen, they quickly followed up with *Loving You, Jailhouse Rock,* (1957) and *King Creole* (1958) all of which allowed the star's sensuality a little more play. *Jailhouse Rock,* one of the greatest rock flicks, shows an Elvis who is totally electric, exuding animal magnetism. While Elvis's later films were once again toned down as his management attempted to broaden his audience appeal, the early Elvis films are milestones in showing the explosive raw energy of rock at its best.

In retrospect, two separate lines of development can be seen in rock films. One line is that of the "good time" movies, where everyone smiled and played the guitar; these films, although fun, were innocent to the point of fantasy. The darker side occurred, in the "teens in trouble" films, many of which were *Blackboard Jungle* set to music; the teens carried knives, wore black leather, and spoke with snarls of rebellious rage. The plots and the music were decidedly dangerous in mood.

The Big Beat

Company: Universal International, 1958
Color, 81 minutes
Category: Musical
Screenplay by: David P. Harmon
Directed by: Will Cowan
Produced by: Will Cowan
Starring: William Reynolds and Gogi Grant
Bands: Fats Domino, the Del Vikings, and the Diamonds
Choreographer: Kenny Williams
Composer: Henry Mancini

16

Plot: After graduation from college, John Randall (Reynolds), a pop music enthusiast, begins working for his father's recording company which makes albums of conservative type music. Before taking off on a trip to Europe, his father agrees to set up a subsidiary company to make pop records, and leaves Johnny and Danny Phillips in charge. Although many top recording artists are signed, including Danny's girlfriend Cindy (Grant), their records just don't sell. But Johnny is able to get his eccentric friend Vladamir, a sculptor who is also the head of a large chain of grocery stores, to sell the records in his markets. Business booms and Johnny's future is assured.
Music: Bands include the Del Vikings, the Diamonds, Fats Domino, the Lancers, Freddy Martin, the Mills Brothers, the George Shearing Quintet, the Bill Thompson Singers, the Cal Tjader Outfit, the Four Aces and Harry James. Songs include "As I Love You," "You're Being Followed," "Can't Wait," "You've Never Been in Love," "The Big Beat," "I'm Walkin'," "It's Great When You're Doing a Show," "Little Darlin'," "Lazy Love," "I Waited So Long," "Take My Heart," "Call Me."

Moves: Fifties style, down-and-out rocking. Choreography by Kenny Williams.
Outfits: Fifties style dresses, jackets, ties, and sportshirts.
Social Significance: One of the first rock movies, featuring lots of music—just what the kids wanted. There was a teenage audience out there that was going bananas for these kinds of flicks and Hollywood responded.
Awards/Records: Both "Little Darlin' " (the Diamonds) and "I'm Walkin' " (Fats Domino) were big hits on the radio.

The style is rather quaint but the enthusiasm is genuine in *The Big Beat*.

Blackboard Jungle

Company: MGM, 1955
Black and white, 101 minutes
Category: Drama
Screenplay by: Richard Brooks
Directed by: Richard Brooks
Produced by: Tandro S. Berman
Starring: Glenn Ford, Anne Francis,
Sidney Poitier, Vic Morrow,
Paul Mayursky, and Jamie Farr

Plot: A young teacher, Richard Dadier (Ford), goes to a large, urban high school to teach English and Social Studies. His pupils greet him rudely, calling him "Daddy-o," and answering his questions sarcastically. Dadier is idealistic and wants to help his juvenile delinquent students, but fellow teacher Jim Murdock (Louis Calhern) tells him that the students are all animals and must be treated as such. Dadier tries to get through to a black teen, Greg Miller (Poitier), but his attempts appear to fail. He discovers that one of the students has been calling his wife (Francis) and threatening her. A classroom fight ensues between Dadier and the class toughie Artie West (Vic Morrow). Artie pulls a switchblade but Dadier is able to win bare handed. Showing his physical prowess, he at last gains the respect of the students who respond to him.
Music: Not in the film, Bill Haley and the Comets play on the soundtrack. First film with rock and roll ever made. "Rock Around the Clock" is the theme song.
Moves: Nobody dances but they snap their fingers and act cool when Dadier goes by.
Outfits: Toughboy circa 1955—cuffed pants, leather jackets, slicked back hair, switchblade optional.
Social Significance: The first gang in high school film, setting the theme for future films. Created a tough juvenile delinquent image that has been emulated ever since. Also, words like "Daddy-o" came into usage.
Trivia: First movie ever that used rock and roll in the soundtrack. Caused an uproar, and was attacked by media and famous personages as being a bad influence on America's youth. Nearly banned, causing tremendous publicity and overflowing crowds. After this, Hollywood saw that rock could make money and began churning out films by the truckload to cash in on this new phenomenon.

Richard Dadier (Glenn Ford) is a new teacher in a tough high school in *The Blackboard Jungle*.

17

Gidget

Band: The Four Preps
Composer: Fred Karger

Company: Columbia, 1959
            Color, 95 minutes
Category: Comedy with music
Screenplay by: Gabrielle Upton
Directed by: Paul Wendkos
Produced by: Lewis J. Rachmil
Starring: Sandra Dee, Cliff Robertson, and James Darren

Sandra Dee portrayed the young and amazingly pretty _Gidget_.

18

Plot: While on a summer vacation, 16-year old Francie Lawrence (Dee) joins some older girls on a "manhunt" to Malibu Beach. They meet a group of college surfers, also on vacation, led by a disillusioned ex-Air Force officer and pilot called Kahoona. He wants nothing more from life than a chance to be a "surf bum." Although Francie is much shyer than the other girls, she gets the most attention when she is saved from drowning by Moondoggie, one of the guys. Soon she has been adopted as the surfers' mascot and called Gidget—short for girl midget—and introduced to surfing. Her parents, aghast at her enthusiasm for surfboarding and its followers, try to get her to go on a date with respectable Jeffrey Matthews, the son of a friend. But Francie is after Moondoggie. She uses Kahoona as bait and goes to his cottage where she tries to get him to come on to her. Too much the gentlemen, he asks her to leave. At this moment, an insanely jealous Moondoggie arrives with the police who have been called by Gidget's parents. Francie is forced to date Jeffrey who turns out to be Moondoggie. The happy pair drive off to the beach and discover that Kahoona has destroyed his beach house and planned to return to flying.
Music: "Gidget" (James Darren and The Four Preps), "The Next Best Thing To Love" (Darren), "Cinderella" (The Four Preps). Composed by Fred Karger.
Moves: Beach jumping, surfing. One of the flicks that started it all.
Outfits: Bikinis, flesh, drops of water rolling down cleavage.
Social Significance: The first of the Gidget movies and it had a tremendous effect on American audiences. One of those movies that defined the teenagers of a generation (or how they'd like to be). Made Dee a teen idol loved by millions of youth.

The Girl Can't Help It

Music: Lionel Newman
Additional Performers: Little Richard, Fats Domino, the Platters, the Treniers, the Chuckles, Eddie Cochran, Gene Vincent and the Bluecaps, and others

Company: 20th Century Fox, 1956
Color, 99 minutes
Category: Comedy with music
Screenplay by: Frank Tashlin and
Herbert Baker
Directed by: Frank Tashlin
Produced by: Frank Tashlin
Starring: Jayne Mansfield, Tom Ewell,
and Edmond O'Brien
Group/Singer: Bobby Troup sings the
title song

Plot: Tom Miller (Ewell) is an agent who hasn't found talent for a long time. Slot-machine magnate Fats Murdock (O'Brien) hires him to make a star of his girl, the untalented, but outstanding, Jerri Jordan (Mansfield). The statuesque Jerri just wants to be a wife and mother, not a star. Miller

19

Jayne Mansfield is outstanding as the girl who would rather be a mother than a star in *The Girl Can't Help It.*

figures a way to accomplish Fat's dream for her. He arranges for her to cut a record called "Rock Around the Rock Pile." Ray Anthony and his band provide the back-up and vocals; all that Jerri does is scream on cue. Jerri and Miller are now in love, and complications ensue. There is a jukebox war between Wheeler (John Emery) and Murdock. Wheeler is determined to keep Jerri's record off the charts and the jukes. Murdock's hoods get his jukes and Jerri's record in the stores by pressure tactics, and the record is a hit. At a rock and roll concert, Jerri sings a love song (she can sing after all), and Murdock, pursued by Wheeler, goes on stage and sings the "Rock Pile" song and is a hit. Wheeler signs him instead of killing him. Murdock isn't angry at Jerri and Miller being a couple, and he acts as best man at their wedding .

Music: There's lots of opportunity in this loose plot to have a bunch of top teen favorites perform here. Notable is Gene Vincent and his Bluecaps, an early influence on the Beatles. Performers include Little Richard, Fats Domino, the Platters, the Treniers, the Chuckles, Eddie Cochran, Abbey Lincoln, Johnny Olenn, and Nino Tempo. Songs include "The Girl Can't Help It," "She's Got It," "Blue Monday," "Be Bop A Lula," and "Twenty Flight Rock." Music by Lionel Newman.

Outfits: Standard 1950s, with some performers in their bright duds. Jayne is in low-cut black and a huge black hat. She leans forward a lot, pouring your coffee, etc.

Social Significance: This was a comedy and spoofed, in a way, the music. But it planted rock and roll more solidly in America, and made Jayne a household word. The two milk-bottles shot of Jayne imbedded itself into many a teenage boy's unconscious. This was the era of the padded bra, but there's no padding on Jayne.

Trivia: The great Eddie Cochran died, as did Jayne, in a car crash. The director was, according to some, taking a gentle slap at society's insistence on pursuing success. He

would rather we lead a personally more satisfying life. Edmond O'Brien's only comedy role. Re-issued in the 1970s by a studio that realized its "cult" value. Director Tashlin directed a number of early WB cartoons and Jerry Lewis films.

Girl's Town (Also *The Innocent and the Doomed*)

Company: MGM, 1959
Black and white, 92 minutes
Category: Drama/musical
Screenplay by: Robert Smith
Directed by: Charles Haas
Produced by: Albert Zugsmith
Starring: Mamie Van Doren, Mel Torme, and Paul Anka
Group/Singer: The Platters and Paul Anka
Composed by: Van Alexander

Plot: Loose-living, tough, and cynical Silver Morgan (Mamie Van Doren) is falsely accused of killing rich Chip Gardner and is sent to Mother Veronica's "Girl's Town" for punishment and rehabilitation. Totally uncooperative with the sisters, she smokes in the dorm, refuses to get out of bed, and shows total disrespect for everyone. A short time later, her look-alike sister Mary Lee arrives at Girl's Town after being arrested for being in a drag race with Fred Alger, the

20

man who identified Silver as Chip's killer. When Alger realizes that it was Mary Lee and not Silver who was with Chip the night he died, he refuses to clear Silver and instead kidnaps Mary Lee. Silver, her cellmates, and the sisters raid Alger's hideout and rescue Mary. Alger is forced to confess that Chip accidentally fell to his death while attempting to attack Mary Lee. With both sisters cleared, Silver vows to mend her ways and become a respected citizen.

Music: Paul Anka, the Platters, and even Mamie sing in this one. Songs composed by Paul Anka include "Girl's Town" (Van Doren and Anka); "Time to Cry" (Anka); "I'm Just a Lonely Boy" (Anka); "Hey Mama" (Van Doren); "I Love You" and "Wish it Were Me" (the Platters); "Ave Maria" (Anka).

Outfits: Juvenile delinquent, nun black.

Social Significance: To quote *Variety*— "Blatantly crude and vulgar, not a mitigating ounce of artistry in it. The screenplay is as flimsy as a G-string and designed for somewhat the same purpose. Scenes of Miss Doren in the tightest of costumes exchanging badinage with nuns are in dubious taste to say the least . . ."

21

Mamie Van Doren is outstanding in *Girls Town*.

Go, Johnny, Go!

Company: Hal Roach Release, 1958
Black and white, 75 minutes
Category: Drama/musical
Screenplay by: Gary Alexander
Directed by: Paul Landres
Produced by: Alan Freed
Starring: Alan Freed, Jimmy Clanton, Sandy Stewart, Chuck Berry, and Herb Vigran
Singer/Group: Chuck Berry, Eddie Cochran, the Flamingos, Jackie Wilson, the Cadillacs, Ritchie Valens, and Jo-Ann Campbell

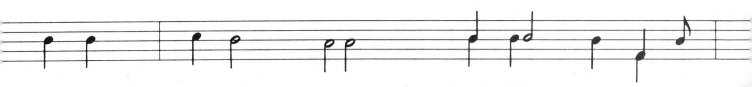

Plot: Orphan boy Johnny (Clanton) goes to New York after he got in trouble for jiving up the organ music in church. Since the great rock and roll disk jockey Alan Freed produced this, we can expect the best stars, and we get them: Chuck Berry, Eddie Cochran, Jackie Wilson, and the Cadillacs are here. Back to the plot: Johnny cuts a record with his new girl Julie (Stewart) and sends it to Alan Freed (playing himself). Freed plays it on the air and it's well received, to say the least. But there's no name or address, so he just plays it and plays it in the hopes that the singers will call him. Julie hears it but has lost track of

Johnny. He is out stealing a pin for her as a Christmas present. Freed hears from Julie and they rescue Johnny from a life of crime. Success looms near!

Music: "My Love is Strong" and "Angel Face" (Jimmy Clanton); "Once Again" (Clanton and Sandy Stewart); "You'd Better Know It" (Jackie Wilson); "Memphis Tennessee," "Go, Johnny, Go," and "Little Queenie" (Chuck Berry); "Jay Walker" and "Please, Mr. Johnson" (the Cadillacs); "Jump Children" (the Flamingos). "Mama, Can I Go Out" (Jo-Ann Campbell).

Outfits: Almost zoot-suited, the male groups are sleek, slippery songsters; Jo-Ann Campbell has that come-on tight sweater look; Jimmy Clanton has that unique combination of d.a. and flattop for a hairdo. Freed must have lent his clothes to Woody Allen.

Social Significance: The usual, you know. Box office triumph, congressional investigations of payola and movieola, parents picketing theaters, and so on and so forth.

Trivia: Often double-billed with *The Ghost of Zorro* and other notable films.

22

Jackie Wilson performs along with the Cadillacs, Flamingoes, Chuck Berry and many more in *Go Johnny Go*.

High School Caesar

Company: Filmgroup, 1959
Black and white, 72 minutes
Category: Drama
Screenplay by: Ethelmae Page and Robert Slaven. Original story by O'Dale Ireland and screenwriters
Directed by: O'Dale Ireland

Produced by: O'Dale Ireland
Starring: John Ashley, Gary Vinson, and
    Lowell Brown
Group/Singer: Monty Pearce

Plot: Matt Stevens (John Ashley) is a rich
teenager who "buys" friendships. He forms a
gang and sells protection to the kids at the
high school. Wanda (Judy Nugent), the new
girl in town, is pushed around by his gang.

**Tough high school kids, led by Matt Stevens (John
Ashley), are out looking for trouble in *High School
Caesar*.**

There is the mandatory drag-race scene,
where Wanda's friend Bob (Gary Vinson)
and Matt force each other off the road, and
the race is won by Bob's friend, the mad-
driver Kelly (Lowell Brown). Matt, always
the spoiled kid/sore loser, gets into a hot rod
and chases Kelly. Kelly's car goes over a cliff
and he dies. His death makes everyone see
that Matt isn't so cool at all and they shun
the guy, providing a moral to this typical
tale of teen trouble, car racing, and
frustrated romance, the mandatory tragedy
that brings teenagers to their senses. The
movie is predictable, and the music is
nothing to rave about, either.
Music: "High School Caesar," "Date Bait
Baby."
Moves: Teen hop, lindy.
Outfits: Teen tough. Filmed in Missouri
where it's strictly Sears.
Social Significance: None except
perpetuating stereotypes about 1950s
teenagers that somehow were true by this
time.

23

High School Confidential

Company: MGM, 1958
        Black and white, 85 minutes
Category: Drama
Screenplay by: Lewis Meltzer
Directed by: Jack Arnold
Produced by: Albert Zugsmith
Starring: Russ Tamblyn and Mamie Van
    Doren

Plot: With the aid of a switchblade and a
lot of macho, young, jive-talking Tony Baker
(Tamblyn) takes over the leadership of the

hot rod/tough boy set at a California high school. Among his fellow students are J.I. Coleridge (John Drew Barrymore), who peddles drugs, and his girl Joan (Diane Jergens), a marijuana addict. Tony's teacher, Miss Williams (Jan Sterling), tries to find out what lies beneath his wise-ass surface but is rebuffed by Tony's "Aunt"

Russ Tamblyn plays Tony Baker, a teenage undercover narcotics cop in *High School Confidential*.

24

Gwen (Van Doren), a near nymphomaniac who acts like a deranged teenager. J.I. introduces Tony to Mr. A (Jackie Coogan) who agrees to supply him with heroin. But Mr. A and his thug Bix find out that Tony is, in fact, a vice-squad cop. Before they can kill him, the teenagers stage a riot and keep the drug thugs at bay until the cops arrive.
Music: Jerry Lee Lewis appears and sings "High School Confidential" at the start of the film, riding by on a truck past a high school. He slams away at his piano in the manic style that made him so famous.
Moves: Teen hop, spinning, lindy.
Outfits: Middle-class gang kids, circa 1950s. Bozo shoes, khaki pants, button sweater. But oh that Mamie in her skin tight sweaters and capri slacks.
Social Significance: One of the first, great teen high school exploitation flicks, with jive talk, crazy kids out for kicks, hooked on marijuana. Set the stage for a decade of bad boy/tough girl movies. Super anti-drug even as it depicts world of hipsters, with teens so hooked on grass that one girl turns her boyfriend in to cops just to get a "stick."
Trivia: Mamie Van Doren was the sex-goddess of the B movie. Zugsmith used her in a lot of his teen flicks to spice up the action. With her rather large bosom, Mamie made a rather powerful impression on the teenage male (ourselves included).

So disturbed some reviewers that. . .well, see for yourself. "There is no surer way to keep people away from the movies than the production, distribution and exhibition of venalties such as this movie. Zugsmith protests that it is an exposé of a social evil. This film itself is a social evil. Plants the suggestion, later explicitly reiterated, that the primitivism of urban youth has become the American norm. The ghastly nihilism that life affords nothing of value greater than a 'kick' is asserted explicitly and defiantly in an existentialist poem. The film's purpose seems to be to provide a 'philosophical' rationalization for bop-jabber, juvenile delinquency and dope addiction."

Hound-Dog Man

Company: 20th Century Fox, 1959
Color, 87 minutes
Category: Drama
Screenplay by: Fred Gipson and
Winston Miller
Directed by: Don Siegel
Produced by: Jerry Wald
Starring: Fabian and Stuart Whitman
Music: Cyril Mockridge

25

Plot: Ne'er-do-well Blackie Scantling (Whitman) arrives at the country farm of the McKinney family, quickly becoming the idol of the two McKinney boys, 16-year-old Clint (Fabian) and 8-year-old Spud. Mrs. McKinney thinks Blackie is a "shiftless hound-dog man" but allows the boys to go with Blackie on a hunting trip. The only thing young Clint doesn't like about his hero is his obvious romantic feelings for pretty Dony Waller. When the party finds a wounded neighbor, they stop their trip to bring the man home. At a party celebrating the man's recovery, Blackie pays too much attention to another man's wife, and her drunk husband takes pot shots at him until Mr. McKinney takes away the gun. Clint, filled with pride for his dad, realizes that the pleasures of fishing, hunting, and loafing are not all there is in this world. He promises to change and stop emulating Blackie, and concentrate on his school and housework. Blackie, too, sees the light, promises to mend his ways, and proposes marriage to the ecstatic Dony.
Music: Songs include "Hound Dog Man," "What Big Boy?," "This Friendly World," "Pretty Little Girl," "Single," "I'm Growing Up," "Hill-Top Song," and "Hay-Foot, Strawfoot."

Clint (Fabian) performs for a crowd in *Hound-Dog Man.*

Moves: Country style twirling and whirling.
Outfits: Mountain gear, circa 1912; thick jackets, boots, rifles.
Social Significance: Shows that right around us and within our own family and circle of friends we can find the qualities of strength and heroism that we look elsewhere to find.
Trivia: 20th Century Fox tried to get a hit (a la Presley) with pretty teen idol Fabian but it didn't do too well at the theaters.

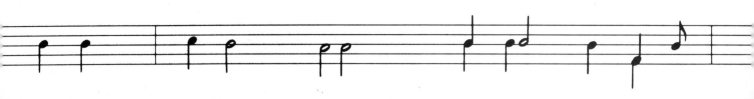

Jailhouse Rock

Directed by: Richard Thorpe
Produced by: Tandro S. Berman
Starring: Elvis Presley
Score by: Leiber-Stoller

Company: MGM, 1957
Black and white, 96 minutes
Category: Musical
Screenplay by: Guy Troster

Elvis Presley is Vince Everett, an ex-con who becomes a national hit in *Jailhouse Rock*.

26

Plot: Vince Everett (Elvis) is a happy-go-lucky country boy who gets in a fistfight defending a woman in a bar. He accidentally kills the man and is put in prison for manslaughter. In jail, he meets Hank Houghton (Mickey Shaughnessy) who likes Vince's singing. He sets up a lavishly produced prison show which Vince stars in. Upon release, Vince forms a record company with Peggy (Judy Tyler) and he quickly becomes a national hit with his recordings. But his fame changes his personality and he becomes self-centered, selfish, an egomaniac. He fires Hank who had been his manager and gets nasty with Peggy. Hank shows up later, gets in a fight with Vince who is finally brought back to his "good guy" senses, and marries Peggy.
Music: "Jailhouse Rock," "I Want To Be Free," "Baby I Don't Care," "Don't Leave Me Now," and "Young and Beautiful." Elvis sang all the tunes, backed up by the Jailbirds.
Moves: Some highly imaginative dances are performed, particularly the jailhouse dance, wildly energetic, sliding up and down prison bars. Elvis's dancing is great, hip-swinging, jumping from level to level of the prison.
Outfits: Prison garb; Elvis wears fancy 1950s rock garb later in film as he becomes more and more famous.
Social Significance: The film was created just for Presley who got to act out his tough, hard loving, fighting country boy image to the hilt. Also set the stage for his woman-protecting, heroic image that has become one of the cornerstones of male macho, particularly in the south and west where Elvis had his most fanatical fans.
Trivia: Made Elvis hunks of dough and proved that he could draw crowds like no other, in this his third film. Set the basic

plot format of many of Presley's later flicks, namely hero turns bad turns good, protecting and falling for a woman.

knows the ropes, a friend of racket-boss Maxie Fields (Walter Matthau). The capable performers in this film flesh out a routine story of rags to riches.

King Creole

Danny Fisher is a successful performer at the King Creole nightclub.

Company: Paramount, 1958
Black and white, 116 minutes
Category: Musical/drama
Screenplay by: Herbert Baker and Michael V. Gazzo. Based on a book by Harold Robbins
Directed by: Michael Curtiz
Produced by: Paul Nathan
Starring: Elvis Presley, Carolyn Jones, Dolores Hart, and Dean Jagger
Group/Singer: Elvis, backed by the Jordainaires; duet with Kitty White on "Crawfish"
Choreographer: Charles O'Curran
Composer: Title song by Jerry Lieber and Mike Stoller

27

Plot: Danny Fisher (Elvis Presley), a busboy in a dive on Bourbon Street in New Orleans. He's a dropout and, to help support himself and his dissolute father, he helps Shark (Vic Morrow) and his hoods pull a robbery. Then, defying his dad, he takes a job as a singer at the King Creole, a dying joint owned by Charlie LeGrand (Paul Stewart). Now there's woman trouble. First, there's pristine good girl Nellie (Dolores Hart), a salesclerk in a dime store. Then there's Ronnie (Carolyn Jones), a girl that

Elvis rocks with a New Orleans back-up band at the King Creole.

28

Danny, of course, is a big success as a singer, the club revives, and Maxie wants him for his joint. Danny refuses and Maxie has his father (Dean Jagger) attacked and robbed by Shark. Danny beats up Maxie, knifes Shark to death, and is seriously injured. He's saved by the nursing of Ronnie, and for that Maxie kills her. Maxie in turn is killed by a friend of Danny's. Danny continues to sing, reunited with Nellie and dad.

The only Presley movie based on a novel by Harold Robbins (*A Stone for Danny Fisher*), this was really the last rocky Elvis. He wiggles, has mixed good and bad emotions, and so on. After this he's so cleaned up it's hardly the same. Maybe that's why it's Elvis's favorite role.

Music: Elvis, backed by Jordainaires, sings "Hard Headed Woman," "As Long As I Have You," "King Creole," "Trouble," "Dixieland Rock," "Don't Ask Me Why," "Crawfish" (with Kitty White), "Steadfast, Loyal, and True," "Turtles, Berries, and Gumbo," and "Lover Doll." Lilliane Montevecchi sings "Banana."

Moves: Elvis does his thing. Choreography by Charles O'Curran.

Outfits: Very New Orleans. Black musicians in light-colored bowler hats, light suits.

Social Significance: *Variety* thought this was the best Elvis flick up till this time. They liked the fact that there were lots of melodic, slower numbers, but this dismayed the followers of Elvis's more frantic numbers. Elvis was even more recognized as an actor, not just a performer, after this film.

Trivia: Gazzo and Baker changed the locale of the Robbins novel to New Orleans from New York's Lower East Side and the story became a singer fighting to the top instead of a fighter.

Awards: The album reached #2 on *Billboard*'s chart, and sold over a million copies, according to RCA. "King Creole" appeared on at least 3 other albums, including *Elvis In Hollywood*.

Let's Rock!

Company: Columbia, 1958
Black and white, 79 minutes
Category: Musical drama
Screenplay by: Hal Hackady
Directed by: Harry Foster
Produced by: Harry Foster
Starring: Julius LaRosa, Phyllis Newman, Conrad Janis, and Joy Harmon
Group/Singer: Paul Anka, Della Reese, Danny and the Juniors, the Royal Teens, Roy Hamilton, the Tyrones, and Julius LaRosa
Choreographer: Peter Gennaro

Plot: It's another vehicle for the great rock and roll teen stars of the fifties and one of the greatest. A washed up forties singer gets on the rock and roll express and resuscitates his moribund career. Helping him along are the rock greats of the era, or some of them at least. This picture had Kathy Abbott, a composer (Phyllis Newman), convince Tommy (Julius LaRosa) to redo his act, to get with it. He does. He records a rock and roll song she penned, and he gets her hand too.
Music: Danny and the Juniors, the ultimate (almost) a capella rock and rollers of the era, sing "At the Hop"; Julius LaRosa gets to sing "There are Times," and some other ditties; the great Paul Anka belts out "Waiting There for You;" "Lonelyville" is sung by Della Reese; "Blastoff" is sung by the Tyrones. The Royal Teens and Roy Hamilton also perform.
Moves: Sock-hop stuff. Lindy. Peter Gennaro choreographed the movie.

Outfits: The ginchiest.
Social Significance: Rock and roll was tied to riots worldwide, nations in panic. This film added fuel to the rock fire that was heating the world at the time. Spawned a new generation, putting barbershops out of business, destroying moral values and other good things.
Trivia: Released as *Rock and Roll Concert* in France. Also known as *Keep It Cool*.

When Paul Anka sings the girls swoon in *Let's Rock*.

29

Love Me Tender

Company: 20th Century Fox, 1956
Black and white, 89 minutes
Category: Drama
Screenplay by: Robert Buckner
Directed by: Robert D. Webb
Produced by: David Weisbart
Starring: Elvis Presley, Richard Egan, and Debra Paget

Plot: Elvis is cast as a backwoods farm boy who, during the Civil War, falls in love with his brother's (Richard Egan) sweetheart, Debra Paget. Egan, a Confederate soldier, is off leading a band of rebel soldiers who raid northern convoys and wreak havoc, including robbing the U.S. Mint. Word gets back to the farm that Egan has been killed and Presley wastes no time making his move and marries Paget. All seems wonderful until Egan returns home. Amidst stolen gold, double- and triple-crosses of his Confederate pals, Egan tries to get back his sweetheart. Presley, alas, is killed near the end but reappears in ghostly form in the sky.
Music: Elvis sings four songs in this Civil War sage: "Poor Boy," "We're Gonna Move," "Let Me," and the huge hit "Love Me Tender."
Moves: Elvis bumps and grinds somewhat in a twilight-zone-type time warp.
Outfits: Farm clothes, Civil War army uniforms, Southern gentlemen's garb.
Social Significance: Presley's first film and it was a smash. Kids went wild when they

30

Elvis struts the stuff that made him famous in *Love Me Tender*.

saw Presley on the screen. He was already a top recording artist, but this gave teens the chance to see him and begin emulating their idol. His hairstyle, mannerisms, slightly nasty but lovable expressions could now be studied up close and imitated by millions of American males searching for a role model in the vacuum of the 1950s.

Trivia: Presley was hot, hot, hot from records and appearances on the *Ed Sullivan Show*. 20th Century Fox wanted to star Elvis in a flick but was somewhat nervous about the "respectable" public's reaction as Pres was already somewhat controversial for his unrestrained sexuality. The studio saw *Love Me Tender* (originally titled *The Reno Brothers*) as a vehicle to show a more restrained Presley in a dramatic role and in this way deflate some of the negative reaction around the country. It worked! Presley became a major film star as well as singer. The rest is history.

Mardi Gras

Company: 20th Century Fox, 1958
                 Color, 107 minutes
Category: Musical
Screenplay by: Winston Miller and Hal
                 Kanter
Directed by: Edmund Goulding
Produced by: Jerry Wald
Starring: Pat Boone, Tommy Sands, and
                 Gary Crosby
Band: V.M.I. Band
Choreographer: Bill Foster
Music Coordinator: Lionel Newman

Plot: The Virginia Military Institute (VMI) Band is invited to the annual New Orleans Mardi Gras. Cadet Paul Newell (Pat Boone)

wins a student lottery which gives him the funds to attend the festivities and invite the Mardi Gras movie queen, Michelle Marton (Christine Carere), to be his date at his graduation prom. But Michelle, exhausted by publicity appearances, disguises herself and sneaks away from her publicity boss, Hal Curtis. During the parade, Paul meets her and, unaware of her identity, falls in love. Meanwhile, Paul's pals, Tony (Gary

Barry (Tommy Sands) is a member of the V.M.I. band which finds fun and romance at the Mardi Gras.

31

Crosby), Barry (Tommy Sands), and Dick (Richard Sargent) also find romance—Tony with Eadie, Michelle's publicity companion; Barry with Torchy Larue, an intellectual stripper; and Dick with Sylvia, a midwestern girl on vacation. Upon learning of Michelle's identity, Paul feels he has been played the fool and when studio PR plays up the romance he calls off their prom date. But Michelle extracts a promise of no more publicity from Curtis and goes to the prom.

Music: Written by Sammy Fain and Paul Francis Webster, songs include "The Mardi Gras March," "I'll Remember Tonight," "Loyalty," "Bigger Than Texas," "A Fiddle, a Rifle, an Axe, and a Bible," "Bourbon Street Blues," "Stonewall Jackson," "That Man Could Sell Me the Brooklyn Bridge," and "Shenandoah." Musical coordination by Lionel Newman.

Moves: Lots of hoofing and wild dancing as the Mardi Gras parade goes by. Choreography by Bill Foster.

32

Outfits: Military uniforms and wildly colorful garb in parade.

Social Significance: Furthered the super clean-cut image of Pat Boone and a boon for tourism to New Orleans as well as recruitment for V.M.I.

Trivia: The real V.M.I. band appeared in film.

Awards: Nominated for an Academy award.

A Private's Affair

Company: 20th Century Fox, 1959
Color, 92 minutes
Category: Musical comedy

Luigi (Sal Mineo) enjoys himself at a USO dance in *A Private's Affair*.

Screenplay by: Winston Miller
Directed by: Raoul Walsh
Produced by: David Weisbart
Starring: Sal Mineo, Christine Carere, Barry Coe, Barbara Eden, Gary Crosby, Terry Moore, and Jim Backus
Composer: Cyril J. Mockridge

Plot: Three young men, college graduates Jerry Morgan (Barry Coe), musician Luigi Maresi (Sal Mineo), and wealthy playboy Mike Conroy (Gary Crosby), become pals after they enter the army. At a recreation hall dance the three find romance—Jerry with a French girl, Marie (Christine Carere); Luigi with Louise Wright (Terry Moore), a childhood friend of Jerry's; and Mike with a WAC sergeant, Katey Mulligan (Barbara Eden). While on KP duty the boys sing a satirical song about army life which is overheard by television MC Jim Gordon (Jim Backus). He gets the boys to agree to do an all-army TV show. Just before they're scheduled to leave for New York, Jerry comes down with laryngitis and is confined to the infirmary. Also there is a dying Dutch businessman whose daughter is in danger of being deported by Immigration. To prevent this, the Assistant Secretary of the Army, Elizabeth T. Chapman, offers to marry the dying man and thereby get custody of the child. But a disastrous mistake is made, and she is married to the soundly sleeping Jerry. When he dimly recalls the ceremony, his rantings land him in front of a psychiatrist. The enraged Mrs. Chapman finally gets the mess straightened out and Jerry is allowed to leave for New York and the TV show where the boys perform and are a great success.

Music: Among the show's songs are "A Private's Affair," "It's the Same Old Army," and "Warm and Willing." Composed by Cyril Mockridge.
Moves: Fast, snappy, lively dance numbers.
Outfits: GI uniforms, suits; women wear tight dresses.
Social Significance: Glamorizes the army in a mocking way.

33

Luigi Maresi (Sal Mineo) and Mike Conroy (Gary Crosby) mull things over in *A Private's Affair*.

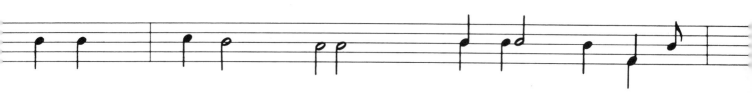

Rock Around the Clock

Company: Columbia, 1956
Color, 77 minutes
Category: Drama/musical
Screenplay by: Robert E. Kent and
James B. Gordon
Directed by: Fred F. Sears
Produced by: Sam Katzman
Starring: Alan Freed, Bill Haley and the
Comets, Alan Dale, and Lisa
Gaye
Group/Singer: Bill Haley and the
Comets, the Platters,
Freddie Bell and his
Bellboys, and Ernie
Freeman

Plot: This, the classic first rock and roll movie (*Blackboard Jungle* had the song in it, but this had the rock and roll group on stage), begins classically: City Slicker Alan Dale scouts up Bill Haley at a small town sock hop and tells him, "I like your sound." He sees the dollar potential and helps launch Haley into the big time. Their new sound, called rock and roll, sweeps the world. Influential DJ Alan Freed (playing himself) pushes Haley on the air. The rest is history.
Music: Bill Haley and the Comets sing "Rock Around the Clock," "See You Later, Alligator," "Rudy's Rock," "Rock, Mambo, Rock," "Rock-a-beatin' Boogie," and "Razzle Dazzle." The Platters do "Only You" and "The Great Pretender."
Moves: Yes. Lindy in socks.
Outfits: That spit curl on Bill's forehead drove girls mad. Pegged-at-the-ankle pants and padded shoulder jackets.
Trivia: Freed was accused and convicted of taking payola, money from record companies to play their "hits", but many believe his

34

Bill Haley and the Comets are launched into the big time in *Rock Around the Clock*.

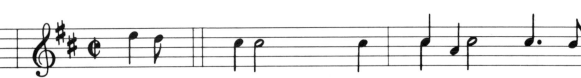

association with black performers—introducing "race music" and idolation of black performers to white teenagers—(and hatred of rock and roll by the establishment) led to his being brought up on charges and dismissed as a DJ.

Rock, Pretty Baby

Company: Universal International, 1956
Black and white, 98 minutes
Category: Drama/musical
Screenplay by: Herbert Margolis and
William Raynor
Directed by: Richard Bartlett
Produced by: Edmund Chevie

Starring: Sal Mineo, John Saxon, and
Luana Patten
Group/Singer: The Rod McKuen Group

Plot: This film has Sal Mineo in it. Sal was so hot at the time he didn't need a plot (and he didn't really get one in this turkey either). This squeaky clean teen film is about a high school's rock and roll bands trial-and-error rise to the top. True fans of rock and roll movies—like Alan Freed's extravagant smorgasbords of delight—should beware.
Music: The Rod McKuen group sings "Rock, Pretty Baby," a truly rotten song. Yes, your eyes are not deceiving you—Rod McKuen, heartthrob poet of the next generation, is one of the erstwhile "teen" musicians. Research has failed to produce the true names of Sax, Ox, and Fingers.
Moves: Yes, they lindy.
Outfits: Bikinis and bobby sox.
Social Significance: If this couldn't kill Sal in the box office nothing could.

35

The teenagers, led by Sal Mineo, cavort on the beach in the basically plotless *Rock, Pretty Baby*.

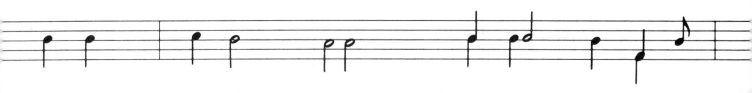

the Sixties

Rockin' Reels

The Explosion (1960-1969)

By the early 1960s, the post-war babies were well into their teens. As their parents prospered, these non-working teenagers. Had plenty of spending money. Whole new industries sprang up to welcome these new members.

The teenage film market was now a major industry; rock films were being turned out with production-line regularity. The only real problem was keeping up with the teenagers' changing tastes—or trying to create them.

The first innovation of the early sixties was the beach party movie, introduced with the big budget ($3,000,000) *Where the Boys Are* (1960). The film (remade in 1984 with a lot more flesh showing) tells the tale of four girls on the make in Ft. Lauderdale during college spring break. While the idea was hardly new, the picture caught hold of teen psyches. The success of the film generated a new wave of similar movies.

Beach Party (1963) introduced to the world the immortal team of Annette Funicello (Dee-Dee) and Frankie Avalon (Frankie). There ensued a series of enormously successful sand rockers—*Muscle Beach Party* (1964), *Bikini Beach* (1964), *Beach Blanket Bingo* (1965), and *How to Stuff a Wild Bikini* (1965)—that were not only quintessential beach party films but blatant self-parodies, filled with a madcap quality and a real *joie de vivre*. The beach party movies were sunny, sexy, and totally amusing. The genre expanded in several directions, including monster movies and *Ski Party*, where the beach theme was transferred to the ski slopes. But on the horizon was a phenomenon that would once again stand

rock music, and rock films, on their heads. This phenomenon was, of course, the Beatles.

Nothing in the history of pop music can compare to the appearance on the scene of the four from Liverpool. The hysteria that swept not just England and the United States but the entire world was more than a little religious in its fervor. One writer reports seeing the first Beatles film in Dar es Salaam, Tanzania, among an audience composed predominantly of local Africans and Indians, few of whom spoke English. When the film began, virtually the entire audience began screaming wildly and waving their hands as if the Rock Messiah had finally come. The appeal of the Beatles was universal.

The Beatles, with their new sound, their wit and intelligence, their boyish good looks and their mod clothing and haircuts, almost instantly changed the face of Western teenage society. Their first film, *A Hard Day's Night*, burst onto the scene with the force of a hurricane. Under the extremely innovative direction of Richard Lester, characterized by skillful editing and a powerful kinetic sensibility, the film was applauded by teenagers and serious critics alike. Shot in black-and-white using highly mobile, lightweight cameras and a *cinéma vérité style*, Lester introduced a new sub-genre, the mock-rocker, that was truly witty, frantically Chaplinesque, and full of good-natured self-ridicule. The Beatles followed up with other concert films—*Help!* and *Let it Be*, which were live, and the animated *Yellow Submarine* and *Magical Mystery Tour*. Each was received by the public with fascination and enthusiasm at the evolving musical and visual concepts of this exceptionally talented group. The legend the Beatles left behind after their breakup in 1970 is still as strong as ever; their albums continue to sell in the millions each year and their films are shown regularly at movie theaters and on television.

Inevitably, a virtual avalanche of English rock groups and films starring them followed. The Dave Clark 5, the Animals, the Beau Brummels, Gerry and the Pacemakers, Herman's Hermits all made films which they hoped would turn them into superstars. Films like *Ferry Cross the Mersey* (1965) and *Having a Wild Weekend* all did fairly well, but neither the films nor the groups that made them ever approached the Beatles in success.

On the darker side, inspired by Marlon Brando in The Wild One, the juvenile delinquent hero of the 1950s films was being slowly replaced by the biker hero. The good-bad boy now was a member of a motorcycle gang, the way paved by Roger Corman's 1966 film *The Wild Angels.* This sub-genre might have gone on forever were it not for the limited number of combinations possible using only the four words Hell, Devil, Wild, and Angel. The genre did not so much culminate as transmute with the landmark *Easy Rider,* which brought the biker hero into the hippie generation of drugs, communes, and easy sex. The teen *noir* saga continued with *Hallucination Generation* (1967), *The Trip* (1967), *Wild in the Streets* (1968), and *Psych-Out* (1968), all of which depicted the downside of the drug-and-rebellion lifestyle and the increasing polarization of the generations wrought by the hippie invasion and the Vietnam war.

With *The Graduate* (1967), a new type of film was born—the serious film with the rock score. Although not a musical, the Simon and Garfunkel songs were used as a device to carry the story forward by reflecting the thoughts and feelings of the youthful hero, Benjamin. A number of hits, including the theme song, "Mrs. Robinson," came out of *The Graduate,* and director Mike Nichols and Dustin Hoffman became instant superstars.

The 1960s, certainly one of the most inventive and explosive eras in every art form, produced yet another addition to the cinematic rock lexicon—the rockumentary. The first filmed concert was *The T.A.M.I. Show* (1964), which was a gathering at the Santa Monica Civic Auditorium of some of the best musical acts in the world, including the Rolling Stones, James Brown, the Supremes, Smokey Robinson and the Miracles, Jan and Dean, the Beach boys, and Lesley Gore. The film was simple enough in its staging and presentation, but enlivened by dance numbers, on and around plastic TV-type sets, that were as wild and well choreographed as any rock numbers ever staged—jazzy, explosive, and kinetic.

Alice's Restaurant

Company: United Artists, 1969
Color, 111 minutes
Category: Drama
Screenplay by: Venavle Herndon
Directed by: Arthur Penn
Produced by: Joe Manduke and Hillard Elkins
Starring: Arlo Guthrie
Composer Arranger: Garry Sherman

Plot: Arlo Guthrie registers with his local draft board and then goes to Rocky Mountain College in Montana from which he gets "educational draft deferrence." Soon disenchanted with the administration of the school (they, likewise, don't appreciate his long hair and eccentric behavior), he drops out and hitches to New York where he visits his father Woody Guthrie, America's greatest folksinger, who is dying of an incurable disease of the nervous system that Arlo may have inherited genetically. (All of this is, by the way, is true.) Arlo travels to Stockbridge, Massachusetts, where friends Alice and Ray Brock (Pat Quinn and James Broderick) have bought a run down, deconsecrated church and turned it into a waystop for homeless hippies. Following a trip to Greenwich Village and a short lived career as a folk singer in a coffee house, Arlo

40

Arlo Guthrie holds his girlfriend Mari-Chan as they wait for Alice's wedding to start in *Alice's Restaurant.*

returns to the church commune and helps set up a restaurant for Alice so the community can support itself. But the responsibilities of running the restaurant plus being surrogate mom to the commune is too much and she splits from Ray, thinking him incapable of physical and emotional support. She has an affair with Shelley (Michael McClanathan), a young heroin junkie who is trying to kick the habit but she and Ray get together again. To celebrate she throws a huge Thanksgiving party. After the meal, Arlo and his buddy Roger (Geoff Outlaw) dispose of trash in a gulley next to the town dump. They're arrested and thrown in jail by Police Chief "Obie" Obanhein, fined $50 for the "crime" of littering. After driving all the way to New York and dumping the garbage onto a sanitation pier, Arlo must report to the army, which rejects him because of his "garbage arrest." Then, within a few days, Shelley dies from a drug overdose, and Arlo's father passes away. Ray persuades Alice to get married in their own church. During the gala celebration, a slightly drunk Ray suggests they sell the church and move to Vermont. Arlo, sensing a note of desperation in Ray's suggestion, moves on once again. Alice stands sadly in front of the church and watches them as they disappear into the horizon.

Music: "Alice's Restaurant," "Songs to Aging Children," "Pastures of Plenty," "Car Song," "Amazing Grace."

Outfits: *Anna Hill Johnstone*, hippie garb, circa 1960s, beards, beads and bangles.

Social Significance: Arlo Guthrie's song, "Alice's Restaurant," on which the film was based, inspired an entire generation with its satirical jabs at the government and the draft, and its pro-hippie freedom beliefs.

Trivia: Penn, the director, actually used many of the real locals in Stockbridge, including William (Obie) Obanhein, the real police chief.

Awards: One of the few folk songs to make it big.

Beach Ball

Company: Paramount, 1965
Color, 83 minutes
Category: Comedy with music
Screenplay by: David Malcolm
Directed by: Lenny Weinrib
Produced by: Bart Patton
Starring: Edd Byrnes, Chris Noel, and Robert Logan
Bands: The Supremes, the Four Seasons, and others
Composer: Frank Wilson

Plot: Dick Martin (Edd Byrnes), manager of the musical group the Wigglers (composed of Jack, Bango, and Bob), is notified by Mr. Wolf that the band still owes him $1,000 for their instruments. To get the money Dick tells Susan (Chris Noel), credit union manager of their college, that he needs some cash to continue his research in African tribal rhythms. The truth is that he and the Wigglers have dropped out of school and are taking it easy among the surfers and racers of Malibu. Susan and finance committee members Augusta, Samantha, and Deborah decide to deliver the money in person but when they get to the beach they discover that they've been tricked and rip up the check. The women then put on bikinis and join the party in hopes of persuading the men to return to college. Mr. Wolf, unable to collect, calls in the cops but the band avoids them by appearing at the "Hot Rod and Musical Show" dressed up as women. The group wins first prize, natch, and the musicians pay back their debts and return to college having won the hearts of the four girls.

Music: Bands include the Supremes, the Four Seasons, the Righteous Brothers, the Hondells, and the Walker Brothers. Some of

41

Dick Martin (Edd Byrnes) romances Susan (Chris Noel) at Malibu in *Beach Ball*.

the songs were "I Feel So Good," "Surfin' Shindig," "Wiggle Like You Tickled," "We've Got Money," "Come to the Beach Ball with Me," "Surfer Boy."
Moves: Lots of beach wiggling to the surf sound.
Outfits: Tan tummies.
Social Significance: Furthered the teen love affair with the beach—utopia for all troubles.
Trivia: Paramount's attempt to imitate American International Pictures' super success with their beach movies but the kids didn't buy it as well.

Beach Blanket Bingo

Company: American International Pictures, 1965
Color, 98 minutes
Category: Musical comedy
Screenplay by: William Asher and Leo Townsend

42

Directed by: William Asher
Produced by: James H. Nicholson and
    Samuel Z. Arkoff
Starring: Frankie Avalon, Annette
    Funicello, Buster Keaton, Paul
    Lynde, Harvey Lembeck, and
    Don Rickles
Band: The Hondells
Choreographer: Jack Baker
Composer: Les Baxter

Plot: Dee Dee (Funicello) and Frankie
(Avalon) and their surfing buddies watch a
parachute jump set up by press agent Bullets
as a publicity stunt for singer Sugar Kane.
The whole crowd loves the show and
becomes interested in skydiving themselves.
They arrange to take lessons at Big Drop's
school. At a party given later for Sugar
Kane, Bonnie flirts with Frankie, making
Dee Dee fly into a jealous rage. Their
fighting is interrupted, however, when Eric
Von Zipper (Lembeck) and his Rat Pack
motorcycle gang crash the party. In the
meantime, Bonehead, one of the surfing
group, is rescued from drowning by Lorelei,
a beautiful mermaid. He falls in love with
her. Meanwhile, believing that Bullets has
set up another publicity stunt, Sugar Kane
allows herself to be kidnapped by Von
Zipper. The surfers go on a wild chase to
save her with the aid of Lorelei and
Bonehead. They succeed. As the mermaid
returns to the ocean, Bonehead finds some
solace with Sugar Kane. Frankie and Dee
Dee patch things up.
Music: Frankie Avalon, and the Hondells
perform. Songs include "I Think," "These
Are the Good Times," "Beach Blanket
Bingo." Composed by Les Baxter.
Moves: More of that good old fashioned
sand-slapping, beach-frugging nonsense that
we all love so dearly. Choreography by Jack
Baker.
Outfits: Bathing suits, bikinis, parachute
gear.
Social Significance: Another step in the
glorification of the beach, beach bums,
surfing, and Annette Funicello.
Trivia: Four of the American International
Pictures beach series.

43

**Frankie (Frankie Avalon) is about
to go on his first skydiving jump
in *Beach Blanket Bingo*.**

Beach Girls and the Monster

Company: U.S. Films, 1965
     Black and white, 70 minutes
Category: Horror with music
Screenplay by: Joan Gardner
Directed by: Jon Hall
Produced by: Edward Jarvis
Starring: Jon Hall, Sue Casey, and
     Walker Edmiston
Composer: Chuck Stagle

The Monster scans the area for some beach girls to mutilate in *Beach Girls and the Monster.*

44

Plot: Otto, an oceanographic professor at the Ocean Research Laboratory, wants his son Richard to be an oceanographer too, but all the young man does is party with girls on the beach. One night he finds the mutilated body of a girl on the shore. Later, at a beach party, his friend Mark discovers that a friend Tom has been murdered. Mark is suspected by the police of disguising himself and committing the murders. He investigates on his own and finds sea monster footprints that lead to Richard's house where Vicki, Otto's very young and attractive wife, tries to seduce him. Suddenly the monster appears and rushes in. It kills Vicki but in its struggle with Mark, its face comes off revealing the insane Otto. Otto escapes by car, but the police chase him through Hollywood Hills. He crashes and dies in a ball of fire.

Music: Frank Sinatra, Jr. sings "Monster in the Surf," "More Than Wanting You. . . ."
Moves: The monster wiggles horribly as it walks.
Outfits: Nubile cuties in wet fabric.
Social Significance: Marks the lowest I.Q. level ever reached in a teen film.
Trivia: Still shown on TV from time to time; try to catch it.

Beach Party

Company: American International
     Pictures, 1963
     Color, 101 minutes
Category: Comedy/musical
Screenplay by: Lou Rusoff
Directed by: William Asher
Produced by: James H. Nicholson and
     Samuel Z. Arkoff

Starring: Frankie Avalon and Annette
Funicello
Band: Dick Dale and the Deltones

Plot: Frankie (Frankie Avalon) takes his
girl friend Dolores (Annette Funicello) to a
beach house in Southern California where
they find a whole crew of their friends. In an
adjoining house their teenage interactions
are observed by Prof. Sutwell (Bob
Cummings) and his secretary, Marianne
(Dorothy Malone), who are doing a study of
the sex play of teens. Frankie becomes angry
at Dolores and feigns a romance with
voluptuous Ava, who works at the local
dance hall. The Professor rescues Dolores
from the aggressive advances of motor cycle
gang leader Eric Von Zipper (Harvey
Lembeck) and a friendship develops between
the two. Frankie gets jealous and, as the film
progresses, the teens discover that Sutwell is
really studying them. At the dance hall, the
irate youths confront Sutwell as the cyclists
show up at the same time. A huge brawl
follows which settles everything and Frankie
and Dolores are together again while Prof.
Sutwell discovers that his secretary is just
the girl for him.
Music: Frankie and the Deltones. Songs
include "Beach Party," "Surfin' and
Swingin'," "Treat Him Nicely."
Moves: Lots of strong hip wriggling and
twisting to the surf sound. Candy Johnson
(who became legendary in these films),
dancer extraordinaire, made her beach party
debut here as the frugger who could make
men's eyes pop and their bodies crash
through walls. Her hip thrusts are something
to behold.
Outfits: Beach garb, bikinis, goofy beach
hats, and, of course, a beach blanket.

45

**Frankie plots to get Dee Dee back
as his buddies look on in *Beach
Party*.**

Social Significance: American International Pictures became image conscious and also realized that their bad boy pictures were starting to fade. A whole new image—wholesome and innocuous—was presented in the beach party movies which depicted teens as smiling goofheads devoid of complexity or problems.

Trivia: Beach Boy Brian Wilson has bit part. Also introduced Harvey Lembeck as Eric Von Zipper, a comedic, satirical character who poked fun at the many motorcycle films of the previous years.
Awards: A big, big hit at the box office. Set the stage for a series of beach party movies to follow.

Annette, the premier beach girl, shows her talents on the bongos in *Beach Party*.

46

Because They're Young

Company: Columbia, 1960
Black and white, 102 minutes
Category: Drama
Screenplay by: James Gunn
Directed by: Paul Wendkos
Produced by: Jerry Bresler
Starring: Dick Clark, Michael Callan, Tuesday Weld, and Victoria Shaw
Group/Singer: James Darren, Bobby Rydell, Duane Eddy, and the Rebels

Plot: Neil Hendry (Dick Clark) is a new history teacher at Harrison High School. He is a get-involved teacher, which irks the principal. Griff (Michael Callan), a delinquent-type, is in his class. Also in the class are Anne (Tuesday Weld), who has been taken advantage of by Griff, and popular football star Buddy (Warren Berlinger). While Hendry romances Joan (Victoria Shaw), he helps out the troubled Griff. Griff, responding to Hendry and the nice classmates, tries to break with the gang but they force him to help commit a

robbery. It goes awry. He escapes but has to face the gang. Hendry comes to the rescue. The principal sees the merit of involved teachers.

Music: James Darren sings "Because They're Young;" Duane Eddy plays "Shazam;" "Swingin' School" is sung by Bobby Rydell.

Moves: Teen lindy stuff goes on at the school dances.

Outfits: Dick Clark always looked cooled out and dressed up. Mr. Straight Dick Clark has been in the rock scene to this day, he's wearing the same suit, I think. Certainly not a flashy dresser like Duane Eddy or Bobby Rydell.

Trivia: *Variety* called it top notch high school drama; *Saturday Review* blasted it as unsuitable for high schoolers. Your move.

The Big T.N.T. Show

Company: American International
Pictures, 1966
Color, 93 minutes
Category: Concert film
Directed by: Larry Peerce
Produced by: Phil Spector
Group/Singer: Roger Miller, Ray
Charles, the Lovin'
Spoonful, Donovan, the
Ronettes, Joan Baez,
Petula Clark, and Bo
Diddley

Plot: David McCallum jumps on stage at Hollywood's Moulin Rouge and introduces the first of the entertainers. He barely

manages to carry this off, because he is beseiged by hysterical teenagers. One after another the acts sing their big hits. The show is dynamite, hence the name. Hot on the heels of the successful (and better)

The great Ray Charles does his thing in *The Big T.N.T. Show.*

47

T.A.M.I. Show, it was slated to be called T.A.M.I. II but you know how these things are. It wasn't.

Music: The Ronettes do "Be My Baby," and Petula Clark does "Downtown." The Byrds sing "Mr Tambourine Man;" Ray Charles does "Georgia on My Mind;" the immortal Bo Diddley does "Hey, Bo Diddley;" Joan Baez sings "Five Hundred Miles," with Phil Spector, at one point, playing the piano with her. Roger Miller sings "King of the Road;" Donovan does some hits; The Lovin' Spoonful do "You Didn't Have to be So Nice."

Moves: The Ronettes corner the market on tight skirt wiggles and bops.
Outfits: Bo Diddley can't wear too tight clothes—he's shakin and strutting so much. Charles is in sunglasses, of course. Strictly sixties.
Social Significance: Records an era of performers.
Trivia: David McCallum was billed as a special guest star.

John Sebastian, lead singer of the Lovin' Spoonful, is one of the many performers in *The Big T.N.T. Show.*

Bikini Beach

Company: American International Pictures, 1964
Color, 100 minutes
Category: Musical comedy
Screenplay by: William Asher, Leo Townsend, and Robert Dillon
Directed by: William Asher
Produced by: James H. Nicholson and Samuel Z. Arkoff
Starring: Frankie Avalon and Annette Funicello
Choreographer: Tom Mahoney
Composer: Les Baxter

Plot: Frankie (Avalon), Dee Dee (Funicello), and their surfing pals vacation at Bikini Beach where they meet the Potato Bug, a British recording star. Huntington Honeywagon (Keenan Wynn) threatens the youngsters' fun on the beach by claiming that they have all sunk to animal level and tries to secure the beach for a senior citizens retirement community. The teens have allies in Vivien Clements, a teacher, and Big Drag (Don Rickles), the operator of a teenage hangout. Potato Bug is interested

in drag racing and when Frankie expresses a similar interest, Dee Dee angrily makes friends with singer.

Eric Von Zipper (Harvey Lembeck) and his motorcycle gang have joined Honeywagon's campaign against the surfers even while Honeywagon is attracted to Vivien who slowly manages to change his conservative views. When Frankie and the Potato Bug compete in a drag race, Von Zipper sabotages what he thinks is the Britisher's car, hoping to blame it on Frankie. But the car is Frankie's and he barely manages to escape when the car crashes at the finish line in a dead heat with Potato Bug. Von Zipper is found out and he and his gang are defeated in a huge brawl at Big Drag's place and are sent packing. Potato Bug leaves, Frankie and Dee Dee are reunited, and Vivien and Honeywagon get together.

Music: The Pyramids and the Exciters are backup bands. The title song "Bikini Beach" is sung by Frankie and Little Stevie Wonder does his first hit "Fingertips." Composed by Les Baxter.

Moves: Wriggling flesh, gyrating beach dances, twisting, and the hip-snapping, electric moves of Candy Johnson, whose body can destroy men's minds. Choreography by Tom Mahoney.

Outfits: Beach gear: T-shirts, bathing suits, bikinis galore. Costumes by Marjorie Corso.

Social Significance: Beach party movies glorified clean-living American teens having fun, dancing, enjoying the beach, never cursing, drinking, or smoking. Made the girls love Frankie more than ever and the boys (including myself) love Annette.

Trivia: Chimpanzee Clyde (Janos Prohaska) provides laughs as Harvey Honeywagon's multi talented monkey who can surf, drag race, twist, and fight. Fabian plays two roles.

Awards: A big moneymaker for American International (the third of their beach party movies).

49

Frankie, Dee Dee, and Potato Bug pose with their club sweats at a drag race in *Bikini Beach*.

Blowup

Company: MGM, 1966
Color, 108 minutes
Category: Drama
Screenplay by: Michaelangelo Antonioni
Directed by: Michaelangelo Antonioni
Produced by: Carlo Ponti
Starring: David Hemmings, Vanessa Redgrave, Sarah Miles, John Castle, and Peter Bowles
Group/Singer: The Yardbirds

Plot: A photographer (David Hemmings), whose life is filled with oh-so-routine days of semi-naked models and driving around in a Bentley, inadvertently photographs a murder. The photographer Thomas spots the action in the far edge of a candid picture he took in a park at night. The picture of two lovers kissing once it's blown-up, has the murder in it. Thomas searches his conscience for what to do about it. There's a break-in and some of the pictures, but not the key one, are stolen. Ten models romp and play on the floor with our hero, he goes to a druggy party, plays invisible tennis with hippies. He can't get it together to do anything about the whole affair and so that's the end.
Music: The Yardbirds (so named, the rumor goes, because some members of the group met in a prison yard. Or was that just publicity hype at the time?) sing "Stroll On." They break their guitars a la Who. There is a mad struggle for the pieces at the dance club. Thomas, though, once he's out in the wet streets, immediately throws away the piece he has managed to tear away from the hysterical fans.
Outfits: Teen girls wear pantyhose, that's about all. Lots of colorful, impractical

50

models' clothes are worn by the glamorous women that parade through Thomas's viewfinder. He's cool in casuals.
Social Significance: The first international hit by the director of *Red Desert,* this picture is supposed to have focused on London because it was the symbol at the time of the new amoral civilization of the west.
Trivia: The story is by Julio Cortazar, author of *All Fires The Fire.* This was a very sexy movie at the time. Since then, of course, the sex angle seems less daring, and the story grips one all the more. See it.

Blue Hawaii

Company: Paramount, 1961
Color, 101 minutes
Category: Musical
Screenplay by: Hal Kanter
Directed by: Norman Taurog
Produced by: Hal Wallis
Starring: Elvis Presley, Angela Lansbury, and the Jordainaires
Choreographer: Charles O'Curran
Composer: Joseph J. Lilly

Plot: Chad Gates (Elvis) comes back to Hawaii after two years in the Army. He goes against his domineering, wealthy Southern mother by turning down a job in his father's pineapple business. He works instead as a guide for the tourist agency where his girlfriend, Maile, who is half French and half Hawaiian, works. His first job is taking Abigail Prentace, a cute schoolteacher, and four teenage girls around the island. Chad gets into a fight at a luau with a tourist who makes drunken advances at the teens. He's hauled off to jail and later reprimanded by

mom who blames the incident on Maile's bad influence. Maile suspects Abigail of pursuing Chad, not knowing that it's really Chad's uncle, Jack Kelman, with whom the teacher is in love. All the confusion is finally straightened out, and Chad and Maile make plans to marry and start their own tourist agency. Chad's father agrees to hold his company's next meeting on the island and let the young couple handle the entire thing. Even Mrs. Gates is won over during a vibrant and colorful Hawaiian-style wedding.
Music: Music scored and conducted by Joseph J. Lilly. Vocal accompaniment by

Hawaii was one of Elvis's favorite milieus. Here he is, with a lei and a ukelele, in *Blue Hawaii.*

The Jordainaires. Songs include "Blue Hawaii," "Aloha Oe," "Rock-a-Hula Baby," "Beach Boy Blues," "I Can't Help Falling in Love," "Almost Always True," "Hawaiian Wedding Song," "Calypso Chant," "Slicin' Sand," "Moonlight Swim," "You're Stepping Out of Line," and "Island of Love."

Moves: Hawaiian-style wanna wichees. Elvis was relatively sedate, although he does all of his classic moves.

Outfits: Edith Head designed the Hawaiian gowns, colorful short-sleeved shirts, loose shirts, and flower patterns.

Social Significance: Furthered the more controlled Elvis in films, and moved him away from his more wild hip swinging of earlier days. A boon for Hawaiian tourism as the sunny islands never looked so luscious.

Blues for Lovers

52

Company: 20th Century Fox, 1966
Black and white, 89 minutes
Category: Drama with music
Screenplay by: Burton Wohl
Directed by: Paul Henfied
Produced by: Herman Blaser
Starring: Ray Charles
Group/Singer: Ray Charles

Plot: American jazz pianist Ray Charles goes to the London Institute for the Blind to entertain the children there. He meets David, a blind 8-year-old, and the boy's widowed mother, Peggy Harrison. Ray grows to like the boy but both he and Steve Collins, a young pianist/composer in love with Peggy, worry about her over-protective feelings toward David. Steve does some musical arranging for Ray's band and the great musician asks Steve to come with him and his band to Paris. Steve invites Peggy and David but she is afraid that the excursion would be too hard on David.

In Paris Steve meets up with old flame Gina, a beautiful socialite. Peggy and David fly to Paris because Ray has contacted a world reknowned eye surgeon who thinks that there's a chance to restore David's eyesight with a dangerous operation. Charles tries to persuade Peggy but it is Gina who finally convinces her to allow the operation.

Ray Charles at the ivories in *Blues For Lovers*.

The operation is done on the day Ray is playing Steve's first major composition in concert. He is told that David's fine and there is a very good chance that the operation succeeded. Steve's music goes over well, and he and Peggy, together again, look forward to a happy life together.

Music: Ray Charles plays the piano and, of course, sings. He's backed by a number of regulars from the Ray Charles band. Songs include "Let the Good Times Roll," "Lucky Old Sun," "Hallelujah, I Love Her So," "Talking About You," "Cry," "What'd I Say;" "Unchain My Heart," "I Got a Woman," "Careless Love," and "Light Out of Darkness" (by Stanley Black).

Moves: Ray does his thing at the piano, free and beautiful enthusiasm. The audience dances to the wondrous sounds of one of the true masters.

Outfits: Subdued gray and black suits.

Trivia: Charles's first dramatic movie role. Though the movie wasn't the greatest, the audience got to see one of America's living legends perform some of his greatest hits.

Bye Bye Birdie

Company: Columbia, 1963
Color, 112 minutes
Category: Musical comedy
Screenplay by: Irving Breaker
Directed by: Sidney Lumet
Produced by: Fred Kohlman

53

Ann-Margret and Bobby Rydell are swinging teens in *Bye Bye Birdie*.

Choreographer: Onna White
Composer: Johnny Green
Starring: Ann-Margret, Bobby Rydell, Dick Van Dyke, Janet Leigh, Paul Lynde, Maureen Stapleton, and Ed Sullivan

Plot: Conrad Byrdie, a super rock idol, has been drafted into the army and the news creates hysteria among his legions of fans. It also means poverty for Albert Peterson (Dick Van Dyke) who has written the title song for Byrdie's next film. Adding to Albert's problems is his domineering mom who is trying to end his romance with Rosie DeLeon (Janet Leigh). Trying to help Albert, Rosie gets him to write a special farewell song that Byrdie will sing on the Ed Sullivan Show. The ecstatic girl selected to appear with him is 16-year old Kim McAfee (Ann-Margret) of Sweet Apple. Byrdie's arrival creates virtual riots and problems for everyone. Kim's boyfriend Hugo gets jealous and her father won't let Byrdie in the house. Then Albert's mother arrives. The worst, though, comes when they all learn that Albert's spot on the TV show will be limited to 30 seconds because the Russian ballet troupe on first needs extra time. Desperate, Albert and Rosie slip nerve relaxing pills into a glass of milk that the Russian conductor drinks. He becomes a zombie and the ballet a joke. Conrad Byrdie performs Albert's song but, as he sings to Kim, Hugo shows up and punches the singer in the jaw. It all ends happily though; Kim returns to Hugo, Albert decides to marry Rosie, and Mama finds someone in Sweet Apple to marry her.
Music: "Bye Bye Birdie," "Put on a Happy Face," "One Boy," "Hymn For a Sunday Evening," "One Last Kiss," "A Lot of Living to Do," "Rosie." Composed by Johnny Green.
Moves: Great choreography (by Onna White) throughout, including Presley-type rockers by Byrdie. He can move those hips.

Outfits: Presley-type, ultra flashy duds on Byrdie; everyone else is Middle America down to the charms and the cardigans.
Social Significance: Further mythification of Presley in the American psyche.

Candy

Company: Cinerama, 1968
Color, 115 minutes
Category: Comedy with music
Screenplay by: Buck Henry
Directed by: Christian Marquand
Produced by: Robert Haggiag
Starring: Ewa Aulin, Charles Aznavour, Marlon Brando, Richard Burton, James Coburn, John Huston, Walter Matthau, and Ringo Starr

Plot: After being scolded by her father for her lack of intellectual pursuits, Candy (Ewa Aulin), a naive and extremely attractive adolescent, goes to a reading given by an alcoholic Welsh poet MePhisto, who gets her drunk. She is then assaulted in the gameroom by the Mexican gardener Emmanuel (Ringo Starr). Discovering her in Emmanuel's embrace, her angry father exiles Candy to New York City then suffers a stroke. On the way to the airport, however, Candy is pursued by Emmanuel's three angry sisters. Candy gets on the plane of General Smight how and grants him favors in exchange for a transfusion for her injured father.

In New York her dad is the patient of a megalomaniacal brain surgeon, Krankeit (James Coburn). Following the operation,

the patient wanders off without even being noticed. Candy goes to Greenwich Village and unwittingly gets into a porno film being shot in a public lavatory. She then meets a benevolent hunchback in Central Park who turns out to be an infamous criminal. In the back of a truck, Candy meets Grindl the guru, who teaches her the true secret of life through sex. Searching for the Great Buddha, Candy finds a filthy hermit and they get it together in a temple. But a deluge destroys the temple and cleans the hermit. "It's Daddy!" she exclaims as she jumps back in horror from her apparently amnesiac father. At a love-in Candy is reunited with all her lovers, everyone wearing hippie-type clothing.

Music: Music composed by Dave Grusin. "Child of the Universe" (the Byrds), "Magic Carpet Ride," "Rock me" (Steppenwolf).

Moves: Choreography by Don Lurio. Happy hippie dancing and dancing to the great Buddha ceremony. But lots of hugging, kissing and. . . .

Outfits: Weird. Everything from business suits to Greenwich Village beatnik, from guru to bum. Sounds like New York.

Social Significance: The peak of spaced-out black humor movies of the 1960's. Every star in sight made an appearance in this very funny movie that marked a new freedom in American comedy.

Trivia: Based on the best-selling novel *Candy* by Terry Southern and Mason Hoffenberg.

Awards: "Child of the Universe" was a hit for the Byrds.

Changes

Company: Cinerama Releasing, 1969
           Color, 98 minutes
Category: Musical melodrama
Screenplay by: Hall Bartlett
Directed by: Hall Bartlett
Produced by: Hall Bartlett
Starring: Kent Lane, Michele Carey, Manuela Theiss, Jack Albertson, and Maris Fehr

55

Candy (Ewa Aulin) stares back innocently at the Air Force General who seeks her favors.

Group/Singer: Tim Buckley, Kim Weston, Judy Collins, Condello, and Neil Young

Title Song by: Kim Weston

Plot: Angry at his parents, Kent (Kent Lane) leaves college on the west coast and takes to the road in his sports car. He told his girlfriend Bobbi that he couldn't be responsible for her, and she killed herself so now he's guilt ridden. He loses control of the car, and then hitchhikes aimlessly. Kristine (Maria Strassner) picks him up. She's a reporter on her way to a peace demonstration and they spent the night together. He ditches her, wanders into a carnival, and meets Julie (Michele Carey) who gets him a job. He moves in with her and for a while it's okay until he wants to travel on, and she wants to go with him.

He's off alone, but thinks about what she said about needing people.

Music: Tim Buckley, Neil Young, and Kim Weston perform. Judy Collins does the famous song "Both Sides Now" by Joni Mitchell.

Outfits: Hippie-era.

Social Significance: None, except furthering performers' careers and sales.

Trivia: Location shooting in beautiful Big Sur, California, and vicinity.

Clambake

Company: United Artists, 1967
Color, 97 minutes

56

Everyone has the rockin' pneumonia in the tropics when Elvis sings.

Category: Comedy/musical
Screenplay by: Arthur Brown Jr.
Directed by: Arthur H. Nadel
Produced by: Jules Levy
Starring: Elvis Presley, Shelly Fabares, and Will Hutchins
Singer: Elvis Presley
Choreographer: Alex Romero

Plot: Oil-rich Scott Heyward (Elvis Presley) sets out to make it on his own without all that money. He switches identities with a motorcyclist and gets his job as a water ski instructor in Miami. The real motorcyclist/water skier guy, Tom (Will Hutchins), checks into the most expensive suite upstairs. Determined to impress golddigger Dianne (Shelley Fabares), Scott will race a dangerously inadequate boat owned by Sam Burton. He will do this by using Gooop, a substance he developed in his multi-million dollar lab back home to strengthen the boat. Scott is racing millionaire Jamison (Bill Bixby) and, at the last moment, golddigger Dianne roots for "poor" Scott. After Scott wins they get engaged and she is floored to learn that poor Scott is really rich beyond comprehension.
Music: "You Don't Know Me," "Who needs Money?," "Confidence," "Clambake," "Hey Hey Hey," "The Girl I Never Loved," "A House that Has Everything."
Outfits: Presley has his collar down; heck, it's hot in Miami. He wears a swimsuit, and Shelley looks like a good girl who thinks she should dress sexy but can't.
Social Significance: Elvis was always switching female co-stars, part of his manager's strategy to keep Elvis the star of these movies. Shelley Fabares had a teen following, unlike some of Presley's other female flirts. She was in lots of beach films.
Trivia: The screenplay writer was a recording artist of some note. Elvis and Shelley were rumored to be angry at each other throughout the whole film. Can you spot it in their acting? Look in the clinches.

Don't Knock the Twist

Company: Columbia, 1962
　　　　　　Black and white, 87 minutes
Category: Musical with comedy
Screenplay by: James B. Gordon
Directed by: Oscar Rudolph
Produced by: Sam Katzman
Starring: Chubby Checker, Gene Chandler, Vic Dana, and Linda Scott
Group/Singer: Chubby Checker, Gene (the Duke of Earl) Chandler, Linda Scott, and others
Choreographer: Hal Belfer

Plot: Television executive Ted Haver (Lang Jeffries) must outdo a rival station so he hires Chubby Checker and others. While on vacation with his fiancee, Dulcie Corbin (Mari Blanchard), a greedy rag-merchant femme fatale, Ted finds Madge Allbright (Georgine Darcy) who can do a mean Twist. He falls for her and he hires the woman, who is performing to collect money for orphans, to do the "Salome Twist" on his show. Incensed, Dulcie designs a too-skimpy outfit for the attractive orphan-lover then tips the papers and the censors. The show will be cancelled. The orphans protest, the show goes on, and Chubby, the Dovells, and the Duke of Earl all get to perform!
Music: The Dovells sing "Bristol Stomp" and "Do the New Continental;" "Slow Twist," "Twistin'," "I Love to Twist" are sung by Chubby Checker; "Bo Diddley" is sung by the Carroll Brothers; "Little Altar Boy" and "Mash Potato Time" are sung by Vic Dana.

57

Moves: The Twist, of course, all with a huge backup cast of dancers in this sequel to the ever-popular spine-cracker *Twist Around the Clock*.

Outfits: Chubby Checker wears his checkers, the rest of the cast have that transition-period-of-rock look: The girls have pre-Beatle beehive hairdos, the short skirts not-too-short; the guys wear tight black jeans.

Social Significance: None except that when the executives are drunk, they go into the men's room and try to sing "Duke of Earl" together!

Trivia: "Duke of Earl," written by Eugene Dixon, Bernice Williams, and Earl Edwards, is the all-time favorite a capella-mania song. Hear it in all places that have echoes, including the whispering gallery of Cornell University and the ivied halls of Harvard. The song that drove a generation mad. "Duke, duke, duke, duke of Earl. . . ."

Don't Look Back

Company: Leacock-Pennebaker, 1967
Black and white, 96 minutes
Category: Cinema verité documentary
Directed by: D.A. Pennebaker
Produced by: Albert Grossman and Don Court
Starring: Bob Dylan
Group/Singer: Bob Dylan, Joan Baez, Donovan, Alan Price, and Allen Ginsberg

Plot: Dylan answers reporters questions cryptically. He cavorts and throws down signs printed with lyrics as the song is sung

58

Bob Dylan lost the pounds he displayed in *Don't Look Back* in this later shot of the ultimate crossover from folk to rock.

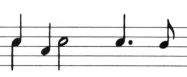

in an alley. Ginsberg cavorts. Joan Baez sings beautifully. Dylan sings. Alan Price, Albert Grossman, and Baez cavort with Dylan, expressing their inner being.

This vehicle was important because it was different, almost hostile to the audience. Dylan's look and demeanor were totally different from previous rock stars, and we were seeing something new. Art meets rock and roll. Check out the scene where Dylan, tired and disgusted, rides in a Rolls with a jokingly money-mad John Lennon. Remember the phrase "put-on?"

Music: Dylan sings "The Times They Are A' Changin'," "Subterranean Homesick Blues," "Death of Hattie Carroll" and others.

Moves: A certain rhythm of action.

Outfits: The Beatles wear their tight, collarless suits, Dylan looks like a beat bum from an alley in the Village, Baez is folksy.

Social Significance: Rock meets art, as it did with the Beatles.

Trivia: Some say Dylan's 'odd' voice was a result of his smoking. He said himself his voice changed for the better when he cut it out. Compare his "hoarseness" in early tracks to the later years' voice.

Double Trouble

Company: MGM, 1967
Color, 90 minutes
Category: Musical/drama
Screenplay by: Jo Heins

59

Singing star Guy Lambert belts out a song at a small club in *Double Trouble*.

Directed by: Norman Taurog
Produced by: Judd Bernard and Irwin Winkler
Starring: Elvis Presley, Annette Day, John Williams, and Yvonne Romain
Group/Singer: Elvis
Composer: Title song by Doc Pomus and Mort Shuman
Choreographer: Alex Romero

Plot: Popular singer Guy Lambert (Elvis Presley) is loved by heiress Jill Conway (Annette Day). Her uncle sends her to Brussels to break up the romance, unaware that Guy has a gig there. Someone is trying to kill Jill; she nearly dies by "accident" several times, and Guy is being watched by thugs who have hidden jewels in his luggage. The Belgian police are on the case but are ineffective, so Guy swings into action. He exposes Uncle Gerald (John Williams) as a would-be killer who wants the fortune. Together with his accomplice Claire (Yvonne Romain), a beautiful woman, he was leading two lives—one as a "protector" of Jill, the other as her stalker. The mysterious stranger seen throughout the film lurking in the shadows is a Scotland Yard inspector. The mystery is solved, and the happy couple set sail for England and a jolly time.

Music: Elvis sings the title song plus "City By Night," "Baby, If You'll Give Me All of Your Love," "There's so Much World to See", "Could I Fall in Love," "Long Legged Girl," "Old MacDonald," "I Love Only One Girl."

The album only reached #47 on Billboard chart. It included five additional songs: "Never Ending," "What Now," "What Next," "Where To," and "Blue River." The title song also was in the *Elvis In Hollywood* album.

Moves: Lots of discotheque dancing, with tamed gyration by, of course, Elvis. Special

60

merit: The festival sequence in Antwerp. Choreography by Alex Romero.
Outfits: At the festival, colorful costumes of Antwerp natives, historical brightness and frivolity.
Social Significance: The New York Times critic thought this movie was better than the three Elvis films before it and put him back on track. But with a #47 album, it isn't much of a track. Elvis fading away to merely great.
Trivia: The song "It Won't be Long" was deleted from final print of film. Ray Charles was in a film of same name; Taurog had directed seven other Elvis flicks by this time. The technical Director was Col. Tom Parker, Elvis's manager for so many years; the Wiere Brothers, as ineffective cops, lend rollicking comedy to an otherwise weak plot.

Dr. Goldfoot and the Bikini Machine

Company: American International Pictures, 1966
Color, 90 minutes
Category: Music-filled comedy
Screenplay by: Elwood Ullman
Directed by: Norman Taurog
Produced by: James H. Nicholson, Samuel Z. Arkoff, and Anthony Carras
Starring: Vincent Price, Frankie Avalon, Susan Hart, and Dwayne Hickman
Title Song by: Guy Hemric and Jerry Styner
Choreographer: Jack Baker

Plot: Dr. Goldfoot (Vincent Price) is determined to get the money of the world's richest man with the aid of his manufactured bikini-clad robots. Diane (Susan Hart), a comely blonde robot, succeeds in marrying playboy Todd Armstrong (Dwayne Hickman) and getting him to sign over his money. Secret Agent Craig Gamble (Frankie Avalon) is in love with Diane until he finds out she's a robot. He's thrown in Dr. Goldfoot's dungeon, and he and Todd evade the fearsome pendulum of death, and they escape in tact. Also featured, in cameo roles, were Annette Funicello and Deborah Walley, then using the name Dorothy.

Music: The Supremes, the premiere girl group (and one that never won any Grammies, for some odd reason), sing the title song. "Wailing" is done by Al Simms.
Moves: Bikini clad robots do the wiggle-jiggle special.
Outfits: Practically nothing. This picture exploits the female body. Remember when sex wasn't passé?
Social Significance: Male arousal.
Trivia: An incredible sequel, full of Italian names, was made, also starring the great Vincent Price, one of our favorite actors. Look for sexy Laura Antonelli in it. It's called *Dr. Goldfoot and the Girl Bombs*.

61

Secret Agent Craig Gamble (Frankie Avalon) begins to suspect something is wrong when the girl he's with springs a leak in *Dr. Goldfoot and the Bikini Machine*.

Easy Rider

Produced by: Peter Fonda
Starring: Peter Fonda, Dennis Hopper, and Jack Nicholson

Company: Columbia, 1969
Color, 94 minutes
Category: Drama
Screenplay by: Peter Fonda, Dennis Hopper, and Terry Southern
Directed by: Dennis Hopper

Plot: Near the California-Mexico border, two motorcyclists, Wyatt (Peter Fonda) and Billy (Dennis Hopper), sell a large quantity of dope to a pusher (Phil Spector) in a Rolls Royce. Wyatt (who is named Captain America because of the stars and stripes on his jacket and bike) hides the money in the bike's gas tank and the two leisurely cycle off across the Southwest, rich for the moment.

62

Captain America (Peter Fonda) looks around at the commune that was his temporary home in *Easy Rider*.

They vaguely intend to reach New Orleans in time for Mardi Gras. Unwelcome at motels because of their hippie appearance—motorcycles, long hair, leather pants—they camp out and smoke grass. They pick up a hitchhiker and take him to the commune where he lives. Despite the friendliness of the people who are working the dry soil and a sexy swim with some of the local females, Billy gets anxious and the two hit the road.

Upon arriving in a small Texas town where a parade is in progress, they get jailed for "parading without a permit." Sharing their cell is George Hanson (Jack Nicholson), an alcoholic civil rights lawyer. A quick friendship grows between the three men and George accepts their invitation to ride with them. George smokes his first joint and happily explicates his theory that creatures from Venus are already living here. But fun turns to tragedy as rednecks get on their trail. First, George is clubbed to death. Then Wyatt and Billy are followed by a pickup truck and blasted off their bikes by shotgun wielding southern trash. They lie dead on the road as the wheels of their upside down bikes spin uselessly in the flick's final, shocking scene.

Music: Background music is used extensively throughout the film. Songs include "The Pusher," "Born to be Wild" (Steppenwolf); "Wasn't Born to Follow" (The Byrds); "The Weight" (The Band); "Ballad of Easy Rider" (Roger McGuinn); "If You Want to be a Bird" (Hody Modal Rounders); "Don't Bogart Me" (Fraternity of Man); "If Six Was Nine" (Jimi Hendrix); "Let's Turkey Trot" (Little Eva); "Kyrie Eleison (Electric Prunes); "Flash Bam Pow" (Electric Flag); "It's Alright Ma I'm Only Bleeding" (Bob Dylan).

Moves: Spaced-out hippie dancing, swinging, waving arms.

Outfits: Motorcycle duds—leather pants and jackets. Fonda's jacket and helmet were decorated with the American flag. Rednecks wear sweat and liquor-stained work shirts and pants.

Social Significance: The first youth breakthrough film, made independently by Fonda. It was a huge hit. Glamorized the hippie generation, footloose with nothing to lose, drugs and hedonism in a way that no movie had before. Fonda captured the mood of America's youth in the late 1960s. Opened up the way for a wealth of independent producers trying to create similar themes. None succeeded but that did not keep the big movie companies from trying.

Ferry Cross the Mersey

Company: United Artists/Suba, 1965
Black and white, 88 minutes
Category: Musical comedy
Screenplay by: David Franden
Directed by: Jeremy Summers
Produced by: Michael Holden
Starring: Gerry Marsden, Fred Marsden, Les Chadwick, and Les Maguire
Group/Singer: Gerry and the Pacemakers, Cilla Black, and others
Music Director: George Warren
Songs: Gerry Marsden

Plot: Screaming fans jam the airport in Manchester, England, to greet Gerry and the Pacemakers on their return from America. (For the uninitiated, this group was a Beatle-clone, part of the British invasion of rock that began with the Beatles). Gerry now recalls the story of the group. He was living with Auntie Lil in a Liverpool boarding house, and took the ferry across the

muddy Mersey river to art classes each day. He was forming a group, with "Chad" (Les Chadwick), also attending art school, and with Fred and Les, factory workers. They sang at local clubs. Gerry's girl Dodie (Julie Samuel) gets the group a good agent, and they get selected in a contest to represent the area in a European Beat contest. After a mixup and the loss of new instruments at the airport, the boys go on to win the contest and are propelled into fame. The end. Prosaic? Well, so are some of the songs, especially the title one. Speeded up camera effects a la *A Hard Day's Night,* youthful exuberance, and cute action pervade the movie. Not bad unless you compare it with the towering achievement of the Beatles.

Music: Gerry and the Pacemakers sing the title song, "I'll Be There," "It's Gonna be Alright," and many others. Cilla Black, the Fourmost, the Black Knights, Earl Royce and the Olympics, Jimmy Saville, and the Blackwells perform.

Moves: Pandemonium of a sort with no real dance numbers, just prancing.

Outfits: Tight Beatle suits, caps, regular duds.

Trivia: Like many other "successful" Beatle spinoffs, Gerry and gang are okay, but not great. That's not to say bad. Almost in the league of The Dave Clark Five. Definitely not the stature of the Animals, yet better than Herman's Hermits.

Festival

Company: Peppercorn-Wormser, 1967 Color, 96 minutes
Category: Rockumentary
Screenplay by: Concept by Murray Lerner
Directed by: Murray Lerner
Produced by: Murray Lerner
Starring: Joan Baez, Theodore Bikel, and Mike Bloomfield
Group/Singer: Joan Baez, Paul Butterfield Blues Band, Mike Bloomfield, Bob Dylan, and many others

Donovan, the ultimate exponent of flower power.

Plot: The Newport Folk Festival was filmed by Lerner over a four year period in the 1960s and this is the result. It shows how folk went rock, among other things. Performers and interviews abound in this free-flowing concert movie. The audience listens attentively even in the rain to the outstanding acts, wanting to know the political and social views of their idols. This film shows all and tells all. It also documents Dylan-gone-electric and some folk fans will never forgive him for becoming a rock star.

Music: See Johnny Cash, Donovan, Odetta, Mimi and Richard Farina, Howlin' Wolf, Jim Kweskin Jug Band—everyone who was anyone in folk, folk-rock, and blues. Also performing were Spider John Koerner, Buffy Sainte Marie, Mike Seeger, Pete Seeger, Staple Singers, Mississippi John Hurt, and Swan Silvertones. All the performers do their hits of the time including Peter, Paul, and Mary doing "Blowin' in the Wind."

Outfits: Folk, folk-rock, casual, country-mod.

Social Significance: Documents a cultural period in America well.

Trivia: The shock on fans' faces when Bob Dylan lets loose from folk music and does an electric-rock "Maggie's Farm" is only partly shown in this important film. The moment passes uncommented upon. Too bad, it's an epic moment in rock. The movie, otherwise, didn't miss much else.

The great Howlin' Wolf performs the Blues in this dynamite film, *Festival.*

Flaming Star

Company: 20th Century Fox, 1960
Color, 101 minutes
Category: Drama
Screenplay by: Claire Huffaker and
Nunnaly Johnson. From
a novel by Claire
Huffaker
Directed by: Don Siegel
Produced by: David Weisbart
Starring: Elvis Presley
Group/Singer: Elvis

Plot: Elvis sings the title song as the credits roll and that's almost the last we hear of his singing. Instead Presley is presented as an accomplished actor.

Pacer Burton (Elvis Presley) is a hot-headed young ranch man in the post-Civil War west. He lives with his mother Neddy (Dolores Del Rio), his father Sam (John McIntire), and his half-brother Clint (Steve Forrest) on a ranch in Texas. The friendly Pacer is tolerated thereabouts, but his mother, a full blooded Kiowa Indian, is shunned. After all there are still simmering hostilities with the Indians.

One day the newly warlike Kiowas attack and kill the Burtons' friends the Howards. A call is made to Sam and Clint to join the whites against the Indian menace but Sam refuses. Trouble with the whites ensues for the Burton family. Buffalo Horn, the chief of the Indians, arrives and asks Pacer to rejoin his people. Pacer doesn't know which way to turn. Neddy and Pacer try to persuade the chief to end hostilities. On the way back from the meeting Neddy is killed by Will Howard, who somehow had survived the massacre at his ranch. Neddy lived for a while, but died when the townsfolk and

66

Pacer Burton is torn by his Indian heritage and his loyalty to the rest of his family in *Flaming Star*.

white doctor refused to help. Pacer joins the Indians. But Sam is killed in a raid by Indians while he is away. Clint vows revenge and kills Buffalo Horn. Pacer, wronged by both sides, returns to his brother. However, he still wants to avenge his father, and rides off. He comes back on horseback some time later, mortally wounded, and says that "I saw the flaming star of death . . . you live for me." He dies as an Indian, yet reaffirming his kinship.

Music: Presley sings "Flaming Star" and "A Cane and a High Starched Collar" in this film. An album with the same title as the film contains more songs.

Outfits: Western, Indian.

Social Significance: Financially this was a flop (compared to Elvis's enviable ability to make producers rich). They had him sing a lot more in films to come. He acted well in the film but it wasn't what the public wanted of Elvis.

Trivia: Don Siegel, the director, did the incredibly wonderful film *Invasion of the Body Snatchers* and was to go on to do *Dirty Harry*.

Follow That Dream

Company: United Artists, 1962
Color, 110 minutes
Category: Musical/drama
Screenplay by: Charles Lederer
Directed by: Gordon Douglas
Produced by: David Weisbart
Starring: Elvis Presley, Arthur O'Connell, Anne Helm, Joanna Moore, Jack Kruschen, and Simon Oakland
Group/Singer: Elvis
Music: Hans J. Salter
Composer: Title song by Fred Wise and Ben Weisman

Plot: Pops Kwimper (Arthur O'Connell) is an old wanderer and he lives off relief

67

Toby Kwimper entertains his father and the four orphans in *Follow that Dream.*

checks, but his son Toby (Elvis Presley) kicks in his army disability money and they support and care for four orphans. One of them, 19-year old Holly (Anne Helm), is in love with Toby but he's shy. Pops and his crew run out of gas and are forced to spend the night in a Florida beach. There are giant tarpon in the water, and Toby and the others decide to homestead there and start a fishing dock. Their enterprise works and, as they are outside of restrictive jurisdiction of a nearby town, they soon attract competition. This includes two mean gamblers, Nick (Simon Oakland) and Carmine (Jack Kruschen), who set up crap games in their trailer. There are lots of settlers now, and they elect Toby "sheriff" of their little ramshackle community. He manages against the gamblers, but soon Alicia Claypoole (Joanna Moore), a welfare investigator, makes trouble. She says Pops is an unfit guardian for the brood. However, the judge is convinced by Pops and the others that all is warm and loving, and they are let go. Holly gets Toby at this point to admit that he loves her, and all is well. Lots of singing make this spotty plot move like a rocket.

Music: In this, Elvis's ninth movie, he sings "What a Wonderful Life," "I'm Not the Marrying Kind," "Follow That Dream," "Sound Advice," "Angel," and "On Top of Old Smokey" (the great Pete Seeger/Weavers theme).
Composed by Hans J. Salter.

Moves: Standard wiggles toned down. The fish prance about nicely.

Outfits: Fisherman gear, poor folks' duds.

Social Significance: None to speak of, though fans were bewildered by this metamorphosis of Presley into a singer of a less-than-number-one-on-the-charts title song.

Trivia: This film was shot close to the home of then eleven-years old Tom Petty, who grew up to form the Heartbreakers. The single was released in May, 1962 and reached #15 on the chart.

Get Yourself a College Girl

Company: MGM, 1964
Color, 88 minutes
Category: Drama/romance vehicle for songs
Screenplay by: Robert E. Kent
Directed by: Sidney Miller
Produced by: Sam Katzman
Starring: Mary Ann Mobley, Chad Everett and Nancy Sinatra
Group/Singer: Dave Clark Five, the Animals, Stan Getz, Astrud Gilberto, and Freddie Bell
Choreographer: Hal Belfer

Plot: Terry (Mary Ann Mobley) writes sexy songs under a phoney name, a trick that might get her expelled from her all girls college if found out. She is discovered and put on probation. She spends the holiday at Sun Valley Ski resort with her friends and ballet teacher Marge (Joan O'Brien). There she meets a young, rich, and handsome publisher, named Gary (Chad Everett). He wants her to pose in a nightie to promote her songs, and, incensed as any pure person would be, she refuses. A senator, the grandson of the college founder, arrives in the valley. He wants to understand youth so the students organize a big rock and roll show for the nice senator. He is sure to be re-elected now. Huh? Anyway, Gary and Terry get over their tiff and make out fine.

Music: Roberta Lynn, the Jimmy Smith Trio, The Rhythm Masters, and Freddie Bell perform their current hits. The title song (composed by Sidney Miller and Fred Karger) was not a winner. The Dave Clark

Five, who almost rivaled the Beatles in popularity once, sing "Whenever You're Around" and "Thinking of You." The Animals sing "Around and Around" and "Blue Feeling."

Moves: The frenetic swaying to the beat is a bit confusing and what are the jazz guys doing in this film? Anyway, there's teen sock-hop fever here, and Mary Ann Mobley looks good just standing still. When she does the Watusi, watch her go-go-go.

Outfits: Ski-outfits, S-t-r-e-t-c-h-e-d out Stretch pants on the females, and goggles complete the picture.

Social Significance: Mary Ann was worshipped by you and me and so many others.

Trivia: This film, a mixed up hodge-podge that delivers a good set of songs, had several titles. In Britain, it was *Swinging Set*, and it's been called *Watusi-a-go-go* and *The Go-go Set* at various times.

69

Even college girls manage to have fun.

Ghost in the Invisible Bikini

Starring: Tommy Kirk, Deborah Walley,
Nancy Sinatra, Boris Karloff,
and Basil Rathbone
Band: The Bobby Fuller Four
Composer: Les Baxter

Company: American International
Pictures, 1966
Color, 82 minutes
Category: Comedy with music
Screenplay by: Louis Heyward
Directed by: Don Weis
Produced by: James H. Nicholson and
Samuel Z. Arkoff

Plot: Cecily, the ghost of Hiram Stokely's sweetheart of 30 years ago, visits him in his coffin. She tells him that if he can perform a good deed within the next 24 hours he will get into heaven and also become young again. The good deed is to prevent his attorney, Reginald Ripper, from cheating Hiram's young heir, Chuck Phillips, out of his inheritance. As Chuck, his girlfriend Lili Morton, and Aunt Forbush wait for the

70

Leers for the girl in the visible bikini.

reading of the will, the swinging nephew Bobby arrives at the Stokely mansion to spend the weekend. Also appearing on the scene are Eric Von Zipper and his Rat Pack. The evil Ripper finds it hard to carry out his plans to get rid of Chuck in the middle of all this madness. When he makes a last murderous attempt in the mansion's chamber of horrors, Hiram and Cecily thwart the plot. Hiram is given his heavenly reward but it is more than he had bargained for. As Cecily leads him up, he turns younger and younger until he's only three.
Music: Composed by Les Baxter and performed by the Bobby Fuller Four and Nancy Sinatra. The songs include "Geronimo," "Swing-A-Ma-Thing," "Don't Try to Fight it Baby," "Stand Up and Fight," and "Make the Music Pretty."
Outfits: Clean teen.
Trivia: Didn't do too bad at the box office.

G.I. Blues

Company: Paramount, 1960
               Color, 104 minutes
Category: Musical/drama

Elvis plays Tank Gunner, Tulsa McCauley, who is in love with beautiful dancer Lili, played by Juliet Prouse, in *G.I. Blues*.

Screenplay by: Edmund Beloin and Henry Garson
Directed by: Norman Taurog
Produced by: Hal B. Wallis
Starring: Elvis Presley, Juliet Prouse, Robert Ivers, and Leticia Roman
Group/Singer: Elvis Presley and the Jordainaires
Composer: Sid Tepper and Roy Bennett (title song)
Choreographer: Charles O'Curran

Plot: Tank Gunner Tulsa McCauley (Elvis, as in real life) is serving with the U.S. Army in Germany together with Rick (James Douglas) and Cookie (Robert Ivers). They form a musical group, and during their off-time play small clubs. They are saving money to open a nightclub back in the U.S.A. when their tour of duty is over. They are still short so when a group of soldiers bet $300 that no one could spend the night with beautiful but pristine dancer Lili (Juliet Prouse), Elvis takes them on. He rescues her from an attacker, befriends her, and they go off sightseeing. They visit historic Frankfurt, and Tulsa finds he is sorry he took the bet, now that he is in love. He won't try to spend the night, money or no money. Pressed into baby sitting for Rick and fraulein Marla (Sigrid Maier), Tulsa has to call Lili when the baby gets difficult. She tells him to bring the baby to her so, quite innocently, he spends the night. He wins the bet but Lili, finding out about it, thinks it was a trick and drops Tulsa. Later, at a musical show, they confess love for one another and they reunite.

Music: The Jordainaires back Presley who sings the title song and also "Pocketful of Rainbows," "Didja Ever," "Frankfurt Special," "Shoppin' Around," "Tonight Is So Right for Love," "Big Boots," "Doin' the Best I Can," and the ballad "Wooden Heart," an old German favorite re-worded.

Moves: Juliet does some dancing and Elvis wiggles. The whole thing comes alive, with this first movie after the army being one of his most popular. Choreography by Charles O'Curran.

Outfits: Lots of uniforms. Juliet wears a slit-skirt, leg-revealing, sparkling gown and regular dresses. Presley's hair is tamer now than in *Loving You* or *Jailhouse Rock*.

Social Significance: The Communist East Germans were upset, to put it mildly, to have such a teen idol on the American side. They called it a provocative act of calculated warmongering to have Elvis in an American uniform so close to East German teens who idolized him.

Trivia: The album remained on the charts of *Billboard* longer than any other Elvis record—111 weeks. "Blue Suede Shoes" is heard on the jukebox in the movie. Three sets of twins played the single infant in the film.

Awards: Gold Album R.I.A.A., #1 album 10 weeks Billboard. Long before Elvis's death sold millions more, it had topped 2,000,000 in sales.

Gidget Goes Hawaiian

Company: Columbia, 1961 Color, 102 minutes
Category: Comedy with music
Screenplay by: Ruth Brooks Flippen
Directed by: Paul Wendkos
Produced by: Jerry Bresler
Starring: James Darren, Michael Callan, and Deborah Walley
Choreographer: Roland Dupree
Composer: George Dunning

Plot: Gidget Lawrence (Deborah Walley) has a fight with her surfer boyfriend, Jeff Mather (James Darren), when she tells him that her parents are taking her on vacation to Waikiki Beach and, instead of being unhappy about the separation, he wishes her fun. On the plane her family becomes friendly with Monty and Mitzi Stewart and their snotty teenage daughter, Abby. In Hawaii, Gidget just mopes around despite the attentions of big TV dancer Eddie Horner (Michael Callan) who himself is being pursued by Abby. Upset by his daughter's depression, Lawrence sends for Jeff. At that point, of course, Gidget decides to have fun, and enjoy Hawaii and Eddie. Jeff shows up just in time to see Eddie kissing Gidget. He counteracts by going after

Deborah Walley poses as Gidget in *Gidget Goes Hawaiian*. She takes over the role of Sandra Dee.

Abby. Further insanities occur when the teens think their parents are playing extracurricular games. But in the grand finale all the misunderstandings are cleared up and Gidget is back with Jeff.

Music: "Gidget Goes Hawaiian," "Wild About That Girl."

Moves: Sand frugging.

Outfits: Bathing suits, regular suits, *lauaus, wanawichees.*

Social Significance: The picture somehow lost a little of its libidinous zest with the replacement of Sandra Dee by Deborah Walley.

Trivia: Location scenes were filmed in Hawaii. The sequel to *Gidget* (1959). Also in the film were Peggy Cass and Carl Reiner.

Gidget Goes to Rome

Company: Columbia, 1963
Color, 101 minutes

Category: Romantic comedy with music

Screenplay by: Ruth Brooks Flippen, K. Eunson, and D. Eunson

Directed by: Paul Wendkos

Produced by: Jerry Bresler

74

Gidget (Cindy Carol) admires the hat of chaperone Albertina (Jessie Royce Landis) in *Gidget Goes to Rome.*

Starring: Cindy Carol, James Darren, Jessie Royce Landis, and Cesare Danova
Singer: James Darren
Musical Score: Johnny Williams

Plot: Gidget Lawrence (Cindy Carol) goes to Rome with her boyfriend Jeff (James Darren) and a group of teenagers chaperoned by Albertina (Jessie Royce Landis), the aunt of one of the teens. The aunt leaves them pretty much alone, otherwise this film would never get anywhere! Gidget falls for Paolo (Cesare Danova) who introduces himself as a journalist doing a story, and shows her all the sights of Rome. Jeff gets jealous but it all turns out well in the end, as usual.
Music: James Darren, occasional teen heartthrob of the era, sings "Big Italian Moon" and "Gegetta." Musical score by Johnny Williams.
Moves: When Gidget goes to Roma, the rocking teen takes on a spaghetti-like hip movement in the dance spots of the ancient city.

Outfits: Gidget's teen duds by Sorelle Fontana of Roma and the fashion show clothes are by Landis and Carol. Otherwise, standard teens-on-vacation fare in 1960s.
Social Significance: Clean-teens-meet-sexy-Romans myth perpetuated. Stick to gauche American hood types.
Trivia: This is hardly a rocking movie, but James Darren for a while, at least, was considered a "rocker."

Go Go Mania (Also *Pop Gear*)

Company: American International, 1965 Color, 70 minutes
Category: Pseudo-rockumentary
Directed by: Frederic Goode

75

The Animals go wild in *Go Go Mania*.

Produced by: Henry Field
Starring: The Beatles and many other bands

Good Times

Plot: Sixteen of Britain's top pop groups were filmed in a staged setting designed to make the viewer think he was seeing live shows. London disc jockey Jimmy Savile, sporting a shoulder-length blonde wig, introduces each group (in an attempt to add some sort of cohesiveness to the flick). In effect a mock concert film is created using brightly lit backdrops, dubbed in audience screams, and lip-syncing by the bands to their pre-recorded hits. Each band performs a few of their tunes to the appreciation of fake audiences. Though much of the footage is visually bland, the Beatles, one of the few who actually perform live (from a previous concert), come off pretty good—but don't they always?

Music: The Beatles, the Animals, Matt Monro, the Nashville Teens, Susan Maughan, the Rockin Berries, the Honeycombs, Herman's Hermits, the Four Pennies, Peter and Gordon, the Fourmost, Sounds Incorporated, Billy Davis, the Spencer Davis Group, Billy J. Kramer and the Dakotas, and Tommy Quickly and the Remo Four all perform. Songs include "Twist and Shout" (the Beatles); "House of the Rising Sun" and "Don't Let Me be Misunderstood" (Animals); "World Without Love" (Peter and Gordon); "Little Children" (Billy J. Kramer); and "I'm into Something Good" (Herman's Hermits).

Moves: Fairly routine: swinging guitars around, low level moves by band members.

Outfits: English pop/mod outfits circa 1965. Same color suits, Nehru jackets, bell bottoms, long hair.

Social Significance: Captured a moment in pop history—the British Invasion of the mid 1960s when English rock and roll totally dominated American music, fashion, even art.

Company: Columbia, 1967
Color, 91 minutes
Category: Fantasy/drama/musical
Screenplay by: Tony Barrett
Directed by: William Friedkin
Produced by: Lindsey Parsons
Starring: Cher and Sonny Bono
Group/Singer: Sonny and Cher
Choreographer: Andre Tayir
Arranger and Conductor: Sonny Bono

Plot: Sonny has fantasies: First he and Cher are a stereo-type cowboy and dancehall girl; then he's Tarzan and she's Jane in a treehouse; finally he's a tight-jawed private investigator. These daydreams are the result of his longing to achieve Hollywood stardom. Sonny and Cher (as in real life) are successful rock stars with millions of fans. A film mogul called Mr. Mordicus (George Sanders) tries to sell them on a bogus film project. That's why Mordicus always popped up in those fantasies as a party-pooping badguy perhaps as a warning to Sonny to take heed of Cher's desire to just stay happy rock stars. Sonny refuses Mordicus at the end and the singing couple live happily ever after.

Music: Sonny and Cher belt out "I Got You Babe," "It's The Little Things," "Good Times," "Trust Me," "I'm Gonna Love You," "Just a Name," "Don't Talk to Strangers."

Moves: Great fantasy dance numbers, especially Cher as a dancehall dame in the West.

Outfits: Does Cher *ever* wear clinging outfits! She must have had some of her intestines removed to fit into them. Costumes by Leah Rhodes do much to

76

stylize this handsome couple, and they wear extravagant fantasy-clothes throughout.
Social Significance: None. These favorite love-birds that teased one another got divorced in real life, but still functioned as an act.
Trivia: What would a rock film book be without one of Sonny and Cher's triumphs?

The Graduate

Company: Avco, 1967
Color, 105 minutes
Category: Black comedy with music

Screenplay by: Calder Willingham and Buck Henry
Directed by: Mike Nichols
Produced by: Lawrence Turman
Starring: Dustin Hoffman, Anne Bancroft, and Katharine Ross
Band: Simon and Garfunkel scored and played all the music

Plot: Benjamin Braddock (Dustin Hoffmann) returns to his Los Angeles home after graduating from college and his parents throw a party to boast of his academic achievements and set up good business contacts. One of the guests, Mrs. Robinson (Anne Bancroft), gets Ben to drive her home and tries to seduce him, but they're stopped by the sound of her husband. Quite aggressive, she soon has the inexperienced and nervous Ben meeting her regularly at

77

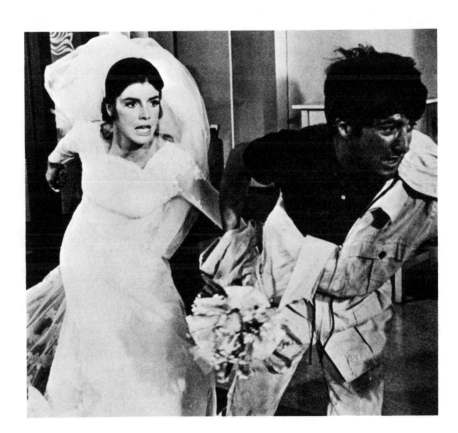

Benjamin manages to pull Elaine away from her impending marriage in *The Graduate*.

the Taft Hotel. As summer goes on he becomes more and more listless and strange. His parents arrange a date with Elaine (Katharine Ross), Robinson's daughter. The two soon grow close and Mrs. Robinson demands that Benjamin stop seeing her. Instead he tells Elaine the truth and she returns to Berkeley. Ben follows her and tries to get her to marry him but Elaine's parents intervene and she agrees to marry another fellow student. Ben learns of the wedding and arrives at the church just as the final vows are being spoken, screaming out Elaine's name over the heads of the shocked guests. Elaine sees how much her parents hate Ben and how they've influenced her. She fights her way free of the clinging guests. She and Benjamin lock the guests inside the church and escape aboard a passing bus.

Music: All the material in the film was written and performed by Simon and Garfunkel. Songs include "Sounds of Silence," "Scarborough Fair," "Mrs. Robinson," "The Big, Bright Green Pleasure Machine," "April Comes She Will."

Outfits: Respectable, late 1960s; weejies, shirts, ties.

Social Significance: *The Graduate* made a large impact on the youth (and adults) of America. Hoffman literally brought a new type of anti-hero into existence with his portrayal of Benjamin. It also made him and director Nichols immediate superstars.

Trivia: "Mrs. Robinson" was a big hit on the radio. Simon and Garfunkel were at the peak of their popularity.

Awards: Mike Nichols won an Oscar for Best Director.

A Hard Day's Night

Company: United Artists, 1964
Black and white, 85 minutes
Category: Drama/semi-documentary
Screenplay by: Alun Owen
Directed by: Richard Lester

The Beatles cavort on a field while escaping from the world in *A Hard Day's Night.*

78

Produced by: Walter Shenson
Starring: The Beatles, Wilfred Brambell,
and Victor Spinetti
Group/Singer: The Beatles
Composer: John Lennon and Paul
McCartney

Plot: Twenty-four hours in the madcap life of the "Fab Four" is recounted in an arty, imaginative way. Critics raved, for everyone expected a meaningless, dull movie capitalizing on the popular songs of the group.

It opens with the Beatles running for their lives down an English street. They are not far ahead of thousands of hysterical fans, mostly girls. The great title song is playing on soundtrack. The Beatles board a train and as, the song ends, it pulls away and we hear the insane, high pitched, shrill scream of 10,000 female hysterics—the sound of Beatlemania. Soon the boys are in the baggage car keeping company with Paul's grandfather (Wilfred Brambell)—a real troublemaking gent. They play cards in a surrealistic scene where "I Should Have Known Better" is on the soundtrack. They reach their destination and there are more fans, a hotel room, annoying managers, and hangers-on. They revolt by slipping away to a dance club. Finally rounded up, they rehearse for a TV appearance the next day. Told to wait in a room while matters are cleaned up, they escape out a side door and cavort away. Youth untamed, looking for a way to duck the adult world of squares seems to be the theme. They frolic in a field as "Can't Buy Me Love" plays. They are kicked off the field. "Sorry we hurt your field, mister," sneers George.

Grandfather, back at the studio, is bored and restless too. Ringo and he go to a canteen and, as they have tea, the old man provokes Ringo to go out and explore the world. Disguised, Ringo slinks about the city. He wanders around sad and profound, and winds up being arrested for "malicious

intent." He escapes, and there follows a great police chase. This, of course, with all four Beatles in front of a frantic police constabulary. They run straight to the studio and into the set just in time to do their songs on live telly. They flee again from their hysterical fans (via helicopter) and the film dissolves.

Music: The Beatles, of course, singing the title song plus "Can't Buy Me Love," "I'm Happy Just to Dance With You," and so on. The soundtrack album was on Capitol and later Apple labels.

Moves: The Beatles cavort in a wild scene in the field. It's like a modern dance to freedom, with stop- and slow-camera action and lots of trick shots.

Outfits: They're very mod in this film, and of course they are mop-topped, as you know.

Social Significance: Are you kidding? John Lennon wanted to be bigger than Elvis and he is and so are the others. The world went from short hair to mop-top overnight, the famous Beatle cut replacing flattops and crewcuts. The Beatles' imitators and spin-offs came out like weeds in a cornfield, and the Motown sound, much of which, along with Gene Vincent and Buddy Holly, influenced the Beatles, was replaced by the English Beat. The most famous singing group ever!

Trivia: Lester won the rave of the intellectuals with this film, a tour-de-force of misé-en-scene.

Awards: Applause at nearly every theatre but no Academy Awards.

79

Having a Wild Weekend

Company: Warner Bros., 1965
Black and white, 91 minutes

Category: Comedy with music
Screenplay by: Peter Nichols
Directed by: John Boorman
Produced by: David Deutsch
Starring: Dave Clark Five, Barbara Ferris, Lenny Davidson, and Rick Huxley

Plot: The Dave Clark Five, shucking commercials for a meat-packer, aim to go on the road. Dave Clark plays Steve, who has a girl named Dinah (Barbara Ferris) who convinces him to take the film company's white Jaguar and travel to an island she wants to buy. They meet beatniks, ride into an army training ground, nearly get hit, and, sans the car (it was blown up), get picked up by a couple, Guy and Nan (Robin Bailey and Yootha Joyce). They go to an Arts Society high-dress ball, get tracked down by a columnist, and found by the studio and the media. (Steve was a minor star until his "kidnapping." Now he's major, and so's she.) She wants the limelight, but he chucks the whole thing. Confused? Don't be. Dig the music.

Music: Dave Clark Five do "I Like It," "It's Gonna Be Alright," "Move On," "Catch Us If You Can," "Sweet Memories," "Time," "When," "I Can't Stand It," "Sol," and "Having a Wild Weekend."

Moves: High-society balling.
Outfits: Carnaby Street influenced togs. English invasion boots.
Social Significance: Can Dave make it like the Beatles? No, but he makes some money too. This group is not half bad.
Trivia: Opened in London in 1965 as *Catch Us If You Can*. This was the first feature film directed by John Boorman who later did *Deliverance*.

80

The Dave Clark Five take a ride on their *Wild Wild Weekend.*

Head

Company: Columbia, 1968
Color, 86 minutes
Category: Comedy
Screenplay by: Jack Nicholson and Bob Rafelson
Directed by: Bob Rafelson
Produced by: Bob Rafelson, Jack Nicholson, and Bert Schneider
Starring: The Monkees—Mickey Dolenz, David Jones, Mike Nesmith, and Peter Tork

Plot: *Head* is a free-form series of vignettes involving the Monkees. Also included are footage from classic Hollywood films such as

Gilda and *Golden Boy*, and newsreel clips on Vietnam.

After leaping off the Golden Gate bridge to escape from Mayor Feedback and his cronies, the Monkees perform an underwater ballet and then reappear in the middle of the desert in some Eastern country. There they attack a Coca Cola machine, follow a sheik and his brain-damaged Arab horsemen, and watch a World War II regime surrender to a single Allied soldier. The four then head to a Columbia Pictures studio where they get into a television commercial as dandruff in the hair of Victor Mature. The boys escape to have more adventures and finally tear apart a huge studio set. At the end they are once more falling from the Golden Gate bridge.

Music: "Porpoise Song" composed by Carole King and Gerry Goffin; "As We Go Along" composed by Carol King and Toni Stern; "Daddy's Song" composed by Nilsson; "Can You Dig It" composed by Peter Tork.

Moves: Choreography by Toni Basil. Surrealistic dances and movement throughout the movie, including an underwater ballet and a mad dash through Victor Mature's hair.

Outfits: Primarily white outfits, Beatles-type look.

Social Significance: The Monkees were a created-for-TV rock group, an imitation of

The Monkees were one of the more successful Beatles clones.

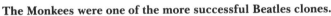

81

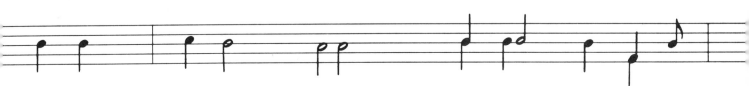

the Beatles. Surprisingly, not only did they do well on TV but they became stars and musicians in their own right, even writing some hit songs like "Last Train to Clarksville" and "I'm A Believer."

Trivia: Bit parts for such diverse talents as Sonny Liston, Frank Zappa, and Victor Mature and Annette Funicello.

The Hellcats

Company: Crown International, 1969
Color, 90 minutes
Category: Drama with music
Screenplay by: Tony Houston

Directed by: Robert Slatzer
Produced by: Anthony Cardoza
Starring: Ross Hager and Dee Duffy
Music by: Jerry Roberts

Plot: When his brother, a detective, is killed while on the trail of a female motorcycle gang called the Hellcats, Monte Chapman (Ross Hager) decides to get the murderer no matter what. Accompanied by his dead brother's girl Linda (Dee Duffy), Monte manages to get in good with the biker girls at a "freak-out/love-in." He discovers that the Hellcats are working with a narcotics smuggler called Mr. Adrian. Linda is invited to join the leader of the Hellcats, Sheila, and another girl, Betty, on a journey to Mexico to pick up some drugs which they'll hide in their motorcycle headlights. On their trip back the police become suspicious and follow them. Betty is killed when her bike goes out of control. Sheila and Linda deliver the dope

82

The Hellcats **are a female motorcycle gang.**

but are held captive by Adrian for letting themselves be trailed. Monte is also taken prisoner. As Adrian tries to make his getaway on boat, the tied and gagged Monte and Linda are taken down to the docks. Sheila manages to escape and calls both the Hellcats and the cops, who rush to the rescue. During the dockside free-for-all, Adrian is killed, the drug ring is destroyed, and Monte and Linda are together.

Music: Davy Jones and the Dolphins and Somebody's Children perform. Songs include "I Can't Take a Chance" and "Mass Confusion" (Davy Jones and the Dolphins); "I'm Up" and "Marionettes" (Somebody's Children).

Moves: Psychedelic arm waving; motorcycle stomp.

Outfits: Motorcycle chic—black leather.

Social Significance: Considered by some as the worst biker movie ever made. A motorcycle gang calling the police for help???

Help!

Company: United Artists, 1965
Color, 90 minutes
Category: Comedy/drama/musical
Screenplay by: Marc Behm and Charles Wood
Directed by: Richard Lester
Produced by: Walter Shenson
Starring: The Beatles, Leo McKern, Eleanor Bron, Victor Spinetti, and Roy Kinnear
Group/Singer: The Beatles

Plot: Clang (Leo McKern) is a devotee of great mothergoddess Kaili, a Far Eastern idol of death. He is about to sacrifice a female to the goddess when the Priestess Ahme (Eleanor Bron) points out that the sacrificial victim is not wearing the ring that signifies her as a "worthy" and the rite can't go on. Where is the ring? Back in England with Ringo, so the great chase is on. The cultists of Kaili will stop at nothing in pursuit of their religious duties and are intent on sacrificing Ringo.

The Beatles are in a recording studio when there is a buzzing noise and Ringo suddenly drops through the floor. He's attacked by Clang but rescued by Ahme who wants to meet Paul. The group enlists the aid of the Army to protect their musical sessions with tanks as they play their hits on the fields near Stonehenge. Then the four moptops are attacked by Clang's forces and they run to the Alps. Clang follows but not before the Beatles can do a wonderful performance with a piano in the snow. Then John, Paul, George and Ringo are off to Bermuda, and there Clang traps Ringo once again but Ahme appears and points out that the ring is off Ringo and on his finger instead. The devotees, the constables, and the Beatles are in a mad scramble on the beach as the film ends.

Music: The Beatles sing the title song, "Night Before," "Hey! You've Got to Hide Your Love Away," "Ticket to Ride," "Another Girl," and others. The score by George Martin, genius of the studio, and creator (aside from the Fab Four) of that Beatle sound, keeps the audience in the action.

Outfits: The Beatles get a bit more to wear in this one (compared to the tight suits of *A Hard Day's Night*). Especially cute are the caped black overcoats in the Alps' sequence. Lots of casual clothes in Bermuda.

Social Significance: This film is far less "arty" than *A Hard Day's Night*. A disappointment to some but with color and even better songs than the first film, it's another hit.

Trivia: "Help!," as are most of the Beatles' songs, is written by John and Paul. Some say

83

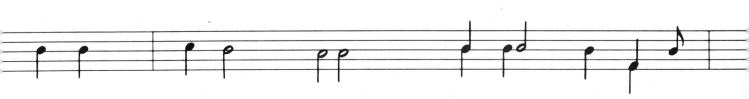

The Beatles are all ready to go skiing and performing in the snow in *Help!*

84

it is Lennon's first cry for help, for spiritual rescue. It is somehow like the Lennon solo songs years later (refer to "Mother You Left Me" on the *Imagine* album).

Especially poignant now are the final cuts of the film, with alternate Beatles appearing in twists of ruby-like gems. John seems to stand out. . . .

Hold On

Company: MGM, 1966
Color, 86 minutes
Category: Musical
Screenplay by: James Gordon
Directed by: Arthur Lubin

Produced by: Sam Katzman
Starring: Peter Noone and Herman's Hermits
Musical Score by: Sue Anne Langdon and Fred Karger

Plot: When the children of American astronauts vote to call a new spaceship after Herman's Hermits, NASA has intellectual Edward Lindquist follow the British pop stars to see if they're worthy of such an acclamation. Among the thousands of hysterical young girls after the Hermits is Cecilie Bannister, a publicity-minded movie starlet. In Los Angeles, Herman and his band slip away from the snoopy Lindquist to have fun at an amusement park. There Herman meets cute Louisa Page who invites him to a party her mother is giving to help charity. The party virtually turns into a riot when the Hermits sing and Cecilie and a

group of teens crash through police gates. The Hermits' appearance at the Rose Bowl is such a tremendous success that NASA decides to go ahead and name the spaceship after them. Holy cow!

Music: Herman and his Hermits sing "Hold On," "A Must to Avoid," "Leaning on the Lamppost," "All the Things I Do for You, Baby," "Where Were You When I Needed You," "Make Me Happy," "The George and Dragon," "Got a Feeling," "We Want You, Herman," "Wild Love," and "Gotta Get Away."

Moves: Choreography by Wilda Taylor, who helps the boys to move with a little bit of life.

Outfits: The Hermits always dressed English Mod mixed with slightly sloppy schoolboy for that oh-so-innocent look.

Social Significance: Peter Noone's further attempts at establishing himself as a major pop sex symbol. Although he graced the covers of magazines for months, somehow he faded away rather quickly after the initial brouhaha was over.

How to Stuff a Wild Bikini

Company: American International Pictures, 1965
Color, 90 minutes
Category: Comedy with music
Screenplay by: William Asher and Leo Townsend
Directed by: William Asher
Produced by: James H. Nicholson and Samuel Z. Arkoff
Starring: Frankie Avalon, Annette Funicello, Harvey Lembeck, Dwayne Hickman, Buster Keaton, and Mickey Rooney.

Herman's Hermits introduced ten new songs in *Hold On,* **the comedy "with a beat."**

85

Plot: Frankie, on a Naval Reserve assignment in Tahiti, comes to Bwana, a witch doctor, to keep his girl friend Dee Dee (Annette Funicello) safe from male competition. Bwana sends out a magic pelican to keep an eye on her until a handsome rogue, Ricky, goes after her, and Bwana decides to use more powerful magic. He sends his own mysterious beauty, Cassandra, to get Ricky. Peachy Keane, an adman, is looking for the "Girl Next Door" for an advertising campaign. He enlists the aid of Eric Von Zipper (Harry Lembeck) and the Rat Pack who are getting ready for a motorcycle race. Cassandra wins the "Girl Next Door" contest but Peachy Keane discovers that she's totally uncoordinated. Von Zipper and his crew meet with numerous difficulties in their motorcycle race and he trades in his black jacket for a grey flannel suit. Ricky falls for Cassandra and Frankie keeps Dee Dee. Everyone is happy.

Music: The Kingsmen, Frankie Avalon, and Annette Funicello. Songs include "Give Her Loving," "After the Party," and "How to Stuff a Wild Bikini."

Moves: Beach fun, witch-doctor dances with smoke, shrunken heads, and magic incantations.

Outfits: Navy outfits, bikinis, and the ever-popular black leather of Eric Von Zipper and his gang. Also witch-doctor masks.

Trivia: Brian Wilson has a bit part in the fourth of the American International Pictures.

I Love You Alice B. Toklas

Company: Warner Bros., 1968
Color, 93 minutes
Category: Drama/comedy
Screenplay by: Paul Mazursky and
Larry Tucker

Does anyone really know How to Stuff a Wild Bikini?

A favorite cult movie of the 1960's, Peter Sellers stars in *I Love You Alice B. Toklas.*

Directed by: Hy Averback
Produced by: Charles Maguire
Starring: Peter Sellers and Leigh Taylor-Young
Group/Singer: Harper's Bizarre

Plot: A middle-aged lawyer, Harold (Peter Sellers), is about to marry proper Joyce (Joyce Van Patten) and make his mother (Jo Van Fleet) happy. At the altar he realizes he cannot live by set patterns, and is off into the street where he meets the "flower people" or hippies. Before long he has beads, long hair, and paisley-psychedelic duds. He sells the *L.A. Free Press* on street corners and enjoys "free love" with hippie goddess Nancy (Leigh Taylor-Young). They smoke pot, party, and generally enjoy a free lifestyle. But, she sleeps around—free love is really free and he's uptight. "Isn't there anybody you don't love?" he asks. He wants his own apartment too, not a communal crash pad. He wants some peace and quiet, not non-stop Grateful Dead songs. He returns to squaredom. But when he is again poised at the altar with his conventional bride, he again bolts for the street, yelling he doesn't know where he's going this time.

Music: Harper's Bizarre sings the title tune. Grateful Dead songs are also interspersed.

Outfits: L.A. hippie outfits. Headbands, beads, pseudo-Indian, peace symbols.

Social Significance: For the first time, a film that neither extolls or abuses the hippie world.

87

Just for Fun

Company: Columbia, 1963
Black and white, 84 minutes
Category: Musical drama
Screenplay by: Milton Subotsky
Directed by: Gordon Flyming
Produced by: Milton Subotsky

Starring: Mark Winter, Cherry Roland, Richard Vernon, and Reginald Beckwith

Group/Singer: Dusty Springfield, Bobby Vee, the Crickets, Freddie Cannon, Johnny Tillotson, the Tremeloes, Brian Poole, Sounds Inc., Jimmy Saville, and Ketty Lester

Plot: A thin plot to get the music on screen. Two main political parties in England try to capture the enthusiasm of the young to no avail. The young run their own candidates on the Just for Fun party line and win. (Sounds like *Wild In the Streets*.) Anyway, this film documents what was going on just before the Beatles invasion. Not much, according to New York City teens, who rioted for their money back.

Music: Dusty Springfield (with the Springfields), in rare appearance on film, sings the title song. Brian Poole and the Tremeloes do "Twist and Shout." Bobby Vee, the Crickets, Freddie Cannon, Johnny Tillotson, Sounds Inc., Jimmy Saville, and Ketty Lester contribute uninspiring numbers in this clunker.

Moves: Pre-Beatle bopping.

Outfits: Imitation American rock-and-roll duds.

Social Significance: Now you can see why the Beatles made such a hit, with such drek (except for the Tremeloes, Springfield, and the Crickets sans Buddy Holly), around.

Trivia: Photographed by the great Nicholas Roeg, who later directed *Performance* and *The Man Who Fell to Earth*. Plus lots of foreign-to-rock goodies.

Let's Twist

Freddie Cannon shown here in a light moment with Bobby Rydell and Chubby Checker in *Just for Fun.*

Company: Paramount, 1961
Black and white, 80 minutes

Category: Musical drama/comedy

Screenplay by: Hal Hackady

Directed by: Greg Garrison

Produced by: Harry Romm

Starring: Joey Dee, Teddy Randazzo, Kay Armen, and Zohra Lampert

Group/Singer: Joey Dee and the Starlighters, Jo-Ann Campbell, and Teddy Randazzo

Plot: Papa Dinato is putting his two sons through college but Joey Dee (as himself) and Rickey (Teddy Randazzo) start a small combo and drop out. Papa has a stroke, the boys take over the family restaurant, and, with the help of widow Angie (Kay Armen),

Hey, the music's cool, so *Hey Let's Twist*.

they turn it into the Peppermint Lounge. A society dame, Sharon (Zohra Lampert), takes a shine to Joey and she gets society's teens to frequent the joint. On her advice, Joey redecorates elegantly and only allows those with pull to get in. The joint nosedives and Sharon leaves. Joey meets Piper (Jo-ann Campbell) and the place is restored to a club for the masses. It finally succeeds.

Music: Joey Dee and the Starlighters sing Twisting songs; Jo-ann and Teddy bounce out a hit or two. Songs include "Mother Goose Twist," "Let's Twist," and "I Wanna Twist."

Moves: Need we say the Twist?

Outfits: Twistable, waistbanded casual wear.

Social Significance: Really started the Twist mania worldwide. A boon to chiropractors.

Trivia: Most people agree that Joey Dee started the Twist craze with the "Peppermint Twist" song at the Peppermint Lounge though Chubby Checker personified

Twistism. Some people claim that Dee and Checker were mad at each other. Both claimed to have started the craze, and there was money to be made in being the original. However, accounts we have heard confirm that Dee and Checker never argued and were the best of friends, sharing the glory. The story was strictly movie-fan-magazine hype which both encouraged.

89

The Lively Set

Company: Universal, 1964
Color, 95 minutes
Category: Drama
Screenplay by: Mel Goldberg
Directed by: Jack Arnold
Produced by: William Alland

Starring: James Darren and Doug McClure
Band: Surfaris
Composer: Bobby Darin

Plot: After two years service in the army, Casey Owens (James Darren), a racer and builder of racing cars, goes to college where he meets Chuck Manning (Doug McClure), another car enthusiast. Casey falls in love with Eadie, (Pamela Tiffin), Chuck's sister. Realizing he is more interested in cars than anything else, Casey quits college and goes to work in his father's garage. He competes in races and becomes a celebrity in racing circles.

A young millionaire racing enthusiast, Stanford Rogers, hires Casey to build two cars for him. Scorning scientific testing on the cars, Casey wrecks one and Rogers fires him, but Casey's parents, with the help of Chuck and Eadie's parents, raise enough money to buy the car's engine from Rogers. Following scientific advise this time around, Casey builds a new car around the engine, enters and wins the Tri-State Endurance race. He pays back the money invested in the engine with his winnings. Casey marries Eadie, Chuck marries Doreen Grey, and both men enroll at Michigan Tech Center.

Music: "The Lively Set" and "Look at Me" (Randy Newmaul); "If I love You" and "Casey Wake Up" (Bobby Darin); "Boss Baracuda" (Terry Melcher).

Outfits: Racing car outfits—helmets, plastic coveralls for driving. Otherwise, extremely clean, preppy look.

Social Significance: Film propaganda that being young is just one big fun time a la Pat Boone.

Trivia: Real race cars were used in the flick.

90

Casey Owens (James Darren), Chuck Manning (Doug McClure), and Eadie Manning (Pamela Tiffin) share a happy moment outside a race track, for a change, in *The Lively Set*.

Magical Mystery Tour

Company: Apple Films, 1967
Color, 60 minutes
Category: Fantasy
Directed by: The Beatles
Produced by: The Beatles
Starring: The Beatles
Group/Singer: The Beatles
Choreographer: The Beatles

Plot: A wonderful rock-opera fantasy journey to Beatle-consciousness. The Beatles and assorted old friends take a tour of Britain by bus and in their heads. The surreal love-wonder-paranoid-ambivalent-happy-sci-fi nature of this film plus the incredibly blurry film quality made this unacceptable for years in America. Never were the Beatles more cute, more psychedelic, more elegant, and more menacing to the crewcut mind.

Music: The Beatles sing "I Am a Walrus," "Fool on the Hill," "Flying," "Blue Jay Way," the title song, and "Strawberry Fields Forever." Other acts appearing were the Bonzo Dog Band, Mal Evans, and Mike McGear (Paul's brother). George Martin the genius was music producer.

Moves: The Beatles *are* a dance. They flit about in Merlin outfits, or parade around like killer fairies.

Outfits: They dress up like the walrus, Eggman, and so on in one performance, while Bobbies parade. Military uniforms, mafioso-style hats, Nehru-collared, psychedelic paisley jackets.

91

The Beatles pose together in the surreal rock fantasy *Magical Mystery Tour.*

Social Significance: Some of the public thought the Beatles had gone mad. Mostly, the public was so for the Beatles that they could do no wrong. This film, "In Colour, Made for Tellie" when it was released on the cult-movie circuit in the U.S., started making money so you'll see it around. Don't miss it for the cute Beatles and the great soundtrack.

Trivia: Sort of a rock *Un Chien Andalou*. Dig the scene where the Beatles, resplendent in white tuxes, descend the stairs in a huge musical-type number that's sort of Busby Berkeley. The number where the fat lady eats shovelfuls of food is like the (much later) Monty Python scene in *Monty Python's The Meaning of Life*. The Capitol album contains a nice booklet of color stills.

Midnight Cowboy

92

Company: United Artists, 1969
Color, 113 minutes
Category: Drama with music
Screenplay by: Waldo Salt
Directed by: John Schlessinger
Produced by: Jerome Hellman
Starring: Dustin Hoffman and Jon Voight

Plot: Dissatisfied with his nowhere life as a dishwasher in a small Texas town, Joe Buck (Jon Voight) gets himself a flashy cowboy suit and jumps on a bus to New York City, sure that his fortune will be made by selling his handsome face and body to rich, lonely, sex-starved Manhattan women. On the bus he flashes back to his unhappy childhood—his father abandoning his mother, the stream of men who visited his grandmother Sally, and the sexual experiences during his teens,

including a gang rape of Joe and his girlfriend Annie. Joe arrives in New York and checks into a cheap hotel. He hits the streets and picks up Cass, a rich, coarse woman. Though they have sex, Joe not only doesn't make any money but has to give her a twenty for cab fare. A super hustler he is not. At a rundown bar Joe meets Ratso Rizzo (Dustin Hoffman), a tubercular, half-crippled, low-level con man and thief who volunteers to be his manager. They share a common situation and somehow are drawn to one another. At first Ratso tries to rip off Joe, but soon offers to let him stay at his room in a condemned building. Almost in spite of themselves and their armor, their experiences lead to a genuine friendship. Ratso tells Joe his fantasies of someday living a life of luxury in Miami Beach. Things pick up a little when Joe meets Shirley, a swinger at an underground party in Greenwich Village, and earns $20 for spending a wild night with her. But winter takes its toll on Ratso and he gets sicker and sicker until he no longer is able to walk. Determined to get his pal to Florida, Joe beats up an old homosexual in a hotel room and steals his cash. He manages to get Ratso on the bus but the poor man dies just as they reach Miami. Joe puts his arm around the dead body of the only real friend he's ever had.

Music: "Everybody's Talking" (Harry Nilsson); "A Famous Myth," "Tears and Joys" (The Groop); "He Quit Me" (Lesley Miller); "Crossroads of the Stepping Stones" (Elephant's Memory); "Jungle Jim at the Zoo," and "Old Man Willow" (Elephant's Memory).

Moves: Wild glitter-doll dancing at an underground party in Manhattan.

Outfits: Cowboy stud and down-and-out.

Social Significance: Huge success with audiences around the country who appreciated its superb writing and acting and realistic action. The use of rock music was exceptional, adding much to the story line.

Trivia: The party filmed in the Village was actually stocked with real characters of the time, largely from the Andy Warhol crew: Viva, Ultra Violet, Taylor Mead, Paul Morrissey, and others.

Monterey Pop

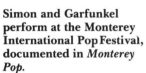

Company: Foundation-Leacock
Pennebaker, 1969
Color, 88 minutes
Category: Rockumentary

Directed by: D.A. Pennebaker
Produced by: D.A. Pennebaker
Group/Singer: Janis Joplin with Big Brother and the Holding Company, Jefferson Airplane, the Mamas and the Papas, the Animals, the Who, Country Joe and the Fish, and others

Plot: This film account of the great, seminal Monterey International Pop Festival is notable in three ways. One, it marked the appearance of the inimitable Janis Joplin in a film for the mass listening audience; two, it recorded the historical mood of the performers and the period comes out; three, it was a benchmark for all future concert

Simon and Garfunkel perform at the Monterey International Pop Festival, documented in *Monterey Pop.*

films and showed how much money they could expect to make. Praised by critics, this cinema verité film did much to cast the die for the next decade's rock development. The festival actually lasted 72 hours in June 1967. One of the most organic-orgiasmic rock songs ever, "Wild Thing" (also done by many other groups), is performed by Jimi Hendrix. He even literally sets fire to the guitar during the performance. Ultimate psychedelic white rock by a black performer. No message except "smile, you're the new generation."

Music: Janis does "Ball and Chain" and "Combination;" "California Dreamin' " is done by the Mamas and the Papas; Otis Redding sings "I've Been Lovin' You Too Long;" the Animals sing "Paint it Black;" the Who sing "My Generation." Other performers include Hugh Masekela, Canned Heat, and Scott McKenzie.

Outfits: Really, really hippie; cool, surreal, naked, wild, real. Also practical stuff like camping gear.

Social Significance: Acid was catching on, flower power was turning into fire-power, but still had a few buds, the hippies had completely displaced the squares and the beat by now. This film documents a fast lived time in America, when it was young and possible again, when people tried to get out of the money bag and partly succeeded.

Trivia: Not so trivially, D.A. Pennebaker also made Dylan's great *Don't Look Back* film.

94

Mrs. Brown, You've Got A Lovely Daughter

Company: MGM, 1968
Color, 95 minutes
Category: Musical comedy
Screenplay by: Thaddeus Vane
Directed by: Saul Swimmer
Produced by: Allen V. Kline

Jimi Hendrix was perhaps the greatest "natural" guitarist ever. The guitar was part of his being and he was part of *Monterey Pop.*

Herman's Hermits' hit song *Mrs. Brown You've Got a Lovely Daughter*, made them international singing stars.

Starring: Herman's Hermits—Peter Noone, Karl Green, Keith Hopwood, Barry Whitwam, and Derek Leckenby
Group: Herman's Hermits
Musical Supervisor: Mickie Most

Plot: Herman (Peter Noone) inherits a greyhound racing dog named Mrs. Brown and his band, the Hermits, all decide to race the dog and get rich. The dog wins the Manchester race and the National Derby. Now Herman meets wealthy Judy Brown (Sarah Caldwall). Herman wants to keep seeing her, but comedic situations erupt wildly. Judy is difficult to pin down but she has something he just can't put his finger on.

The whole movie is a vehicle for the Hermits to sing their British hearts out in this British-Invasion era film. The songs are good. Judy's mom is played well by Mona Washbourne.
Music: Herman's Hermits sing the title song plus "There's a Kind of Hush," "I'm Into Something Good," "A Must to Avoid," "Daisy Chain," "Lemon and Lime," "The World Is for the Young," and "Holiday Inn."
Moves: Wiggles, hippy-shakes, hair-do woggles.
Outfits: British Carnaby Street look.
Social Significance: Herman's Hermits were one of the better Beatle-clone acts. Had a style and method of their own.

Muscle Beach Party

Company: American International Pictures, 1964
Color, 94 minutes

Category: Comedy
Screenplay by: Robert Dillon
Directed by: William Asher
Produced by: James H. Nicholson and Robert Dillon
Starring: Frankie Avalon and Annette Funicello
Band: Dick Dale and the Deltones

Plot: Surfers Frankie, Dee Dee (Annette Funicello), and pals feel nervous when muscleman Flex Martian and his friends from Jack Fanny's gym invade their part of the beach. Meanwhile, on a yacht offshore, rich contessa Julie arranges for her business manager S.Z. Watts to get her Flex for the latest of her long string of boyfriends. Julie is happy with Flex until she meets Frankie. He responds to her love, angering Dee Dee, the surfers, and the musclemen. S.Z. tells Frankie about Julie's numerous and disastrous past affairs, and he breaks up with her and goes back to Dee Dee. The surfers and the musclemen battle until the fight is stopped by Mr. Strangdour, who convinces Flex to work on his muscles and forget Julie. Julie gets S.Z. Watts, Dee Dee gets Frankie.
Music: Frankie and Annette both sing such songs as "Beach Party," "Running Wild," "Muscle Bustle," "My First Love," "Surfin' Woodie," "Surfer's Holiday," "Happy Street," and "A Girl Needs a Boy."
Moves: Beach wiggling and more frenetic shimmying by Candy Johnson, who bumps and grinds her way into every teenage male's heart. Lots of musclemen shine their bulk and flex their biceps to the big beat.
Outfits: Bathing suits by Marjorie Corso, suntan oil, and muscle.
Social Significance: Another film directed right at the teen market, giving youth another role model—happy-go-lucky surfing rocker.
Trivia: Film also features cameos by Buddy Hackett and Morey Amsterdam. Second of the very successful American International Pictures beach party movies. Some good shots of real surfing.

Annette puts an appreciative hand on Frankie's
bicep—not too bad but you should see the muscle guys.

97

Pajama Party

Company: American International
Pictures, 1964
Color, 85 minutes
Category: Sci-fi/musical comedy
Screenplay by: Louis Heyward
Directed by: Don Weis

Produced by: James H. Nicholson and
Samuel Z. Arkoff
Starring: Tommy Kirk, Annette
Funicello, and Buster Keaton
Band: Nooney Rickett Four
Choreographer: David Winters
Composer: Les Baxter

Plot: Mars decides to invade Earth and Go-
Go (Tommy Kirk) is the advance scout sent
down to pave the way. He lands in Aunt
Wendy's (Elsa Lanchester) garden and

98

**It may supposedly be a Pajama
Party, but the kids still manage to
have fun on the beach.**

meets Big Lunk, her musclebound nephew, and his friend Connie (Annette Funicello). Aunt Wendy, a strange bird who owns a dress shop, is rumored to be hiding a small fortune in her house. She is the object of a robbery plan by hoods J. Sinister Hulk and Fleegle. There are also problems with motorcycle gang leader Eric Von Zipper (Harvey Lembeck) who is jealous of Big Lunk's affections for Connie. Helped by Chief Rotten Eagle (Buster Keaton) and Helga, a sexy Swede sent to get information from Big Lunk about the hidden money, the con men crash a pajama party given by Aunt Wendy for the teens. Go-Go saves the day by teleporting the would-be thieves to Mars. Von Zipper and the bike gang are also taken care of. Go-Go persuades Mars to call off the invasion and decides to stay on Earth because he has fallen in love with Connie. Big Lunk wins Helga's love even though she does not understand English.

Music: Songs include "It's that Kind of Day," "There Has to be a Reason," "Where Did I Go Wrong?," "Pajama Party," "Beach Ball," "Among the Young," and "Stuffed Animal." Composed by Les Baxter.

Moves: More of that teen sand jerking and oh that Candy Johnson, renowned for her hip snapping moves from the other beach pictures. Men go mad when they see her dance. Choreography by David Winters.

Outfits: Bathing suits, pajamas, spacesuits.

Trivia: One of the few early sci/fi musicals.

Palm Springs Weekend

Company: American International
Pictures, 1964
Color, 82 minutes

Category: Musical comedy
Screenplay by:
Directed by: Norman Taurog
Produced by: Michael A. Hosy
Starring: Troy Donahue and Connie Stevens
Music Composed by: Frank Perkins

Plot: Every Easter, Palm Springs in California is inundated by teens searching for fun and adventure, often to the distress of Police Chief Dixon and his wife Cora. On a bus headed for the famous vacation resort is a college basketball team and its captain, medical student Jim Munroe (Troy Donahue), and Coach Campbell. On the same bus is Gail Lewis (Connie Stevens), a senior at Hollywood High School who pretends to be a wealthy college girl. The bus breaks down and Gail gets a ride to the resort with playboy Eric Dean, the spoiled son of a millionaire. On the way they run into Stretch Fortune, a Hollywood stuntman from Texas to whom Gail becomes attracted. In Palm Springs Jim meets Chief Dixon's daughter Bunny, who works in a local record store. He takes her to a party which is invaded by young hoods. After a fight that ends up at the police station, everyone is let go with a warning, but Chief Dixon forbids Jim from seeing his daughter again. In the meantime, Eric tries to force his attentions on Gail, but she is rescued by Stretch who teaches Eric a lesson. Stretch is chased by the enraged Eric who sideswipes Stretch's car, causing it to overturn. Jim, who has been trailing them, pulls Stretch from the burning crash. Gail visits Stretch at the hospital and confesses that she is only a high school student and he forgives her. As the students leave Palm Springs, Bunny promises to wait for Jim until he finishes medical school. Even Chief Dixon loosens up enough to say they can all come back next Easter.

Music: "Live Young" and "Palm Springs Weekend" were all sung by Donahue.

99

Outfits: Early teen, upper-class clothes. Pre-Beatle, pre-drugs, pre-pulsing rock and roll. What did they used to do in those days?

Social Significance: One of Troy Donahue's earliest vehicles, which made him one of the most popular of the teen idols.

Produced by: Hal Wallis

Starring: Elvis Presley, Suzanna Leigh, James Shigeta, and Donna Butterworth

Group/Singer: Elvis, the Jordainaires, and Donna Butterworth

Choreographer: Jack Regas

Paradise, Hawaiian Style

Company: Paramount, 1966
Color, 91 minutes

Category: Drama/musical

Screenplay by: Allan Weiss and Anthony Lawrence

Directed by: Michael Moore

Plot: Unemployed pilot Rick (Elvis Presley) returns to Hawaii and with his friend Danny Kohana (James Shigeta) he starts a charter helicopter service. He hires secretary Judy Hudson (Suzanna Leigh), an aloof woman who intrigues him. Other girlfriends working in hotels send business Elvis's way. He is grounded, though, when he was forced to ditch a chopper near an FAA man's car. He then manages to rescue Danny who went down in the jungle. Later, at a big party, all his girlfriends meet one another and they

100

Elvis comes along shore in a flower-decked Polynesian craft in *Paradise, Hawaiian Style*.

gang up on Rick. He escapes to the arms of Judy and even wins his FAA license back.

Music: Presley sings "Sand Castles," "House of Sand," and other sandy numbers such as "Datin'," a duet with Donna Butterworth. "You Scratch My Back," "This is My Heaven," "It's a Dog's Life," "Drums of the Islands" and the title song are sung by Elvis. "Bill Bailey Won't You Please Come Home" is sung by Butterworth.

Outfits: Island stuff: South-sea ritual costumes, open shirts of bright colors, grass skirts, nice-girl outfits, and bikinis.

Social Significance: Elvis made a lot of money going Hawaiian.

Trivia: Lani, played by Marianna Hill, looks lush too. Donna is one of our favorite Elvis co-stars. Wallis first brought Presley to Hawaii for *Blue Hawaii* in 1961.

Petulia

Company: Warner Bros.-Seven Arts, 1968
Color, 105 minutes
Category: Drama with music
Screenplay by: Lawrence B. Marcus
Directed by: Richard Lester
Produced by: Don Devlin and Raymond Wagner

Petulia (Julie Christie) wants to have an affair with Archie (George C. Scott) but returns to her husband anyway.

101

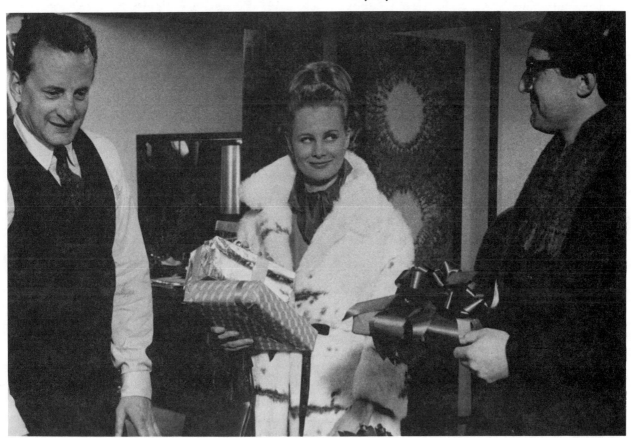

Starring: Richard Chamberlain, Julie Christie, and George C. Scott
Group/Singer: The Grateful Dead and Janis Joplin and Big Brother and the Holding Company
Non-rock Score: John Barry

Plot: Newlywed, Petulia (Julie Christie), disillusioned and half-buggy, attends a San Francisco charity bash where she tries to seduce Archie (George C. Scott). Her bored society husband (Richard Chamberlain) beats her up and has her hospitalized. She decides her husband needs her and she's off to South America with him, intent on becoming pregnant. A year later Archie visits her in the maternity ward. As she is wheeled into the delivery room, she promises to run away with Archie who now loves her. But he never gets around to making the arrangements.
Music: Janis Joplin is great, in a brief appearance, and sings "Take It (Another Little Piece of My Heart)." Jerry Garcia stands out in several Grateful Dead numbers.
Outfits: Hippie for the musicians, standard sixties for the rest.

Privilege

Company: United International, 1967
Color, 101 minutes
Category: Musical fantasy
Screenplay by: Norman Bagner and Peter Watkins
Directed by: Peter Watkins
Produced by: John Heyman

Starring: Paul Jones and Jean Shrimpton
Singer: Paul Jones
Composer: Mike Leander

Plot: The most famous figure in England in the 1970s is pop singer Steven Shorter (Paul Jones). Every one of his performances is attended by thousands of adoring teenagers who release their feelings of anger and rebellion by madly cheering his stage shows where he is chained, beaten, and locked in a cage by sadistic police officers. Realizing the potential of being able to control and channel the emotions of the young, a coalition government of State and Church forces Shorter to change his image from an inspirer of rebellion to leader of a new evangelical crusade. Although he hates his new identity, he is too deeply involved to break with the Establishment. His only chance of salvation comes from Vanessa Ritchie (Jean Shrimpton), a young eccentric artist who has been commissioned to paint him. As she sees his daily life and the way he is coldly manipulated, she realizes that beneath the image is a lost man. She grows close to him and urges him to destroy his manufactured self in public. After a mock demonstration in which he apparently heals the sick, Shorter is ordered to attend a banquet to receive an award. Once there, he screams out in defiance against the system and the public that created him. The outburst is greeted with stunned horror as he is denounced by the State, the Church, and the conformist audience.
Music: Paul Jones sings "Free Me," "Onward, Christian Soldiers," "Bad, Bad Boy," among others.
Moves: Slow Elizabethan-type church-like dances and processions.
Outfits: Very romantic—flowing gowns, dresses, the pageboy look. The fashions of the film are a precursor to the neo-romantic resurgence in the early 1980s.
Social Significance: Interesting prophetic film of the power of the pop star to

manipulate and diffuse genuine, critical, and revolutionary energies of the young. One can see the process in motion today with present day mega-stars having a tremendous influence on the thought and style, not to mention the outright selling of products over television. "Hi, my name's Bob Dylan and I drink Manichevitz."

Vanessa Ritchie (Jean Shrimpton) contemplates the speech that pop idol turned evangelist Steven Shorter is about to give in *Privilege*.

Psych-out

Company: American International Pictures, 1968
Color, 101 minutes
Category: Drama
Screenplay by: E. Hunter Willett and Betty Ulius
Directed by: Richard Rush
Produced by: Dick Clark
Starring: Jack Nicholson, Susan Strasberg, Dean Stockwell, and Bruce Dern
Group/Singer: The Strawberry Alarm Clock, the Seeds, Boenzee Cryque, and Storybook

Plot: This movie of freaked-out hippie land, is exploitative of its theme, yet sensitive, realistic, and wild. Jennie (Susan Strasberg) is a 17-year-old deaf runaway to Haight-Ashbury, in San Francisco. She's looking for her lost brother, a sculptor. She teams up with Stoney, Ben, and Elwood (Jack Nicholson, Adam Roarke, and Max Julien), and she exchanges her square duds for psychedelic wear. Jenny searches through the teeming hippie coffee shops, head parlors, crash-pads (temporary housing), and other in places. Stoney finally gets Steve (Bruce Dern), her lost brother, out of hiding. Thugs want him and Steve is forced to flee them. Dave turns on Jenny to STP and we experience the "trip." Steve barricades himself in a house and sets it on fire. Dave is killed by cars while stoned, as he saves Jenny from same fate. Jennie and Stoney walk away to a new tomorrow.
Music: Strawberry Alarm Clock sings "Rainy Day Mushroom Pillow" and "The World's on Fire;" the Storybook sing "The Pretty Song," "Psych-Out Sanitorium,"

103

"Beads of Innocence," "The Love Children," and "Psych-Out." Seeds do "Two Fingers Pointing on You;" and "Ashbury Wednesday" is sung by Boenzee Cryque.

Outfits: Lots of beads and spangles, tie-dyed things. Headbands, prismatic jewelry, paisley pads, long hair on guys, Madras shirts, Nehru jackets, Indian bedspreads, and so on.

Social Significance: This period of American life is so baroque, it's good someone has gotten a fairly accurate representation of it on film during the rare era. Nobody would believe this was real stuff nowadays.

Trivia: Dick Clark meets Jack Nicholson.

Revolution

Company: Lopert Pictures, 1968
Color, 87 minutes
Category: Rockumentary
Screenplay by: Jack O'Connell
Directed by: Jack O'Connell
Produced by: Jack O'Connell

The fun never stops in Psych-out.

104

Starring: Today Malone, Herb Caen, Lou Gottleib, and Ronnie Davis
Group/Singer: Tracy Nelson and Mother Earth, Country Joe and the Fish, Quicksilver Messenger Service, and others
Choreography by: Ann Halprin

Plot: This rockumentary concerns itself with the once flourishing hippie community in San Francisco's Haight-Ashbury section. This bit of nostalgia is a good insight into a lost lifestyle.

Today Malone (her real name) is a pretty thing who's left her middle-class life to become a hippie. Why not? Among the many fun things they do are "be-ins" in the park, dancing to "acid" rock under a psychedelic light show, Indian religious services, acid, and so on. In the Golden Gate Park there's a discussion about "guerrilla" street theatre. The positive attitudes of hippies (as opposed to "straight" America) are emphasized. Juxtaposed are clips of psychiatrists warning against aberrant behavior, doctors who caution against drugs, and criminologists who note that social problems cause hippies.

Music: "Revolution" (Mother Earth); "Mercury Blues" (the Steve Miller Band); "Revolution" (repeated by Kenny Karen and the Family Album); "Co' Dine" (Quicksilver Messenger Service).

Moves: Lots of naked flower-power girls dancing under strobe lights.

Outfits: Beads, Indian stuff, paisley, long hair. Long earrings, bare asses, bouncing boobs.

Social Significance: A solid film that doesn't portray hippies as evil incarnate. Worthy of another look.

105

The Hippie community of Haight-Ashbury started a musical *Revolution*.

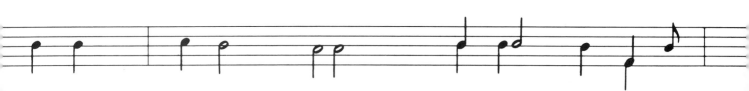

Ride the Wild Surf

Company: Columbia, 1964
            Color, 101 minutes
Category: Drama
Screenplay by: Jo and Art Napoleon
Directed by: Don Taylor
Produced by: Jo and Art Napoleon
Starring: Tab Hunter and Fabian
Band: Jan and Dean and Fabian

Plot: A competition to ride the world's largest waves is held at Oahu Island in Hawaii. Surfers Steamer Lane (Tab Hunter), Jody Wallis (Fabian), and Chase Colton (Peter Brown) come to compete. Steamer falls for Lily Kilua whose mom is against the romance as she thinks surfers are "beach bums." Jody, meanwhile, falls in love with Brie Matthews (Shelley Fabares) who makes him believe he can be more than a surf bum if he really tries. The stuffy Chase falls for out-going Augie Poole (Barbara Eden) who helps him learn to enjoy life.

To fulfill a Hawaiian myth for bringing the giant waves in, Chase takes a perilous 80-foot dive into a small rocky pool. The big waves roll in and the contest starts. Chase almost drowns but Jody saves him. Steamer drops out when his surfboard breaks but he's consoled by being able to marry Lily with mom's consent. Only Jody and a surfer named Eskimo are left, the previous champion. Eskimo finally pulls out and Jody rides a 40-foot wave in for the championship and a waiting Brie.

Music: "Ride the Wild Surf" by Jan and Dean, and other background rock songs.
Moves: Twisting on surfboards.
Outfits: Beach wear by SunFashions of Hawaii—swimsuits, flowered shirts, flesh.
Social Significance: Made a generation want to be surfers with its thrilling surfing scenes.
Trivia: Actual footage from the "World Series of Surfing" was used.

106

Brie Matthews (Shelley Fabares) believes that Jody Wallis (Fabian) could be more than a surf bum if he tried in *Ride the Wild Surf*.

Roustabout

Company: Paramount, 1964
Color, 101 minutes
Category: Drama/musical
Screenplay by: Anthony Lawrence and
Allan Weiss
Directed by: John Rich
Produced by: Hal Wallis
Starring: Elvis Presley, Barbara
Stanwyck, and Joan Freeman
Group/Singer: Elvis Presley and the
Jordanaires
Choreography by: Earl Barton
Music Composed by: Joseph J. Lilley

Plot: Charlie Rogers (Elvis Presley) is an embittered orphan who is a small-time singer. He crashes his motorcycle with a jeep driven by Joe Lean (Leif Erickson) and carrying Joe's daughter Cathy (Joan Freeman) and Maggie Morgan (Barbara Stanwyck). Joe had run Charlie off the highway because Charlie was making remarks to his daughter. This has ruined both the guitar and motorcycle. Maggie cools things by saying she'll have the cycle fixed. She asks Charlie to work with Cathy at her carnival, seeing he's at loose ends. He gets his guitar back and he's happy now to be working near Cathy. The singing is so successful the carnival is brought back from virtual bankruptcy. Charlie is wooed away by promoter Harry Carver (Pat Buttram) but, pursued by Cathy, he returns to again save the carnival, patching things up with Maggie and Cathy.

Music: Elvis Presley sings "Little Egypt," "Poison Ivy League," "One Track Heart," "Carny Town," "Roustabout," "Wheels on My Heels," and "It's a Wonderful World."

Outfits: Carny corny. Colorful, though. In the "Little Egypt" number, cuties of the Nile do a suggestive burlesque.

Trivia: A coup: Barbara Stanwyck in an Elvis movie. At the end Presley says, "Git closah, ah give awff body heat . . . ."

107

Elvis charms them again.

Ski Party

Company: American International
Pictures, 1965
Color, 90 minutes
Category: Musical comedy
Screenplay by: Robert Kaufman
Directed by: Alan Rafkin
Produced by: Gene Corman
Starring: Frankie Avalon, Dwayne
Hickman, and Deborah Walley
Band: Lesley Gore, James Brown, and
more
Composer: Gary Usher

Plot: At a Los Angeles college, cute athletes
Todd Armstrong and Craig Gamble are after
coeds Linda Hughes and Barbara Norris.
The girls, however, like stuffy, intellectual
Freddie Carter. When the whole gang goes
on a skiing holiday at a Sun Valley resort
run by social director Donald Pevney, Todd
and Craig disguise themselves as females
and flirt with Freddie to find out why the
girls find him so sexy and irresistible.
Masquerading as Jane and Nora, the two
join the ladies' ski instruction lesson where
Freddie takes note of the two newcomers.
Freddie goes after Craig disguised as Nora
and chases the whole crew through Sawtooth
National Forest and back to the heated pools
of Los Angeles. Once back at home, the
coeds realize the joke Craig and Todd have
played on Freddie. No longer susceptible to
Freddie's flirtations, the girls give their
hearts to Todd and Craig, where they
belong.
Music: Frankie, the Hondells, James Brown
and the Flames, Leslie Gore. Songs include
"Ski Party," "Lots, Lots More," "Paintin'
the Town," "We'll Never Change Them."
Moves: Ski lodge spectaculars, and lots of
ski antics to music: jumping, hot-dogging,
crashing.
Outfits: Ski gear, colorful sweaters (filled
out nicely, thank you), ski boots, goggles,
parkas.

108

**Stuffy intellectual Freddie Carter
attracts all the girls in *Ski Party*.**

Social Significance: Got the white kids of America to see and hear the king of rhythm and blues—the great James Brown.

Trivia: American International Pictures' attempt to duplicate the success of the beach pics on the ski slopes. It somehow didn't work out the same way, too much flesh covered up.

Spinout

Company: MGM, 1966
Color, 93 minutes
Category: Comedy/musical
Screenplay by: Theodore J. Flicker
Directed by: Normal Taurog
Produced by: Joe Pasternak
Starring: Elvis Presley, Shelley Fabares, Dianne McBain, and Deborah Walley
Group/Singer: Elvis Presley and the Jordanaires

Plot: Singer Mike McCoy (Elvis) is leader of a small combo (as they used to be called). He tours the country, barely making a living. He gets to see lots of women in his travels, and he's not interested in a serious relationship. In Santa Barbara, California, he dates three women all after marriage: Les (Deborah Walley), the drummer of his combo, Cynthia (Shelley Fabares), a rich daughter of a car manufacturer, and Diana (Dianne McBain), a writer who has selected Mike as the ideal male for a new book.

Mike is challenged to a race in Santa Fe by Cynthia's overbearing dad and Mike wins it with his own sports car. At the victory party he finds all the girls have new interests: Les, who he considered a tomboy, has a crush on a cop; Cynthia will marry her father's assistant; and so on. But then comes Mike's new drummer Susan (Dodie Marshall). Ah.

Music: Elvis sings "Spinout," "All that I Am," "Beach Shack," "Adam and Evil," "Smorgasbord," "Stop, Look, and Listen," "I'll be Back," and "Never Say Yes."

Moves: He twitches a bit here, but the shaking pelvis moves seem to be forgotten.

Outfits: Elvis is in casual California wear: white sportscoat and open collar. Deborah Walley dresses a bit like a guy, but those curves . . . .

Social Significance: Elvis was 31 when this film was made and is beginning to look porky. This is his 22nd flick in the ten years after *Love Me Tender*.

Elvis keeps them rockin' in *Spinout*.

109

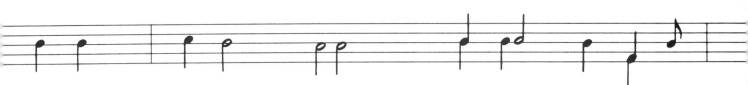

State Fair

Company: 20th Century Fox, 1962
Color, 118 minutes
Category: Musical
Screenplay by: Richard Breen
Directed by: Jose Ferrer
Produced by: Charles Brackett
Starring: Pat Boone, Bobby Darin,
Pamela Tiffin and Tom Ewell
Chorus: Nick Castle
Composer: Richard Rodgers and Oscar
Hammerstein II

Plot: The Frake family arrives at the annual Texas State Fair. Abel is entering his prize hog, Blue Boy, in the grand championship, Melissa hopes to win the mincemeat competition, young Wayne is planning to enter the sports car race, and 17-year old Margie (Pamela Tiffin) dreams of love and excitement. Almost instantly Wayne falls for Emily Porter, a sexy showgirl, and Margie falls for Jerry Dundee, a cocky TV interviewer. Although Blue Boy wins and Melissa's spiked mincemeat creates a sensation when the judge gets drunk, the younger Frakes have problems. Wayne allows someone else to win the race and Emily, positive the Frakes will think she's a tramp, walks out on him. Margie is devastated when Jerry splits. Once back on family farm, however, Wayne quickly forgets his big romance and runs off to see his old girlfriend. Later, Margie is ecstatic when Jerry telephones, and asks to marry her.

Music: "It Might as Well be Spring," "Our State Fair," "It's a Grand Night for Singing," "That's for Me," "Isn't It Kind of Fun," "It's the Little Things in Texas," "More Than Just a Friend," "Willing and Able," "Never Say No," and "This Isn't Heaven."

Moves: Gala, spirited number around the state fair.

Outfits: Rural hip, white shirt opened at collar, loose pants, thin belts.

Social Significance: Welcome to Pat Boone's America.

Trivia: Alice Faye's first film in 17 years. *State Fair* was previously filmed in 1933 and 1945.

110

Wayne Frake (Pat Boone) gives his sister Margie (Pamela Tiffin) money so she could go off and he could meet Emily in *State Fair*.

The T.A.M.I. Show

Starring: The Supremes, Chuck Berry, the Beach Boys, Marvin Gaye, James Brown, the Rolling Stones, and many others

Company: American International Pictures, 1964
Black and white, 100 minutes
Category: Taped concert
Directed by: Steve Binder
Produced by: Lee Savin; executive producer: Bill Sargent

Plot: A rock concert taped at the Santa Monica (California) Civic Auditorium on October 29, 1964 for T.A.M.I., or the Teenage Awards Music International. One of the best and historically the first rock concert film. Here the big rock acts of the time were given a chance to just get up and do their thing. There is a primitive feeling to

111

The Beach Boys, some believe, are America's favorite group, even after the Beatles.

the goings-on with grainy film and straight ahead rocking. The show looks a lot like a TV special complete with plastic looking modern decor and go-go dancers wildly pumping away on scaffolding.

Music: "Where Did Our Love Go?" and "Baby Love" (the Supremes); "Around and Around" and "Off the Hook" (the Rolling Stones); "Please, Please Me" (James Brown); "Maybe I Know" and "It's My Party" (Lesley Gore); "Johnny B. Goode" (Chuck Berry); "Can I get a Witness" (Marvin Gaye); "Little Old Lady from Pasadena" (Beach Boys); "Mickey's Monkey" (Smokey Robinson and the Miracles). Other performers were Gerry and the Pacemakers, Billy J. Kramer and the Dakotas, Jan and Dean, and the Barbarians.

Moves: Bands and singers do their moves the way they were meant to be done, and can't be done anymore. Backed up by different costumed watusi dancers wildly frugging on platforms that adds a fun, surreal quality to this great show.

Outfits: Mod, colorful clothes that are just now starting to come back again.

Social Significance: One of the best (some say the best) of all rock concert films. The people who got together during these few hours at the T.A.M.I. Show may well have been the best single group of rock musicians ever to assemble.

Trivia: Still shown as an underground cult hit and now available on video cassette.

Tammy and the Doctor

Company: Universal International, 1963
Color, 88 minutes
Category: Drama with music
Screenplay by: Oscar Brodney
Directed by: Harry Keller

112

The unbelievably young looking Rolling Stones appear in the 1965 extravaganza *The T.A.M.I. Show.*

Produced by: Ross Hunter
Starring: Sandra Dee, Peter Fonda,
MacDonald Carey, Beulah
Bondi, and Margaret Lindsay
Singer: Sandra Dee
Music by: Frank Skinner
Plot: Wealthy Mrs. Call (Beulah Bofdi)
needs a serious operation. Tammy, a country
girl from the deep South (Sandra Dee),
accompanies her to the hospital where there
are lots of attractive young doctors around.
Tammy becomes an assistant on the nursing
staff. She's confused but kindly Miss Coleman
(Margaret Lindsay) helps her. Dr. Mark

Cheswick (Peter Fonda) is Tammy's
heartthrob, but he must desist or ruin his
career. The only way that he and Tammy
can get together is to get his superior, Dr.
Bentley (MacDonald Carey), hitched up
himself. Tammy succeeds in pairing Dr.
Bentley off with Miss Coleman and can now
be with Mark.
Music: Sandra Dee sings "Tammy,"
composed by Jay Livingston and Ray Evans
Outfits: Nursing white, doctor bright.
Social Significance: More money for
Sandra, teen idoless.
Trivia: Who played Tammy in *Tammy and
the Millionaire?* Answer: Debbie Watson.
Peter Fonda's first movie!

Tammy (Sandra Dee) works as an assistant on the
nurses' staff before finding love in *Tammy and the
Doctor.*

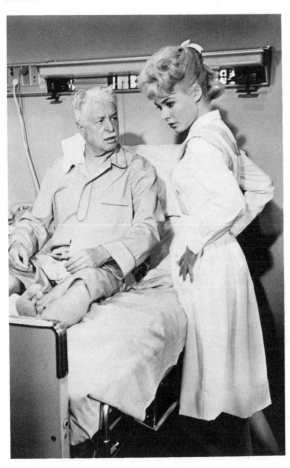

Tammy Tell Me True

113

Company: United International, 1961
Color, 97 minutes
Category: Romance comedy with music
Screenplay by: Oscar Brodney
Directed by: Harry Keller
Produced by: Ross Hunter
Starring: Sandra Dee and John Gavin
Composer: Joseph Gershenson

Plot: Unhappy because her boyfriend
doesn't answer her letters, Tammy (Sandra
Dee), who lives on a houseboat, decides to
attend college herself. Moving her
dilapidated craft down the river to Seminola
College, she is admitted as a special student.
To pay her tuition she gets a job as a
companion to a wealthy eccentric. Tammy's
innocent and bubbly nature so enthuses

Mrs. Call that she moves in with Tammy on her houseboat and gives the young girl an expensive necklace. Meanwhile, Tom Freeman, the handsome speech teacher, has fallen for Tammy. Mrs. Call's conniving niece Suzanne Rook has launched a search for her missing aunt when she sees the necklace around Tammy's neck. She has Tammy arrested and sets up a sanity hearing for her aunt. But the direct honesty of Tammy's testimony so impresses the judge that he dismisses Suzanne's charges and frees Tammy. Tammy realizes that she no longer cares for her old boyfriend and that it is Tom whom she really loves.

Outfits: Late 1950s teens, baggy dresses, funny hats. Strange time.

Social Significance: The Tammy series affected millions of young teens. The girls wanted to be Tammy and the boys fell in love with her.

Trivia: Second in the highly successful Tammy series. Sequel to *Tammy and the Bachelor* (1957). Later films were *Tammy and the Doctor* (1963) and *Tammy and the Millionaire* (1967).

To Sir with Love

Company: Columbia, 1967
Color, 105 minutes
Category: Drama
Screenplay by: James Clavell
Directed by: James Clavell

114

Tammy's in a kissing mood in *Tammy Tell Me True*.

Produced by: James Clavell
Starring: Sidney Poitier, Suzy Kendall, Lulu, and Judy Geeson
Group/Singer: Lulu

Plot: Thackerey (Sidney Poitier) is a teacher in a troubled East End (London) school. The kids curse, smoke in class, have no manners, and take no care in their appearance. They eventually learn to call him sir when he is recognized as one of them and someone desperately trying to reach out to them. The rest of the faculty seem to represent latent racism and fanaticism, as well as hopelessness in their ranks. Thackerey will not be daunted; he has his own way. These children with dim prospects for employment or happiness are guided by Sir to graduation. The deputy head of the school, Mrs. Evans (Faith Brooks) helps Sir in this unenviable task, as does Gillian (Suzy Kendall), a fellow teacher. At a dance at the end of the term, the students thank him. They hand him a package beautifully gift wrapped. The card with it says, "To Sir, With Love" and the signatures of all the students are on it!

Music: The great title song is sung by Lulu. A hit internationally, it was an example of a successful ballad that made it in the rocking sixties.

Moves: A bit of english rocking.

Outfits: These kids are gawky, awkward, and the girls tend to do frumpy things with their clothing and hair till Sir gets there.

Social Significance: Inspiring.

Trivia: Poitier directed *Stir Crazy*, a wild Richard Pryor-Gene Wilder comedy vehicle in 1980. But he'll always be remembered for the role of Sir.

Sir can start with the basics and work up if he has to in order to save the slum kids in *To Sir with Love*.

115

The Trip

Company: American International
Pictures, 1967
Color, 85 minutes
Category: Drama with music
Screenplay by: Jack Nicholson
Directed by: Roger Corman
Produced by: Roger Corman
Starring: Peter Fonda, Susan Strasberg,
Bruce Dern, Dennis Hopper,
and Salli Sachse

116

Plot: The film follows the trials and tribulations of Paul Groves (Peter Fonda), a decent, clean-cut man in the middle of deep personal problems. He and his wife Sally (Susan Strasberg) have recently broken up, and the pressures of his job as a TV commercial director have driven him to his wits' end. He seeks help from his friend John (Bruce Dern), a guru who uses LSD to achieve peace and self understanding. He meets Glenn (Salli Sachse), a beautiful girl who is very attracted to him. Paul takes some acid at John's house and has a wild trip. At first it starts out good with an explosion of colors, a kaleidoscope of swirling shapes that the movie viewer is invited to get dizzy on. But the fun soon turns to horror as the trip gets weirder. He begins to experience all his sexual guilt and anxiety which comes out in images before him—a medieval world with writhing, moaning woman and torturers. He runs away from the house and ends up with Glenn with whom he spends the night. He wakes up the next morning apparently all right. In fact, he feels reborn—ready to change his whole life for the better. But Glenn says "It's okay now, but wait until tomorrow."

Music: Mike Bloomfield and the Electric Flag perform their interpretive background music to augment the swirling trip footage and create an aura of psychedelia.

Outfits: Very straight-looking hippies, all ties and jackets.

Paul Groves (Peter Fonda) and Glenn (Salli Sachse) take a shine to one another as he explains his conception of the universe in *The Trip.*

Valley of the Dolls

Company: 20th Century Fox, 1967
Color
Category: Drama with music
Screenplay by: Helen Deutsch
Directed by: Mark Robson
Produced by: David Weisbart
Starring: Barbara Parkins, Patty Duke,
Paul Burke, and Sharon Tate
Choreography by: Robert Sidney
Music Composed by: Johnny Williams

Plot: Anne Welles (Barbara Parkins) arrives
in New York and accepts a secretarial job
with a big theatrical law firm. On her first
day she is present at a Broadway rehearsal
where hard-boiled comedy star Helen
Lawson fires a newcomer, Neely O'Hara,
because she is so good she threatens to steal
the show. Lyon Burke, a lawyer in the firm,
gets Neely on a TV show that leads to
stardom in Hollywood. At the same time,
beautiful but untalented Jennifer North falls
in love with nightclub singer Tony Polar and
marries him over the objections of his sister
Miriam. Anne and Lyon have an affair but
quarrel over his refusal to get married. Lyon
quits the law firm to write and Anne appears
in a number of TV commercials. As time
passes, Neely finds herself unable to adjust
to fame; two bad marriages have led to
alcoholism and drug addiction. Neely is
persuaded to enter the same sanitarium
where Tony is dying. Jennifer, who has been
paying Tony's bills by making nudist films

119

Neely O'Hara (Patty Duke Astin)
finds it hard to keep off the pills
in *Valley of the Dolls.*

in Europe, learns she has breast cancer and commits suicide. After Anne and Lyon have reconciled and then broken up again, Neely gets the chance for a comeback on Broadway but she is emotionally unable to face an audience. Too drunk to go on, she collapses in the theater alley after her understudy has scored an opening night triumph. By now Anne is at her New England home. One day Lyon visits her and pleads with her to marry him. Anne only kisses him kindly and says no.

Music: Songs written by Andre and Dory Previn. Theme from "Valley of the Dolls" (Dionne Warwick); "Give a Little More," "It's Impossible" (Patty Duke); "Come Live With Me" (Tony Scotti); "I'll Plant My Own Tree."

Moves: Nightclub, Broadway hoofing. Gala performances.

Outfits: Slinky dresses, Hollywood sexy.

Social Significance: Super flick. Top of the trashy. Had a big impact both as a book and as a film. Became retroactively famous with the death of Sharon Tate at the hands of the Manson family.

Awards: Did bonanza business at ticket counter and spawned countless imitations.

120

Village of the Giants

Company: Embassy, 1965
Color, 80 minutes
Category: Sci-fi musical comedy
Screenplay by: Alan Calliou
Directed by: Bert I. Gordon
Produced by: Bert I. Gordon
Starring: Tommy Kirk, Johnny Crawford, Beau Bridges, and Ron Howard
Choreographer: Toni Basil
Band: The Beau Brummels
Composer: Jack Nitzsche

Plot: Four teen couples come to a town after their car is wrecked in an avalanche. Young sweethearts Mike and Nancy are interrupted by Nancy's younger brother, Genius, who tells them he has discovered an

The teenagers listen to the story of the strange substance that makes things grow to enormous proportions in *Village of the Giants.*

edible substance that will cause anyone or anything that eats it to grow to gargantuan proportions. Hearing about the strange food, the eight teens steal some and eat it. Of course, they grow into giants and get some pretty big ideas. They take over the town, terrifying the residents, and hold the sheriff's daughter hostage. But Genius then discovers a gas which can reverse the process and the giant teens are tricked into sniffing it and return to their normal size. The sheriff and townsfolk chase them out of town.

Music: Beau Brummels, Mike Clifford, Freddy Cannon. Songs include "When It Comes to Your Love," "Little Bitty Corrine," "Marianne," and "Nothing Can Stand in My Way."

Moves: Some great scenes as the giants dance among themselves, making the very ground shake. Choreography by Toni Basil.

Outfits: Pre-Beatles teen garb, sports shirts, loafers, dresses.

Social Significance: Showed teenagers fighting back, having power at a time when teens were largely powerless and unheard. Prophetic perhaps of troubled times ahead and the roles that youth would play, making them grow to giants in terms of their influence.

Trivia: Filmed in Perceptovision. Based on the book *The Food of the Gods*, by H.G. Wells. Also made into a monster flick by the same director (See the *Great Book of Movie Monsters*).

What's New, Pussycat?

Company: United Artists/Famous Artists, 1965 Color, 108 minutes
Category: Comedy/musical
Screenplay by: Woody Allen

121

Peter Sellers plays crazy psychiatrist Dr. Fassbender who is jealous of his patient Michael's success with women in *What's New, Pussycat?*

Directed by: Clive Donner
Produced by: Charles K. Feldman
Starring: Peter Sellers, Peter O'Toole, Romy Schneider, Capucine, Paula Prentiss, and Woody Allen
Group/Singer: Tom Jones, Dionne Warwick, and Manfred Mann
Choreographer: Jean Guelis
Music Score: Burt Bacharach

Plot: In Paris, fashion editor Michael James (Peter O'Toole), is involved romantically with Carole (Romy Schneider), but is distracted by the beautiful women he encounters at work. He goes to psychiatrist Dr. Fassbender (Peter Sellers) and the fun begins. Hearing about Michael's success with beautiful women, the doctor goes into a jealous rage, and tries to sneak away from wife Anna (Eddra Gale) to have affairs. Victor (Woody Allen) is also in love with Carole, but she is demanding Michael marry her before her parents arrive for a visit. Michael visits a club where he falls for a suicidal poet-stripper and for Renee (Capucine), though he passes her along to the doctor. It goes on, and is most amusing when we see the shrink throw tantrums.
Music: The title song is sung by Tom Jones, "Here I Am" (Dionne Warwick), "Little Red Book" (Paul Jones).
Moves: Parisian rock steps, hippy-hippy-shake variety
Outfits: Sellers is wont to wear Freud-like outfits, the others are 1960s chic. The women are outstandingly sexy, especially mad parachutist Rita (Ursula Andress).
Social Significance: Proved the Freudian preoccupation of the public with ridiculing psychiatry because they are uneasy with it.
Trivia: Filmed in Paris, and opened there as *Quoi de Neuf, Pussycat?* Also proved that loading a film with sexy women makes good box office. Woody Allen's acting debut.

122

What's Up, Tiger Lily?

Company: American International Pictures, 1966
Color, 80 minutes
Category: Comedy
Screenplay by: Woody Allen and Frank Buxton
Directed by: Senkichi Janiguchi
Produced by: James H. Nicholson and Samuel Z. Arkoff
Starring: Tatsuya Mihashi and Mie Hama
Band: Lovin' Spoonful and others

Plot: The story tells the adventures of Phil Moscowitz, a young Japanese man who is kidnapped by Oriental beauties and taken to an unnamed Asian country to help stop an international plot to steal the recipe for the best egg salad in the world. Despite numerous assassination attempts, Phil always manages to escape narrowly with his

This oriental sex symbol gets Phil Moscowitz involved in international intrigue and espionage in *What's Up, Tiger Lily?*

life. Edited in are intermissions showing the Lovin' Spoonful singing. Moscowitz discovers that the brains behind the operation is Shepherd Wong, a connoisseur of eggs and cigars. In a blazing finale, Moscowitz shoots it out with four villains, killing them with three bullets. The day is saved for egg salad. Woody Allen appears accompanied by China Lee. He explains that he had promised to give her a part in the picture. Allen eats an apple while China Lee takes off some of her clothes. The end.

Music: The Lovin' Spoonful do "Pow, Pow Revisited," "Gray Prison Blues," "Unconscious Minuet," "A Cool Million," "Lookin to Spy," "Phil's Love Theme," "Fishin Blues," "Respoken," "Speakin of Spoken."

Outfits: Japanese gangster.

Social Significance: One of Woody's insanest moments.

Trivia: Originally released in Japan by Toho Co. in 1964, Woody Allen got hold of the film, erased the soundtrack, re-edited it and added several sequences. He redubbed English dialogue, commentary, and music.

When the Boys Meet the Girls

Company: MGM, 1965
            Color, 110 minutes
Category: Comedy/musical
Screenplay by: Robert E. Kent
Directed by: Alvin Ganzer
Produced by: Sam Katzman
Starring: Connie Francis, Harve Presnell, Herman's Hermits, and Louis Armstrong

Group/Singer: In addition to the stars mentioned above, Sam the Sham, Liberace, and others

Choreographer: Earl Barton

Plot: Escaping girl-entanglements, Danny (Harve Presnell) enrolls at Cody College. He falls for Ginger (Connie Francis) whose dad's dude ranch is doing badly. Danny

When the Boys meet the Girls, **Connie Francis is there.**

finds a way to convert it to a swinging divorcee spa. He also hires swell entertainers. Tess (Sue Ane Langdon) tries to mess things up, but morality and honesty come out on top.

Music: "Bidin' My Time" (Herman's Hermits), "Embraceable You" (Harve Presnell), "Treat Me Rough" (Sue Ane Langdon), "Throw it Out Your Mind" (Louis Armstrong), "It's All in Your Mind" (the Standells), "Aruba Liberace" (Liberace).

Moves: Everything they were doing in the student bodies of the mid-sixties colleges is wiggled around here. Still, it's strictly routine stepping to the big beat, with few surprises. Choreography by Earl Barton.

Outfits: Bop clothing, college crewneck sweaters, girls in booster skirts and rah rah blouses. Groups have that English look; Louis has a handkerchief handy.

Trivia: This film is a remake of an MGM 1943 film called *Girl Crazy*.

124

Where the Boys Are

Company: MGM, 1960
Color, 99 minutes
Category: Musical
Screenplay: George Wells
Directed by: Henry Levin
Produced by: Joe Pasternak
Starring: Connie Francis, Yvette Mimieux, Paula Prentiss, and Dolores Hart
Singer: Connie Francis

Plot: This seems to be a vehicle to promote the hit "Where the Boys Are," a love-ballad by Connie Francis. It does little else. Four

Connie Francis and friends wonder *Where the Boys Are*.

near-the-age teenagers embark to Ft. Lauderdale, Florida, for the annual search and revel. There they are, in all their pulchritude and innocence, ready to meet the boys. Ready to make MGM money, in its first foray into the teen market. The company scores big at the box office, as Connie belts out the theme song all kids can relate to. Needless to say, the boys are there. True love after tribulations, sigh.

Music: Connie Francis sings "Where the Boys Are," and other tunes. She was a big star at the time. The lady still is, despite problems.

Outfits: Lots of beach scanties, lots of pajamas for girl-talk.

Social Significance: Studios hit again. They realize that lots of big money can be spent to get top stars, productions, and they'll still have box office bonanza. Rock means money, even quasi-rock ballads like those sung by Connie.

Trivia: Lisa Hartman (of TV soap fame) appeared in a remake of this film in 1984, and she recorded the title song, figuring if it was a hit for Connie. . . .

The Wild Angels

Company: American International Pictures, 1966
Color, 93 minutes
Category: Drama with music
Screenplay by: Charles B. Griffith
Directed by: Roger Corman
Produced by: Roger Corman

125

The townspeople try to stop The Wild Angels from burying their fallen comrade in the local cemetery.

Starring: Peter Fonda, Nancy Sinatra, Bruce Dern, Michael J. Pollard, and members of the Hell's Angels
Band: David Allan and the Arrows

Plot: Heavenly Blues (Peter Fonda) is the leader of the Wild Angels, a gang similar to the Hell's Angels. His girl is Mike (Nancy Sinatra). The gang rides around the West Coast, getting their kicks and scaring the pants off everybody else. Trouble brews when gang member Loser (Bruce Dern) gets his bike stolen by a rival gang. The Wild Angels have a rumble with the other gang and steal a chopper back. But Loser gets shot by the cops during melee. Fellow Angels free him from the hospital but he dies on the run. The Angels pay their last respects and show up at the church where they tie up the minister, rape Loser's widow, and have an orgy. They wrap Loser's body in a Nazi flag with a joint in his mouth. The local citizens attack the group as the Angels bring the body to a cemetery. The cops arrive and a huge fight ensues. The gang members flee on their cycles but Heavenly Blues waits by the gravesite muttering "There's no place to go."
Music: Music performed by David Allen and the Arrows. Songs include "Wild Angels".
Moves: The Angels have their own drunken fisticuffs that pass as dance.
Outfits: Black leather, chains, Nazi helmets, big, big boots.
Social Significance: Caused an uproar everywhere it was shown, antagonizing critics and viewers alike with its graphic, realistic depiction of motorcycle life. Had an indelible effect on American youth, glamorizing the Hell's Angels and setting the stage for all future bike pictures (including *Easy Rider*) to follow. The most controversial picture ever released by American International Pictures and they loved it since the audiences crowded in to see what everyone was yelling about.

126

Trivia: Peter Bogdanovich worked extensively on this flick: as a writer and editor.

Wild in the Streets

Company: American International, 1968
Color, 97 minutes
Category: Drama
Screenplay: Robert Thom
Directed by: Barry Shear
Produced by: James H. Nicholson and Samuel Z. Arkoff
Starring: Shelley Winters, Christopher Jones, Diane Varsi, and Hal Holbrook

Now that rock singer Max Frost (Christopher Jones) is president, everyone over 30 is arrested and fed LSD in *Wild in the Streets*.

Group/Singer: Christopher Jones, Paul Weiler, and the Thirteenth Power
Composer: Score by Les Baxter and songs by Barry Mann and Cynthia Weil

Plot: Rock singer Max Frost (Christopher Jones) digs the fact that over half the U.S. population is under 25 and wants to lower the voting age, singing to hysterical audiences: "Fourteen or Fight". The politicians thought they could capitalize on Frost's appeal to youth and they played along, not realizing how powerful a figure he actually was, hoping to get themselves elected. After the nationwide youth riots, the voting age is changed. Frost becomes President, and everyone over 30 is arrested and fed LSD. But, at the end, the under-10s are starting their own revolution.
Music: "The Shape of Things to Come", "Listen to the Music", "Sally Leroy", "Fourteen or Fight".
Moves: Dancin' in the streets, rioting, wiggling on stage. The dances are incidental but Frost's flipped out girlfriend (Diane Varsi) can shake it.

Outfits: "Youth" styles of the sixties.
Social Signficance: Had sort of a *1984* effect on movie goers. Good idea for a movie, though most dismissed it as social comment. Those in the Nixon White House probably thought it a possibility that the youth of the nation, crazed by drugs, and sex, and rock might actually . . . but they were paranoid and over thirty, man.
Trivia: *The New York Times* called it ". . . the best American film of the year (so far)". Makes you hanker for the movies of the fifties when real rock and roll stars made appearances in films. Chris Jones just isn't one.

Wild Wild Winter

127

Company: Universal, 1966
Color, 80 minutes
Category: Drama

The Beau Brummels appear in *Wild Wild Winter.*

Screenplay by: David Malcom
Directed by: Lenny Weinrib
Produced by: Bart Patton
Starring: Gary Clarke, Chris Noel, Don Edmonds, Suzie Kaye, Les Brown Jr., and Vicki Albright
Group/Singer: Jay and the Americans, Beau Brummels, Dick and DeeDee, the Astronauts, and Jackie and Gayle
Musical Supervisor: Frank Wilson
Music: Jerry Long

Plot: Bert and Perry arrive at a small college in the mountains in order to pursue their main interest—skiing. Dot and Sandy, their female lures, are out-of-bounds because their sorority's leader, Susan (Chris Noel), does not believe in boy-girl affairs. (What does she believe in?) Anyway, Ronnie (Gary Clarke), the frat brother of the two erstwhile suitors, is from Malibu. Natch the guy is irresistible to girls. He attempts to thaw Susan to no avail. Pop music groups try to do so too (this is how they manage to fit into the film, which at 80 minutes, is really just a vehicle for them). Nothing works. Ronnie somehow winds up on the champion ski course. He wins the trophy and Susan, who confesses true love.
Music: "Two of A Kind" (Jay and Americans), "Heartbeats" (Dick and Dee Dee), "A Change of Heart" (Astronauts), "Just Wait and See" (Beau Brummels), "Our Love's Gonna Snowball" (Jackie and Gayle).
Moves: Who can fail to bop and rock when listening to these guys and gals?
Outfits: Strictly ski country duds. Plus some rocker accoutrements.
Social Significance: Here come the Beau Brummels. Can you understand the lyrics? No.
Trivia: If you know this film, you are a trivia expert.

128

Yellow Submarine

Company: Apple Films, 1968
Color, 85 minutes
Category: Cartoon musical
Screenplay by: Lee Minoff, Al Brodax, Jack Mendelsohn, and Erich Segal
Directed by: George Dunning
Produced by: Al Brodax
Starring: Animated Beatles
Band: The Beatles
Animation: Jack Stokes
Animation Director: Bob Balser

Plot: On a peaceful day in the happy kingdom of Pepperland a performance by Sergeant Pepper's Lonely Hearts Club Band is halted by an invasion of Blue Meanies, an army of music-hating nasties who take all the color from their victims with Splotch guns and then knock them unconscious by hitting them on the head with giant green apples. Old Fred, the conductor of the band, escapes in the nick of time in the Yellow Submarine provided by the Lord Mayor. Arriving in Liverpool, Old Fred meets Ringo who helps recruit the other Beatles to help save Pepperland. Heading off in the Yellow Submarine, the five heroes have kaleidoscopic and surrealistic adventures through numerous strange dimensions of time, space, and color—the Sea of Time, the Sea of Science, the Sea of Monsters, and the sea of green, and the sea of holes. The Beatles meet the Nowhere Man and bring him along and are then propelled through the sea of holes and into occupied Pepperland by an enormous sneeze. Disguising themselves as one of the Blue Meanies' Apple Bonkers, they get into the place where all the musical instruments have

been hidden. Armed with love and song, they battle the Blue Meanies and convert them into peaceful creatures. Music, love, happiness, and color are returned to Pepperland.

Music: The speaking voices of the Beatles were done by John Clive, (John), Geoffrey Hughes (Paul), Peter Batten (George), and Paul Angelus (Ringo). The songs, performed by the real thing, include "Yellow Submarine," "When I'm Sixty Four," "Nowhere Man," "Lucy in the Sky with Diamonds," "Eleanor Rigby," "All You Need Is Love," "Sgt. Pepper's Lonely Hearts' Club Band," "A Day in the Life," "All Together Now," and "Northern Snow."

Moves: Many dances by animated Beatles and mystical, psychedelic creatures who waddle, slither, and blip their way through reality.

Outfits: Animated Beatles wear brightly colored, old-time-band style uniforms, high to the collar.

Social Significance: Brought animation into a beautiful, surreal, post-Disney horizon to the point of "hallucinogenic poetry."

Furthered the mythology of the Beatles in the collective unconscious of the western world.

Trivia: Songs written specifically for the movie include—"Only a Northern Song," "All together Now," "It's All Too Much".

Awards: Huge hit at the box-office and constantly brought back for new generations to experience with joy.

You're a Big Boy Now

Company: Warner Bros., 1966
Color, 96 minutes
Category: Drama
Screenplay by: Francis Ford Coppola

129

The Beatles, in animated form, meet the Nowhere Man, yet another strange creature in the Psychedelic world they have entered to battle the blue meanies in *Yellow Submarine*.

Directed by: Francis Ford Coppola
Produced by: Phil Feldman
Starring: Peter Kastner, Geraldine Page, and Rip Torn
Group/Singer: Lovin' Spoonful, led by John Sebastian

Plot: A charming, disarming film by Francis Ford Coppola, a director of some note, as we all know now. Bernard (Peter Kastner) is a virginal, earnest young assistant in the New York Library, and wears rollerskates, as do the other young slaves, to roll down the long aisles and get the public its books. (This was the practice at the time. Really.) Miss Thing (Julie Harris) runs Bernard's boarding house. Barbara Darling (Elizabeth Hartman) captivates young Bernard, who sees her go-go dancing in a Greenwich Village dive. She hates men, and Bernard in particular, when he tries an advance. Rafe, Bernard's sophisticated friend, however, moves in with

Barbara. Crushing to the ego. Bernard runs away. Amy (Karen Black) is truly in love with the introverted guy, though, and this leads to her rescue of the harried Bernard and his pet dog and the kid's father's Gutenberg Bible (which he sort of stole). The whole tale is much more charming than can be portrayed here. Kinda reminds one of *Breakfast at Tiffany's* in its emotional impact.
Music: The Lovin' Spoonful at last on a soundtrack! The nicest, most laid back rock group around sing "Darlin' Be Home Soon" and the title song. They're great, but couldn't they have squeezed in "Do You Believe in Magic?"
Outfits: Good Karen wears goody girl, clean teen stuff. Bad girl Elizabeth is sexy and mean looking in go-go undies.
Social Significance: We used to hang out at the Night Owl cafe where John and the Spoonful got their start. The track reminds one of the good ol' days.
Trivia: Coppola had previous directed two cheepie-nudies. From schlock, to pop, to top.

130

This early film by Francis Ford Coppola really shines, aided by a wonderful Lovin' Spoonful soundtrack.

Coppola also did the Roger Corman bomb *The Terror*. Come to think of it, that wasn't half bad. He wrote the screenplay for *Is Paris Burning?*
Awards: An Academy Award nomination went to Geraldine Page for best supporting actress for this one.

You Are What You Eat

Company: Commonwealth United, 1968
Color, 75 minutes
Category: Docu/musical

Directed by: Barry Feinstein
Produced by: Peter Yarrow and Barry Feinstein
Band: Tiny Tim, Peter Yarrow, and others
Score: John Simon
Musical Director: Peter Yarrow

Plot: The film zeros in on the contemporary youth revolution that was occurring in America. The major sections of the movie are devoted to rock and folk music performers. Shown are scenes of Father Malcolm Boyd, an Episcopal priest and writer who has joined the Love Generation, hanging out with a band of hippies on a beach. The film shows an institution for wayward girls and boys; teenagers rioting and police brutality; Super Spade, the cult hero, murdered by mobsters in San Francisco in 1967 for giving away free marijuana and acid; Anti-war

131

You Are What You Eat **says Tiny Tim. What do the Paul Butterfield Blues Band eat to be so good? Noodles? Blues Noodles.**

demonstrations and advertisements for Nazi helmets; Barry McGuire, the "prophet of doom," dancing in the sun; and shots of hippies sun-worshipping, eating flowers, riding motorcycles, climbing trees, surfboarding, and enjoying the happy pursuits of body painting and love-ins.

Music: "Memphis," "Be My Baby," "Sonny Boy," and "I Got You, Babe" (Tiny Tim); "Family Dog" (Johnny Herald); "You Are What You Eat" (Paul Butterfield); "Moments of Soft Persuasion," "Silly Girl," and "Don't Remind Me of Time" (Peter Yarrow); "The Wabe" (John Simon and Peter Yarrow); "Nude Dance" (Hamsa El Din); "My Name is Jack" (John Simon); "Come to the Sunshine" (Harper's Bizarre); "Teenage Fair" (Rosko); "Freakout" (Electric Flag and John Simon). Other performers were Family Dog, David Crosby and Vito's Group.

Moves: Hippie freakout, acid swirling, beach gyrating, sun worship. And a semi-nude dance by El Din.

132

Outfits: Hippie at its peak: bellbottoms, vests, Ben Franklin shades.

Social Significance: One of the better films documenting an era, its main performers, and the everyday feelings and interactions of the "Love Generation" that already seems a million years away.

Young Animals

Company: American International Pictures, 1968
Color, 89 minutes
Category: Drama
Screenplay by: James Gordon White
Directed by: Maury Dexter

The photo shows the poster used to advertise *The Young Animals.*

Produced by: Maury Dexter
Starring: Tom Nardini and Patty McCormack

Plot: The film examines the subject of school integration and racial problems between Mexican-American and white students in a small border town high school. Nardini, a new student quickly sees the strong prejudice toward the Mexicans by both white students and faculty. He joins a liberal student Patty McCormack, and together they form a grievance committee. But Patty's ex-boyfriend, David Macklin, starts a terror campaign against the Mexicans. When a Mexican girl is raped, the minority students decide that the "gringos" need a good lesson. Racial riots ensue with students fighting it out hand to hand. But Macklin wants more and goes mad, pursuing Patty and Tom around a junkyard in a wrecking machine. Macklin is finally arrested and things quiet down. Patty and Tom lead the students in a massive demonstration for racial equality. The principal, previously prejudiced himself, agrees and gives in to their demands for fair treatment.

Music: "Born Wild" and others sung by American Revolution.

Outfits: Teen garb at a time when teens weren't nearly as fashion conscious as they are now: dirty jeans, sweaty shirts.

Social Significance: Pro-integration picture showing that the different races could and must live together peacefully and that the way to future harmony is through young people who, even when prejudiced, are much more open than adults to change, and even friendship, with other races.

133

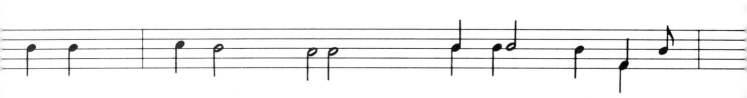

the Seventies

Rockin' Reels

Dance and Darkness (1970-1979)

The 1970s brought many changes to the look of the rock film and made the business of rock and roll itself bigger than ever. This was, after all, the Youth Decade, and everything that looked, acted, or sounded young was in. The Beatles, after an extraordinary series of metamorphoses from "mod moppets" to psychedelic visionaries to Eastern mystics, broke up in 1970, leaving behind a rich legacy that included lyrics of extraordinarily poetic imagery and music that borrowed not only from earlier rock sources but from the Western classical tradition and the Oriental repertory as well. These innovations were not lost on the many performers who now sought to fill the void left by the Beatles' departure.

With new developments in filmmaking technology, including lighter cameras, more sensitive film, and more sophisticated sound-recording equipment, a new form of rock film became possible and instantly popular. The rockumentary finally came into its own. With the new equipment, the filmmaker was now able to freely roam the aisles of the many large, open-air concerts that were appearing everywhere, giving audiences a spectacular, close-up, multi-angled view of the proceedings, both on-stage and off.

Monterey Pop (1969) was one of the first of these loose-jointed concert pictures, filmed by Albert Maysles and directed by D.A. Pennebaker, among others (both Maysles and Pennebaker would rise to the top in rock and counter-culture films as time went on).

Actually filmed in 1967, *Monterey Pop* is an historical record of some of the biggest talents of the day—Janis Joplin and Big Brother and the Holding Company, the Who, the Mamas and the Papas, the Jefferson Airplane, Otis Redding, the Animals, Jimi Hendrix. The film is not entirely successful, due to the fact that the camera crews became so enamoured of their new equipment that the special effects— zooming, panning, quick cuts, blurred focus—detract strongly from the actual performances. On the other hand, the visual effect is not unlike that of a drug trip (which would certainly have been a legitimate artistic device at the time), and the music comes through loud and clear.

The rockumentary allowed audiences to participate in their own time and place in concert expriences that they might have missed entirely. The popularity of the new genre gave birth to a number of examples, some better than others. It was with *Woodstock* (1970) that the genre reached its zenith, capturing with incredible fidelity much of the feeling of actual presence of the historic birth of the "Woodstock generation." The film worked beautifully, using split-screen effects to show the audience interaction with such greats as Joan Baez, Sly & the Family Stone, Joe Cocker, the Who, Jimi Hendrix, Crosby, Stills, Nash, & Young. But it was the audience itself—Woodstock Nation—that was the true theme of the film; the event itself, rather than the performers on stage, was the subject of *Woodstock*.

The other side of *Woodstock*, made the same year, was *Gimme Shelter*, the ugly and notorious documentary of the concert at Altamont, California, starring the Rolling Stones, the Jefferson Airplane, Santana, and the Grateful Dead. The event that marked this film was not planned, but it was as surely a symbol of the era as if it had been scripted. The Stones, possibly with the not-too-well-thought-out idea of forestalling what finally happened, had hired the Hell's Angels to handle security for the event, where drugs were used freely and bad trips were to be expected. The films shows the Angels throughout the concert harassing the audience and pushing people around, and during the Stones' performance of "Sympathy for the Devil" the mood grows palpably ugly. The Angels continue to grow wilder until at last they attack a black man in the crowd who is having a bad trip and, by way of calming him down, knife him to death. All this was captured on film and appears in the movie. At the end, Mick Jagger is shown watching the footage of the murder and shaking his head in disbelief, clearly stunned at the result of his own manipulation of dark energies in his songs of violence.

While *Gimme Shelter* clearly destroyed forever the exuberance and innocence of the Woodstock Nation, it did not stop fans from going to concert films. *Celebration at Big Sur*, (1971), *The Concert for Bangladesh*, (1972) and other rockumentaries continued to proliferate even to this day, with increasingly sophisticated sound recording and bigger and more powerful speaker systems bringing to the film audience the ever truer experience of attending the real thing.

As the movement of Black consciousness became more powerful during this period, a new form of rock film developed to meet it. Although decried by more conservative members of the movement, the so-called "Blacksploitation" film quickly caught on with white and black audiences alike. American got to see a whole new view of their country through the urban black experience and its funky rhythms. *Shaft, Superfly*, (1972) and dozens of other films appeared starring a new kind of hero (or heroine) who was tough, mean, and black, though always, if just barely, on the right side of the law. The soundtracks, with performers like Isaac Hayes, Curtis Mayfield, and Marvin Gaye, reflected this

new and powerful experience.

Inevitably, the audiences began to shy away from the increasing violence portrayed in these films. When the nostalgic *American Graffiti* (1973) hit the screen, it began an entire new trend back to the oldies but goodies of an earlier era. Directors began to use oldies to add mood and texture to their films, whether or not they were set in the present. Rock music took on a deeper meaning for those who had lived through its birth. It had captured moments in our lives, forever linking love and pain with certain melodies, certain singers. It was becoming clear that rock and roll, in its own way, was a form of prayer, a way of being put in touch with something beyond ourselves, filled with the power of the past. *Shampoo* (1975) and *American Pop*, among other films, brim over with early rock tunes. Today, with their constant use in television shows and commercials, they have become cliches, their original intensity lost in the repetition.

Along with passion for the nostalgia came a revived interest in big-budget song-and-dance films, begun with *O Lucky Man* and *Car Wash*, among others, and culminating in the blockbuster *Saturday Night Fever* (1977). The film that made John Travolta a star and the Bee Gees a new recording phenomenon (for the next year, it was impossible to turn on the radio without hearing "How Deep is Your Love," "Stayin' Alive," "More than a Woman") inspired millions of teenage American males to put on white suits, grease back their hair, and practice Travolta-style dance moves. If *Grease* (1978), *The Wiz* (1978), *and Hair* (1979) never created quite the stir of *Saturday Night Fever*, they certainly cashed in on the renewed interest in the rock film musical and the country's desire for instant nostalgia.

Been Down so Long It Looks Like Up to Me

Company: Paramount, 1970
Color, 91 minutes
Category: Musical drama
Screenplay by: Robert Schlitt
Directed by: Jeff Young
Produced by: Robert Rosenthal
Starring: Barry Primus, Linda De Coff,
and David Downing
Music Composed by: Gary Sherman

138

Plot: In 1958, after moving around the country in a mad search for his "identity," a young dropout, Gnossos Pappadapoulis, goes back to college and gets Dean Oeuf to allow him to register for classes. At the snack bar Gnossos runs into old pal Heff, a black man, who is so bored by academic life that he plans to join the Cuban revolution. He won't listen to Gnossos's entreaties that the outside world is a mess and just as depressing. Gnossos gets into various kinds of trouble at school including freaking out a group of fraternity brothers by smoking grass and accusing one of the boys of being a homosexual. Gnossos goes to the only adult he has any good feelings for—Calvin, the art professor who uses acid and mescaline. Gnossos takes some himself and has a bad trip, becoming even more alienated and freaky than ever. He meets Kristin at a drug party and tries to seduce her but she tells him she's a virgin. Eventually, however, she falls for him and they get together in that time honored way. For a while they live in relative happiness, until Kristin leaves following a violent argument. Depressed more than ever, Gnossos goes to join Heff in Cuba where he soon discovers that he has gotten gonorrhea from the "virginal" Kristin. He goes into an alcohol and drug stupor until he finds out that Heff has been shot during a battle. Finding his only friend-in-life's mutilated body, he takes him into the mountains and digs him a peaceful grave in a forest.

Some times it feels like *I've Been Down So Long It Looks Like Up To Me.*

Music: The Five Satins, the Platters, Four Lads, and Linda Hopkins perform. Music and songs composed by Gary Sherman, lyrics by Gene Pistilli. "Been Down So Long" and "Little Boy" (Gene Pistilli); "Play Something Slow" and "Roll Daddy Roll" (the Five Satins); "Be My Love" and "It Was You (the Platters); "Down by the Riverside" (the Four Lads); "God be with You" (Linda Hopkins).

Moves: LSD hand-waving, hallucinatory solos.

Outfits: Hippie, dirty clothes, Cuban guerilla green.

Social Significance: The Richard Farina novel (on which the film was based) was a big hit in the late 1960s, and influenced a whole generation growing up and searching for their own identities. A sort of *On The Road* for the descendants of the beat generation.

Trivia: Murray the K (may his soul rest in heaven rocking thru the millenium) had a bit part.

Billy Jack

Company: Warner Bros., 1972
          Color, 112 minutes
Category: Drama/musical
Screenplay by: Frank and Theresa
          Christina
Directed by: T.C. Frank
Produced by: Mary Rose Solti
Starring: Tom Laughlin, Delores Taylor, and Clark Howatt
Group/Singer: Katy Moffatt, Jinx
          Dawson-Coven, Teresa
          Kelly, Lynn Baker, Gwen
          Smith, and Robbyn
          Etelson
Music Score: Mundell Lowe

Plot: *Billy Jack,* a sleeper hit that won fame for Laughlin, was a real "new consciousness" movie. The concerns of the film were humanity, civil rights, the ecology, animal welfare, organic food, and, that magic word to all Americans, freedom.

Coming back from duty as a Green Beret in Vietnam, Indian Billy Jack (Tom Laughlin) returns to his reservation in the Southwest U.S. Dedicated to preserving his tribal ways, and incensed over the slaughter of wild mustangs for dog food meat, Billy Jack, a rugged loner, takes up with the director of an "alternate" type school. Jean Roberts (Delores Taylor) runs the Freedom School, and teaches peace and love to an integrated class, so naturally the town is up in arms. The townfolk threaten them but Billy karate-kicks his way to peace. Made by the National Student Film corporation, it is a period piece of the Ecology-Peace movement era.

Music: Katy Moffett, as Maria, sings her own "The Ring Song." Sweet, melodic folk-rock compositions comprise most of the soundtrack.

Outfits: Billy Jack sports denim, some Indian adornments on his black porkpie hat, a black T-shirt, and boots. Jean Roberts wears country-hippie styles, organic grain make-up, straw-dry, ecologically safe hair. The students at the school wear non-designer jeans, cast-off army clothes, non-violent sloganed T-shirts, and peaceful expressions. The townfolk wear mean looks and heavy boots, and drive wasteful, guzzling vehicles. The worst of them sport cowboy outfits of polyester and other synthetics.

Social Significance: Surprise! This film was a hit everywhere, and Warner was blown away by the profits. Follow-up lookalikes abounded, but there's only one original *Billy Jack*. People were dying for a film like this to be made, and only the students that made it were aware of that fact.

Trivia: American International was set to

139

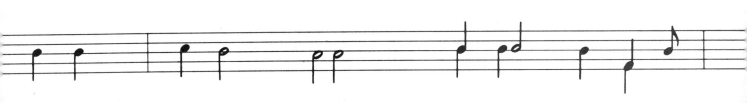

release this film, but Laughlin bought it and sold it to 20th Century Fox. But they wanted to edit it a bit so he bought it back again for $100,000 and sold it to Warner for $1,800,000 plus 45% of the profits. And profit it did! In 1973 Laughlin did *The Trial of Billy Jack* and in 1977 *Billy Jack Goes to Washington*. Director T.C. Frank is pseudonym for Laughlin.

The Blank Generation

140

Company: Poe Visions, 1976
Black and white, 55 minutes
Category: Rockumentary
Screenplay by: Amos Poe and Ivan Kral
Directed by: Amos Poe and Ivan Kral
Produced by: Amos Poe and Ivan Kral
Starring: Blondie, Patti Smith, the Ramones, Talking Heads, the Miamis, Television, and others

Plot: This is the cream of New York's punk/new wave set doing their famous songs. It's just beginning here. The first time we saw Patti, it was a poetry gig she was doing with Allen Ginsberg. She's gone on to rock here. (We'll never forget "Piss Factory," a record you can only get in odd places.) But she does do her thing. So do the Ramones and others. For a glimpse of the scene at this time, see this shorty. Raw and rough-edged as it is blown up from a super-8 home movie, it's appealing in its hostile-friendly sentiments.

Music: Blondie does "He Left Me;" Patti Smith does "Gloria;" The Ramones do "Shock Treatment" and "1-2-3 Let's Go;" Talking Heads do "Psycho Killer." Also performing are the Shirts (of Brooklyn), Harry Toledo, the Marbles, Wayne County, Tuff Darts—with Robert Gordon, the Dolls, and the Miamis. All done at a dive named CBGB on the Bowery.

Outfits: Lots of black, lots of thinness, lots of spitting, drinking, eyes rolling, lots of sound off-sync, as "hostile to the audience" performers do blankness.

Patti Smith stars in *Blank Generation*, a stunning portrait of Patti.

Social Significance: Beginning of a new genre, punk/new wave movies. Lots of these production values (previously thought of as non-values) were taken into video.

The Buddy Holly Story

Company: Entertainment Releasing, 1978 Color, 114 minutes
Category: Biography/concert film
Screenplay by: Robert Gittler. Story by Alan Sawyer, based on a book by John Coldrosen
Directed by: Steve Rash
Produced by: Freddy Bauer
Starring: Gary Busey, Maria Richwine, and Don Stroud
Group/Singer: Busey as Holly, Gailard Sartrain as Big Bopper, others
Choreographer: Maggie Rash

Plot: It's Buddy Holly's life, from just starting-to-rock, to really-rolling. Busey is as good as Holly was and the mood is authentic. Holly was one of the greatest rockers ever. Nearly every song he wrote was a gold hit sooner or later, and twenty years after his death his album was going platinum in England! The Beatles did a Buddy Holly tune, "Words of Love," as one of their first releases.

Like *The Glenn Miller Story*, the Holly legend unfolds, hoked up and simplified a bit. He's portrayed as a moral, anti-racist guy in a time of exploitation of black stars and a hostile establishment. Tastefully, the story ends before his fatal plane crash (along with Richie Valens and the Big Bopper). The soundtrack in this film is a stupendous recreation of the Holly appearances and the big rock and roll sound of the sax-heavy orchestras. Expect to be blown away by Holly's tunesmithing talent, not the story. Best scenes are Holly in a duel of guitars with Eddie Cochran; and Holly at the all-black Apollo Theater in Harlem, winning acceptance and rocking the house apart.

Gary Busey gives an incredible performance as Buddy Holly, one of the premier pioneers of rock and roll, in *The Buddy Holly Story*.

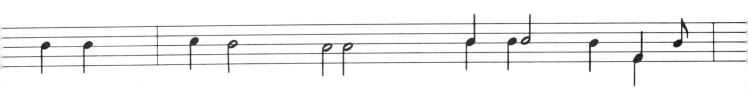

Music: Gary Busey does all his own singing and it is fine, even great. The mimic ry of other performers long dead is realistic. Songs include "That'll Be the Day," "Everyday," "Peggy Sue," "Rave On," "Maybe Baby," and "It's So Easy (To Fall in Love)." Musical Director Joe Renzetti did a fine job of recreating all those great acts. (Holly usually played big shows featuring a half-dozen or more big names. His solo performances were rare.)

Moves: Holly had a way of bouncing bow-legged around a stage that was not usual for the period. He was years ahead with this and it disappointed a lot of people who expected an Elvis pelvis shudder-twitch. Choreography by Maggie Rash.

Outfits: Busey, as Holly, dons those incredibly famous often imitated black hornrim glasses. Proves he's a non-conformist. Glasses were o-u-t back then. He had a style of his own, with a close-to-white sport coat and pink carnation, droopy shouldered suits.

Social Significance: He was devastating audiences everywhere with his white version of black music. The establishment's reaction: This kid could start a riot, even worse he could cause integration of audiences and performing acts.

Trivia: There is much talk of the role of Holly mentor Norman Petty and what he was to Holly, but not in this movie. He's hardly mentioned here! Buddy, we miss you!

A Bullet for Pretty Boy

Company: American International Picture, 1970
Color, 88 minutes
Category: Drama with music
Screenplay by: Henry Rosenbaum

142

Fabian beats up the guy that insulted his new wife in a *Bullet for Pretty Boy.*

Directed by: Larry Buchanan
Produced by: Larry Buchanan
Starring: Fabian Forte and Jocelyn Lane
Music Composed by: Harley Hatcher

Plot: After his wedding reception, Charles "Pretty Boy" Floyd (Fabian Forte), an Oklahoma farmer, demands that Jack Dowler apologize for making sexual advances to his bride Ruby. Charles beats up Dowler when the man refuses. Dowler swears to get revenge for the humiliation and that night he attacks, but accidentally kills Charles's father. Charles goes to Dowler's farm the next morning, the two fight, and Dowler is killed. Charles is tried and sent to prison. He escapes four years later and flees to Kansas City to a brothel. Betty, one of the prostitutes, likes him which infuriates the madame's brother Wallace who is himself in love with Betty. Wallace begins referring to Charles as "Pretty Boy" in contempt. The name becomes nationally known when Charles joins a gang of bank robbers. After several holdups Pretty Boy is captured but he kills the guard accompanying him and escapes from a train. He heads to Oklahoma and meets Ruby. Even though she still loves him, she knows she can't lead his kind of life. "Preacher," a drunkard, goes with Pretty Boy back to the brothel where they join Betty and Ned Short's gang in a widely publicized robbery spree. Short and Preacher are killed in a stakeout, but Pretty Boy escapes with Betty to a shack near his old home. After one last goodbye with Ruby, the two survivors rob Pretty Boy's hometown bank. Betty escapes but Pretty Boy is trapped in a ranch house and is killed in a police fusillade of bullets.

Music: The Source sing the theme Song, "It's Me I'm Running From," "I'm Gonna Love You Till I Die," "Gone Tomorrow," and "Ruby, Ruby."

Outfits: Hick hip, prison stripes, hooker pink, gangster stylish.

Social Significance: Another teen *noir* in a long line of flicks that romanticized the outlaw, the ex-con, the "good" gangster/killer.

C.C. and Company

Company: Avco Embassy, 1970
Color, 88 minutes
Category: Adventure with music
Screenplay by: Roger Smith
Directed by: Seymour Robbie
Produced by: Alan Carr and Roger Smith
Starring: Joe Namath and Ann-Margret
Band: C.C. Ryders
Composer: Lenny Stack

143

Plot: C.C. Ryder (Joe Namath), Crow, and Lizard, gang members of the Heads motorcycle gang, find Ann McCalley (Ann-Margret), a beautiful fashion correspondent, when her limo breaks down. Lizard and Crow try to rape the young woman but C.C. overpowers them and saves her. The next day, while the Heads are disrupting a motorcycle race, C.C. sees Ann taking pictures of Eddie Ellis, one of the racers. To impress her, C.C. steals a motorcycle and wins $600 in the race. Moon, the leader of the Heads, demands that C.C. give the loot to the gang. C.C. refuses and Moon beats him up and takes the money. Later that night, C.C. seduces Pom Pom, Moon's girlfriend, and steals the money back. He moves in with Ann, but the Heads kidnap her and ask for a thousand dollars ransom. C.C. makes an offer of double or nothing in

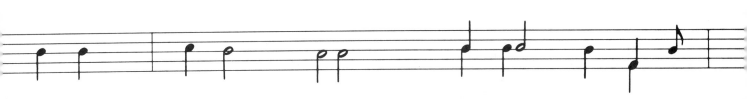

a bike race against Moon. During the contest, Moon's cycle swerves and he's killed. After setting all the Head's bikes on fire, C.C. runs off with Ann.

Music: "Today" (Ann-Margret); "I Can't Turn You Loose" (Wayne Cochran and the C.C. Ryders); "Jenny Take A Ride" and "C.C. Rider" (Mitch Ryder).

Moves: The stomp, the fist, the brass knuckles.

Outfits: Motorcycle down to the tattoos. Some of the more aristocratic racers wear zip-up racing suits.

Social Significance: Sex-symbol Namath's (remember him) biggest contribution to the annals of film history.

Celebration at Big Sur

144

Company: 20th Century Fox, 1971
                Color, 82 minutes
Category: Rockumentary
Directed by: Baird Bryant and Joanna Demetrakis
Produced by: Carl Gottlieb
Starring: Joan Baez, Mimi Farina, John Sebastian, others

Plot: This documentary recorded the 1969 Big Sur Festival in California, which was officially a "performer's festival," an opportunity for artists to perform, relax, and live together in a peaceful outdoor setting on the Pacific Coast near the Esalen Institute. Profits from the festival went to Joan Baez's Institute for the Study of Non-Violence. Interspersed with the acts are interviews with the audience, informal interludes of performers rapping and jamming together, and a sequence where some of the performers and the producer take a bath in the Institute's mineral baths. There are shots of Baez's sister dancing (Farina) on a hill and a brief argument between a spectator and Stephen Stills of Crosby, Stills, Nash, and Young. The film ends with all the performers and the audience performing a rousing rendition of "Oh Happy Day."

Music: Joan Baez, David Crosby, Mimi Farina, Van Morrison, Julie Payne, John Sebastian, Dallas Taylor, Carol Ann Cisneros, Chris Ethridge, Joni Mitchell, Graham Nash, Stephen Stills, Neil Young, the Combs Sisters, and the Struggle Mountain Resistance Band all perform. The songs include "Song For David," "Oh Happy Day," "Get Together," "Mobile Line," "All God's Children Got Soul,"

Some of the biggest rock and folk-rock acts of the 1960's join in a rousing rendition of "Oh, Happy Day."

"Daydream," "Woodstock," "Sweet Sir Galahad," "Everybody Let's Get Together," "I Shall Be Released," and "Malaguena Salerosa," "Oh Happy Day" (All).
Moves: Hippie space dancing, LSD entranced arm waving.
Outfits: Middle to late hippie—vests, ponytails, work clothes, bells.
Social Significance: The peak of the hippie folk music scene. Much happiness and good vibes. Too bad it's all gone now.

A Clockwork Orange

Company: Warner Bros., 1971
Color, 137 minutes
Category: Drama/sci-fi
Screenplay by: Stanley Kubrick
Directed by: Stanley Kubrick
Produced by: Stanley Kubrick
Starring: Malcolm McDowell and Patrick McGee

Head Droog Alex (Malcolm McDowell) has that look in his eye as he goes out for a night on the old ultraviolence in *Clockwork Orange*.

145

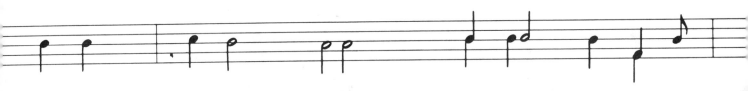

Plot: Sometime in the not too distant future in England, the social order has disintegrated to the point where teenaged gangs roam the rubble-strewn streets, robbing, raping, and killing other gangs and citizens who live in terror behind locked doors. One night, after downing a stimulant drink at the Korova Milkbar, a young gangleader, Alex (Malcolm McDowell), and his three "Droogs," Pete, Georgie, and Dim, set out for another night of the "old ultra-violence." After beating up a bum, they demolish a rival gang in a warehouse and then go joyriding. They invade a rich writer's home, severely beating him and raping his wife. Alex loves to inflict pain while singing "Singing in the Rain." One thing follows another and Alex is captured and put in prison. He volunteers for a new treatment program which, by using behavioral adaptation techniques (electric shocks whenever he sees violence), supposedly gets rid of all his bad qualities. He is released, and at first the treatment works. Others can hit him, do anything they want and if he feels even the slightest anger he becomes violently ill. He is captured by the writer he nearly killed who locks him bathroom and plays Beethoven over and over (Alex's favorite music and the theme that was playing while he was receiving treatment). He nearly goes mad and dives out of the window. When he comes to in a government hospital, he realizes that he has broken through the conditioning and once again will be able to return to "the old ultra-violence."

Music: Electronic music composed and realized by Walter Carlos (now Wendy Carlos). Music for "The Funeral of Queen Mary" is by Henry Purcell, Molly Malone, and James Yorkston; "The Thieving Magpie" and the *William Tell* "Overture" by Rossini; "Singing in the Rain" sung by Gene Kelly; "Ninth Symphony in D Minor" by Beethoven. "Wayward Child" and "Pomp and Circumstance" by Sir Edward Elgar; "Overture to the Sun" by Terry Tucker; "I

146

Want to Marry a Lighthouse Keeper" by Erika Eigen.

Moves: Alex does a somewhat violent tap dance on the face of his victims as he croons "Singing in the Rain."

Outfits: Futuristic and incredibly wild costumes. Alex and his droogs wear all white costumes with codpieces, bowler hats, and canes as weapons. Other gangs have their own unique style including a baseball suited gang, and all leather.

Social Significance: Showed the future of society, teenagers, and rock. This truly apocalyptic film depicts an interesting evolution of rock into a sensual electronic sound. Songs out today on the radio are already in that direction, so . . . ?

Trivia: Made McDowell a superstar and furthered Kubrick's brilliant career as one of the best directors of all time.

Awards: One of the best films of any genre ever made. The mood, the locales, the vision of our world in the future where all spirit has disintegrated and only survival and wealth are left is amazingly familiar. Audiences responded as film was big hit and is constantly brought back to the revival houses. The film was originally X-rated. The version shown today has a few minutes snipped out to make it R-rated.

Cocksucker Blues

Company: Not listed, 1976
Color, 95 minutes
Category: Rockumentary
Screenplay by: Robert Frank and Daniel Seymour
Produced by: Marshall Chess
Starring: The Rolling Stones, Stevie Wonder, and Dick Cavett
Group/Singer: The Rolling Stones

This is the banned, disowned, and sued version of the Rolling Stones' 1972 tour of the U.S. The Stones commissioned it but were outraged by the results—and it takes a lot to outrage Mick! There's a little petting, a bit of violence (a TV set thrown out a closed window), and some drug use, but it's tedious too.

This 16-mm exposé by photographer Robert Frank is a study of the behind-the-curtain lives of the Rolling Stones. They hang out with Stevie Wonder, Truman Capote, Terry Southern, Andy Warhol, and their ilk, and it's boring. These people are downers. We do get to see and hear live "Satisfaction," "Jumpin' Jack Flash,'' and other songs.

Music: "Jumpin' Jack Flash,'' "Satisfaction," "Street Fightin' Man,'' "Honky Tonk Woman,'' and others are sung by the Rolling Stones.

Outfits: Slumped funk.

Trivia: *Cocksucker Blues* was also released as *CS Blues*, for obvious reasons. In 1979, the Stones dropped their suit and allowed limited showings of this underground classic.

Coming Home

Company: United Artists, 1978
Color, 127 minutes
Category: Drama
Screenplay by: Waldo Salt, Robert C. Jones, and Nancy Dowd
Directed by: Hal Ashby
Produced by: Bruce Gilbert
Starring: Jane Fonda, Jon Voight, and Bruce Dern
Group/Singer: Simon and Garfunkel, the Chamber Brothers, Bob Dylan, Jimi Hendrix, the Beatles, and more

147

Luke Martin and Sally Hyde enjoy a happy moment in *Coming Home.*

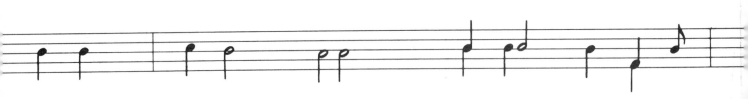

Plot: Jane Fonda plays a woman who falls in love with a paraplegic war veteran (Jon Voight) while her gung-ho husband, played by Bruce Dern, is still away on active duty. Dern eventually comes home and finds out about the whole thing. The message is that war does bad things to people, and we should support our vets, especially those who come to oppose the war. There are lots of touching love scenes, lots of emotional sparks in this well-made film. A must see.

Music: The sound track, sometimes overwhelmingly loud, gives an evocative-of-the-sixties-mood to the whole proceedings. "Hey Jude," and "Strawberry Fields" (the Beatles); "Just Like a Woman" (Bob Dylan); "Sympathy for the Devil" (the Rolling Stones); The Chambers Brothers, Simon and Garfunkel, and Jimi Hendrix are also featured.

Outfits: Sweat shirts, jogging suits, casual wear a la suburbs. Plus crisp military uniforms. Wheelchairs by the score, and partial nudity.

148

Social Significance: Kind of defused complaints that Fonda was anti-veteran. She makes a point that you can be pro-vet and anti-war.

Trivia: The best use of rock, we think, in a Vietnam tale is the Doors on the soundtrack of *Apocalypse Now*. It works here, but not as well.

Concert for Bangladesh

Company: 20th Century Fox, 1972
             Color, 100 minutes
Category: Concert on film
Screenplay by: Saul Swimmer
Directed by: Saul Swimmer

Bob Dylan joined George Harrison to raise funds for Bangladesh emergency aid in *Concert for Bangladesh*.

Produced by: George Harrison and Allen Klein

Starring: George Harrison, Bob Dylan, Ringo Starr, Eric Clapton, others

Group/Singer: In addition to those mentioned above, Billy Preston, Ravi Shankar, Leon Russell, and Klaus Voormann

Plot: This is a film of the 1971 charity concert inspired and organized by George Harrison. The nation of Bangladesh was starving and nobody was doing enough. George and Ravi Shankar put their best effort into raising money for the place, but it's hard to turn a profit when so many people are involved (especially lawyers). The money raised after expenses, and mostly after etceteras, was disappointing, but George gave of his own to help Bangladesh and the concert was certainly spectacular. There is a glimpse of Dylan and Harrison rehearsing, then we are given what in effect was the evening concert in Madison Square Garden. Newsreel images of the Bangladesh refugees are also screened.

Music: "A Hard Rain's A-Gonna Fall," "Blowin' in the Wind," "Just Like a Woman," and "It Takes a Lot to Laugh" (Bob Dylan). "Bangla Dhun" (Ravi Shankar); Ringo Starr does "It Don't Come Easy, and the song didn't—he forgot some of his own lines. "Here Comes the Sun," "My Sweet Lord," "While My Guitar Gently Weeps," "Something" (George Harrison); "Jumpin' Jack Flash" and "Youngblood" (Leon Russell).

Moves: Billy Preston breaks into an improvised dance so enthusiastic is he when he performs "That's the Way God Planned It."

Outfits: Dylan wears the styles of down-home dirt-farmer/super cool Mac-Dougal Street-hipness he's famous for. George is casual too. Ravi wears his collarless essence, and hefts a sitar. Man, don't you get sick of groups that are all hype/dress? Look at these great performers as natural as can be. In the sixties, once the Beatles got rid of their silly tight suits, everyone that was great used to just come as they were and play. The music was the thing, not the special effects. That's why rock went halfway down the tube in the seventies. It concentrated in large part on hype, not musical expression.

Awards: George and the other Beatles should get some humanitarian awards. They did a lot of charity work together and separately. McCartney donated some hits to the Concert For Kampuchea disk; there's Lennon's Spirit Foundation and other charities; Ringo, er . . . always helped along on all these projects as he did here.

Cotton Comes to Harlem

149

Company: United Artists, 1970
Color, 97 minutes

Category: Action with music

Directed by: Ossie Davis

Produced by: Samuel Goldwyn Jr.

Starring: Godfrey Cambridge and Raymond St. Jacques

Choreographer: Louis Johnson

Composer: Galt McDermot

Plot: At an outdoor barbecue in Harlem, con man Rev. Deke defrauds local residents of $87,000 which is intended to transport blacks to Africa. The money is seized, however, by the black crook's white partner,

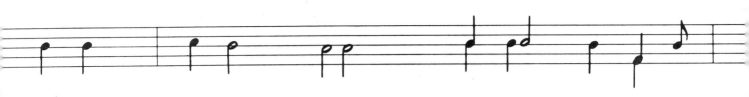

Calhoun, who flees in a meat truck, having hidden the loot in a bale of cotton. Pursued by tough black cops Coffin Ed Johnson (Godfrey Cambridge) and Gravedigger Jones (Raymond St. Jacques), the bale bounces from the truck and is found by junkman Uncle Bud (Redd Foxx) and sold to Mabel, an inventive stripper. After a complex plot in which Deke continues to con women left and right, Coffin Ed gets a mafia don to agree to pay back the money to the people of Harlem in return for allowing him to exploit them. Deke is captured and runs out to the stage where a gospel group is singing. As he begs those in the church who once were his followers to listen, they walk out in disgust as the blathering man is led away by cops. The cops get a postcard from Uncle Bud who has absconded with the loot to Africa.

Music: "Cotton Comes to Harlem," "Goin' Home," "Ain't Now But It's Going to Be," "Down in My Soul," and "My Salvation."

Moves: Lots of stripping and gospel dancing, clapping and carrying on.

Outfits: Harlem pimp, purple dresses, rags.

Social Significance: One of the better of the black cops/robbers flicks with a memorable score, an insane plot, and good acting.

Trivia: Filmed on location in Harlem.

Eraserhead

Company: Libra Films, 1978
                    Black and white, 90 minutes
Category: Fantasy
Screenplay by: David Lynch
Directed by: David Lynch

150

Gravedigger (Raymond St. Jacques, in the middle) and Coffin Jones (Godfrey Cambridge, far right) stare down a local Mafia don in *Cotton Comes to Harlem.*

Produced by: David Lynch (with the cooperation of the A.F.I. Center for Advanced Film Studies)
Starring: John Nance, Charlotte Stewart, Allen Joseph, and Jeanne Bates
Singer: Peter Ivers
Cinematography by: Frederick Elmes and Herbert Caldwell

Plot: This strange, depresso-mucho movie is an unusual horror. Its super-pathetic production qualities do something to add to the weird effect. The sound by Splet (Alan R.) is always distraction-over-noise (Like in real life, other noises constantly impinge when you really want to hear something). Repellant, sadistic, and void, this film is trying to tell the following story: Henry Spencer (John Nance) is a creep with stand-up hair. He lives in a dilapidated building where his window faces a wall and his dresser actually has seaweed growing all over it. Henry's baby by girlfriend Mary X (Charlotte Stewart) is a mutant. We see lots of other disgusting things and visit disgusto people galore, and the hideous baby cries a lot. Surrealistic scenes with a prostitute and the Lady in the Radiator (Laurel Near) round out the non-action, all filmed with inadequate light and meaning.
Music: Peter Ivers wrote and sang the soundtrack "Lady in the Radiator." I guess it's punk.
Outfits: Creepo stuff.
Social Significance: Disgusts one-half the audience, the other half cheers at the end. Gives vent to funko-punko self aggrandizing hatefulness and sloth.
Trivia: Sissy Spacek helped finance this movie. See it on the midnight movie circuit where it is a cult item. One thing: You'll be inspired to dust off that old movie camera or video outfit and get cracking. How could you do worse? Director David Lynch went on to direct the filmed version of *The Elephant Man.*

Fillmore

Company: 20th Century Fox, 1972 Color, 105 minutes
Category: Rockumentary
Directed by: Richard T. Heffron
Produced by: Herbert Decker
Starring: Some of the best bands of the 1960s

Plot: When rock and roll promoter Bill Graham decided to close his six-year old Fillmore West theater, the announcement inspired this documentary on both the famous San Francisco rock palace and the man who made it all happen. To capture the final days, local independent film company Medion Productions got the aid of over 40 filmmakers while Graham picked what he felt best represented the San Francisco sounds. Edited down from forty hours of footage, the film operates on two levels—the music and scenes of Graham making innumerable telephone calls, playing with his young son, and discussing his childhood flight from the Nazis in Germany. He explains his reasons for closing the Fillmore. He was discouraged by an industry he feels has grown too big and inflated egos of musicians who demand exorbitant rates. Graham bemoans the passing of the spirit that moved him in 1965 to open the Fillmore. "Back in those days," he says, "people came to have a good time and the other people were there for the same reasons—everybody won." Finally, in looking back on the flower children era, Graham regrets that "Utopia never came, the streets were never filled with flowers." This footage is interspersed with the performance of numerous of the best bands.

151

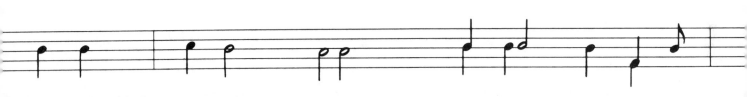

Music: Santana, the Grateful Dead, Quicksilver Messenger Service, Lamb, It's A Beautiful Day, Cold Blood, Boz Scaggs, the Elvin Bishop Group, Hot Tuna, the Jefferson Airplane, the New Riders of the Purple Sage, the Rowan Brothers. Songs include "Incident at Neshibur," "In a Silent Way," "Casey Jones," "Johnny B. Goode," "Fresh Air," "Mojo," "Candy Man," "Uncle Sam Blues," "White Bird," "You Got Me Humming," "I Wish I Knew How it Would Feel to be Free," "Hollywood Blues," "I'll be Gone Long," "Sky Is Crying," "Hello Friends," "River Boulevard," "We Can be Together." Plus rehearsal scenes of the New Riders of the Purple Sage and the Rowan Brothers.

Moves: On stage and in the audience, fans go wild, jumping on the seats.

Outfits: Late hippie—long hair, jeans, sweat shirts, peasant blouses, ethnic jewelry and beads.

Social Significance: Marked the end of an era. The youthful optimism of the flower children and the love/peace/togetherness mythology which would now be replaced by new forms of rock and consciousness such as heavy metal and glitter.

Friends

Company: Paramount, 1971
Color, 101 minutes
Category: Drama
Screenplay by: Jack Russell and Vernon Harris
Directed by: Lewis Gilbert
Produced by: Lewis Gilbert
Starring: Sean Bury, Anicee Alvina, Toby Robbins, and Ronald Lewis
Group/Singer: Elton John
Songs by: Elton John and Bernie Taupin

Plot: Two teenagers, well played by Sean Bury and Anicee Alvina, decide to run away together. They have found a place, a lovely country cottage. This sticky production, full of poetic love scenes, full of the embarrassment and awkwardness of first

152

An era comes to a close as the bands fill the stage of the Fillmore West to play in the finale.

love, is still nonetheless touching. This young couple engage upon the most inevitable, considering their knowledge of love. They have a baby; will the world accept their love now?

Music: Elton John sings his numbers, co-written with Bernie Taupin. One of the most successful teams in rock songwriting, they met through an advertisement.

Outfits: The earnest young girl wears her dark hair in pigtails, and wears a flower-print dress, one of her few possessions. He is in a white shirt usually, with an English schoolboy-type hairdo, and corduroy pants to complete his outfit. In the cottage she lets her hair down, indeed.

Social Significance: Young lovers' stories have been a hit since *Romeo and Juliet*.
Trivia: Poetic treatment. Compare the harsh realities in *Private Lessons*.

G-AS-S-S or It May Become Necessary to Destroy the World In Order to Save It

Sean Bury and Anicee Alvina play two teenagers in love in *Friends*.

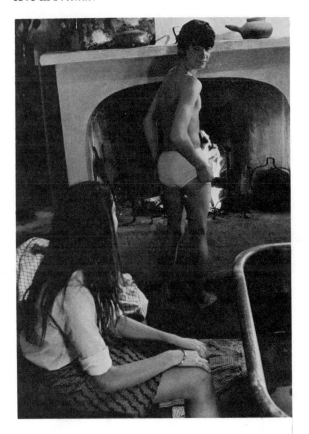

Company: American International
Pictures, 1970
Color, 79 minutes
Category: Sci-fi/musical satire
Screenplay by: George Armitage
Directed by: Roger Corman
Produced by: Roger Corman
Starring: Robert Corff, Elaine Giftos, Ben Vereen, and Cindy Williams
Composer: Barry Metton
Band: Country Joe and the Fish

153

Plot: A strange, satirical film that begins with an accident at a government plant in Alaska. A cask of experimental nerve gas is accidentally released into the atmosphere. It quickly travels around the world causing everyone over the age of 25 to die, within days, of old age. The world is in chaos. Cole and Celia (Robert Corff and Elaine Giftos) flee Dallas in their car hoping to find peace. They run into misadventure after misadventure, first meeting a young weirdo

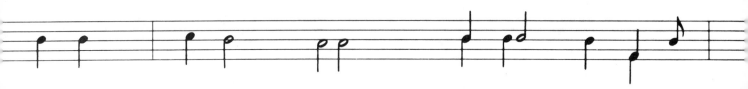

desperado named Billy the Kid. They meet other young pilgrims, Hooper, Bud, Carlos, Marissa. The entire group head for a commune in a pueblo in New Mexico. They stop at a rock concert given by F.M. Radio (Country Joe and the Fish). The group is then captured by a right wing football team, Jason and the Nomads. They escape and run into the last remnants of the money-hungry middle class led by Marshall McLuhan. They escape again and make it to the commune but soon discover that it's not utopia there either. Jason and the Nomads attack but a huge surreal storm strikes and the dead arise, including a procession of famous heroes John F. Kennedy, Martin Luther King, Edgar Allan Poe, even God. Everyone gives their blessings and things will now be okay.

Music: Country Joe and the Fish, Johnny and the Tornados. Songs include "Please Don't Bury My Soul," "Maybe It Wasn't Really Love," "Don't Chase Me Around," "I'm Looking for a World," "World That We All Dreamed Of," "Got to Get Moving," and "This Is the Beginning" (Robert Corff); "Cry a Little," "Gas Man," "The Pueblo Pool," "Bubble Gum Girl," "Juke Box Serenade," "Castles" (Johnny and the Tornados); "First Time, Last Time," "Today Is Where" (Gourmet's Delight).

Outfits: Hippie, football, rags.

Social Significance: Never got into much circulation. An extremely weird flick.

Trivia: Ended Roger Corman's association with American International Pictures, so angry was he at the cuts they made in the film, including, as Corman put it, "They cut God from the movie. Can you imagine—cutting God?"

Getting Straight

Company: Columbia, 1970
Color, 124 minutes
Category: Comedy/drama with music
Screenplay by: Robert Kaufman

Only the young survive when an experimental nerve gas is released on the world in *G-AS-S-S*.

Directed by: Richard Rush
Produced by: Richard Rush
Starring: Elliot Gould, Candice Bergen,
    Robert F. Lyons, and Jeff Corey
Group/Singer: P.K. Limited and the
    New Establishment
Song by: Barry Mann and Cynthia Weil
Music: Ronald Stein

Plot: Vietnam vet and activist Harry Bailey (Elliot Gould) returns to college after six years to earn a master's degree in education. He's assigned to teach remedial English. Black militant Ellis (Max Julien) wants Harry to help demonstrate but he refuses. Harry sexes it up with his students, namely Jan (Candice Bergen) and some black coeds. A guy who has been taking Harry's exams for him reveals all to the hard-assed chairman of the department, Wilhut (Jeff Corey), and thus jeopardizes Harry's career.

Harry gets involved unwillingly as a liason between rioting students and the school president, then is called upon to comment on a paper on *The Great Gatsby* that interprets it as a homosexual theme. Harry dances on the table and denounces the panel of inquisitors, ruining his academic career. He rushes into the hall and joins Ellis and Jan in a student revolt.
Music: The New Establishment sing "I'll Build a Bridge," P.K. Limited sing "Moon Rock," "Talk," "Feelins," and "Shades of Grey."
Outfits: Collegiate student-revolting clothes.
Social Significance: Further established Gould as counter-culture hero.
Trivia: Filmed at Lake Community College, Oregon, on a mini-budget.

A scene from the rear in *Getting Straight*.

155

Gimme Shelter

Company: Cinema V, 1970
Color, 91 minutes
Category: Rockumentary
Directed by: David Maysles, Albert
Maysles, and Charlotte
Zwerin
Produced by: Ronald Schnieder
Starring: The Rolling Stones and others
Band: The Stones, Jefferson Airplane,
and Ike and Tina Turner

Plot: *Gimme Shelter* is a Rockumentary of the wrapup concert of the Rolling Stones' triumphant 1969 tour of the United States. The Stones mounted a gargantuan free concert at Altamont Speedway in Northern California. The Stones, dissatisfied with regular security guards, got the Hell's Angels to "police" the concert. Paranoia, drugs, and bad planning marred the show from the start. The audience was huge, with hundreds of thousands of young people showing up. The Angels began getting increasingly violent and even punched Jefferson Airplane singer Marty Balin who protested their treatment of the audience. The Angels took over the stage, kicking and punching people who got too close. By nighttime, when the Stones came on, the entire scene had taken on a nightmarish atmosphere. Jagger tried to cool the whole thing out but couldn't. A black man, meanwhile, pulled a gun in the crowd. Instantly he was surrounded by Hell's Angels and knifed to death (all of this caught on film). The concert went on as Jagger didn't know until later what had happened. At the end of the film we see Jagger watching the footage of the knifing, shaken, pale, and silent.

Music: Tina Turner does a super hot version of "I've Been Loving You Too Long." Jefferson Airplane does "White Rabbit," among others. The Rolling Stones perform "Jumping Jack Flash," "Satisfaction," "You Gotta Move," "Wild Horses," "Brown Sugar" and, while the Hell's Angels are doing their work yards away, "Sympathy for the Devil."

Moves: Jagger prances and struts around the stage, flashing his amorphous sexuality. In the crowd, the stoned audience whirl and space out.

Outfits: Late hippie, California beacher. Hell's Angels wear black and vests, Jagger a skin-tight (as always) black-leather suit.

Social Significance: Ended the romantic image that motorcycle gangs had had up until that point, largely from glamorizing motorcycle rock flicks. Also effectively marked the collapse of the "Woodstock Generation."

156

The Rolling Stones perform before a huge audience in *Gimme Shelter*. They will later discover that their choice of security had been ill-made.

Grease

Company: Paramount, 1978
Color, 110 minutes
Category: Musical
Screenplay by: Bronte Woodard
Directed by: Randal Kleiser
Produced by: Robert Stigwood and Alan Carr
Starring: John Travolta, Olivia Newton-John, Jeff Conaway, and Stockard Channing
Group/Singer: Cast, Sha-Na-Na, and Frankie Avalon
Choreographer: Patricia Birch
Musical Play by: Jim Jacobs and Warren Casey

Plot: This is a homage to the fifties. Olivia is the new girl at school, John is a leader of the tough rockers. They had an interlude during the summer on the beach, but lost track of each other. Now she's with the nerdy-girl set, he's a real greasy character

Can the twain meet? Well, yes, and they can argue, too. Eventually it's all straightened out. The sounds of rock in this film are more disco than fifties a capella and doo-wop. The one group really doing fifties stuff is Sha-Na-Na. They provide magical entertainment at the 1950s style high school celebration. Frankie Avalon plays a Teen Angel, and Lorenzo Lamas is the high school jock, a familiar figure of the era. *Grease*, for all it's failings, is lively and bright.

Music: "Beauty School Dropout" Frankie Avalon; "Queen" and "Rock and Roll Party" Louis St. Louis; "Sandy" (John Travolta). The title tune (by Barry Gibb) is sung by Frankie Valli; "Hound Dog," "Tears on My Pillow," "Rock and Roll Is Here to Stay," and "Born to Hand Jive (Sha-Na-Na). "Hopelessly Devoted To You" (Olivia Newton-John). "We Go Together," "Summer Nights," and "You're the One That I Want" (Newton-John and Travolta).

Moves: Done around the honey of a car.

Outfits: Fifties-a-la-disco. Gold suits, black T-shirts, duck-tail hairstyles, toreador pants on girls. Convertibles and hair tonic.

Social Significance: Speaks to the disco generation; idealizes as it distorts the fifties generation.

Trivia: A favorite in eastern Europe.

157

John Travolta and his buddies dance to a stylized number in honor of one of the symbols of teenage freedom—the car—in *Grease.*

Groupies

Company: Maron, 1970
Color, 92 minutes
Category: Documentary with music
Screenplay by: Robert Dorfman and
Peter Nevard
Directed by: Robert Dorfman
Produced by: Robert Weiner
Starring: Miss Harlow, Cynthia P.
Caster, and Andrea Whips
Band: Joe Cocker and others

Plot: Shot over a nine-month period in numerous locations across the U.S., including the Fillmore East and Fillmore West, the film looks at the lives of the young fans of rock stars, particularly the girl and gay groupies who offer their services, primarily sexual, to big time rock stars while they're on tour. Scenes include live footage of groups playing, backstage where the real action is going on, in hotel rooms, and in the homes of some of the groupies. The focus of much of the footage is on the sexual interests and aberrations of many of the groupies. The film climaxes with a visit to see Miss Cynthia, whose specialty is making plaster of paris casts of the erect organs of the musicians. One might call the art form "preservus erectus."

Music: Bands that perform in the film include Ten Years After, Joe Cocker and the Grease Band, Spooky Tooth, Luther Grosvenor, Terry Reid, Keith Webb, Peter Shelley, Dry Creek Road. Songs include "Delta Lady," "Good Morning, Little Schoolgirl," "Help Me Baby," "Mister Sun," and "Superlungs." Plus rehearsal material.

Moves: Crowds can be seen cavorting on chairs and doing late hippie writhing. Lots of foot-tapping by offstage groupies.

Outfits: Flower generation chic, gold beads, tight miniskirts.

158

**Groupies follow musicians
around from gig to gig.**

Social Significance: Immortalized the most important parts of some of rock's most famous personalities. Are these in the Smithsonian?

Trivia: Jimi Hendrix's appendage is rumored to be among the plaster casts and is also said to be of mammoth proportions.

Hair

Company: United Artists, 1979
Color, 121 minutes
Category: Musical

Screenplay by: Michael Weller
Directed by: Milos Forman
Produced by: Lester Persky and Michael Butler
Starring: John Savage, Treat Williams, Nicholas Ray, Beverly D'Angelo, and Annie Golden
Group/Singer: Cast

Plot: Czech director Forman was called in to do this paean to the flower-power generation for the screen. Long a hit musical on Broadway, *Hair* hit the screen after the flower-power had wilted. Weller's screenplay

**The Love Generation, "with hair down to there,"
. . . rock-out in Central Park.**

159

grafted a pretty good set of circumstances onto the whole thing. An Oklahoma cowboy arrives in New York City to report to the army for service in Vietnam. He gets involved with hippies, and learns it's okay to let your hair down. They all dance through Central Park, which seems scrubbed up a bit here, and we see paraded before us musically a psychedelic church, a wedding, and a Central Park be-in (remember those?). John Savage is the draftee and Beverly D'Angelo is a wigged-out deb. The whole message here is the great songs and music.

Music: "Ain't Got No," "Black Boys/White Boys," "Flesh Failures," "Sodomy," "Donna," "Air," "Hashish," "I Got Life," "Good Morning Starshine," "LBJ," "Hare Krishna," "Let the Sunshine In," "Don't Put It Down," and "Age of Aquarius."

Moves: Group-grope type togetherness; be-in blessedness; shouting, enthusiastic bead-shaking rhythm.

Outfits: Hippie styles.

Social Significance: The Broadway show was a bit of a shocker and thriller. Here was something new. But by the time the movie came out the novelty had worn off.

160

The Harder They Come

Company: New World, 1973
Color, 98 minutes
Category: Drama
Screenplay by: Perry Henzell and Trevor Rhone
Directed by: Perry Henzell
Produced by: Perry Henzell

Starring: Jimmy Cliff, Carl Bradshaw, and Bobby Charlton
Group/Singer: Jimmy Cliff, the Maytals, and others

Plot: Ivan Martin (Jimmy Cliff) is a rural boy who, seeking fortune, comes to Kingston, the capital of Jamaica, where he is trying to get a record company to cut his reggae compositions. The record industry is dominated by sharpies who would rip off your creations for a few dollars and he's soon shorn of his money and possessions. Disillusioned and hungry, he takes odd jobs. He winds up working for basically room and board for a minister. He gets in trouble fast. He woos the ward of the preacher, Elsa (Janet Barkely), and has to flee. He tries out for a record contract again, singing the title song, and the producer (Bobby Charlton) offers twenty-dollars for all rights. Ivan refuses, stunned. Publicly flogged for fighting the preacher's henchmen, he moves into a slum with Elsa. He joins the ganja (marijuana) sellers. The police control the ganja trade, and he's set upon by several cops when he decides not to pay his boss, Jose (Carl Bradshaw), his exorbitant cut. Ivan kills them, and with a bunch of pistols and a motorcycle and to the tune of his forgotten recordings (because he's now a famous outlaw, the record company digs them out and they become number one), he is off. He taunts the police for their inability to apprehend him, has his photos taken, for publicity, with his guns pointed. Finally, he tries to swim to a freighter which is going to Cuba, which might give him sanctuary. He fails to reach it. Exhausted, he's beseiged on the beach by a whole army, and he fights to the death.

Music: Jimmy Cliff sings "You Can Get it If You Really Want," "Sitting in Limbo," "Many Rivers to Cross," and "The Harder They Come." The Maytals sing "Pressure Drop" and "Sweet and Dandy." Scotty sings "Draw Your Brakes" and the Melodians

sing "Rivers of Babylon." "Johnny Too Bad" is sung by the Slickers and "Shanty Town" is sung by Desmond Dekker.

Moves: We see some undulating, good-time dancing to the reggae beat.

Outfits: Desperate people, they still manage bright colors, mostly green and red with black, and they often wear large caps to hold their dreadlocks, the long braids favored by many men of the Rasta persuasion.

Social Significance: This film is a cult sensation, and the soundtrack has never been even equalled in a film (except by Bob Marley). Jamaica is (or was) such a violent place that two actors died by violence before many people saw the film. The grinding

Jimmy Cliff, the reggae singer in *The Harder They Come*.

161

poverty and exploitation, though, take second place to the exuberance and ingenuity of the people of Jamaica and their good nature and will to live.

Trivia: Players Ras Daniel Hartman, Winston Stona, and Basil Keane do good support work; the whole thing has an air of authenticity. One of the few films in the English language to be partly subtitled in English! This is because the Jamaican accent is difficult for non-Jamaicans to pick up.

Awards: Jamaican awards. Continued showings at midnight movies in USA. The album, on the Mango label, distributed by Island Records, sells steadily years after the film was made.

Imagine

162

Company: Apple Films, 1972
Color, 81 minutes
Category: Rockumentary
Screenplay by: John Lennon and Yoko Ono
Directed by: John Lennon and Yoko Ono
Produced by: John Lennon and Yoko Ono
Starring: John Lennon and Yoko Ono
Group/Singer: John Lennon, Yoko Ono, and others

Plot: John and Yoko do their thing, seen in TV clips, home movies, and concert clips. It's a menage-a-collage. Documents a period in Lennon's life when he was doing Power-to-the-People type political stuff. That didn't last long. Settled down in New York's Dakota apartment, he and Yoko quickly moved on to esoteric spiritual practices and gooey ruminations about love.

Why not? Yoko is still in her well, let's call it "screaming" stage. She was more lyrical, and quite good, a bit later on than shown here. However, her scream medleys seemed to spawn a whole bunch of experimentation with music form that's still going on (Nina Hagen, and others). John Lennon seemed to invite everyone in all the time. Witness an odd collection of celebrities, plus George Harrison and Phil Spector, in this erratic production. Worth seeing for the hearing.

Music: Lennon does "Crippled Inside," "Imagine," "Jealous Guy," "Power to the People," "Oh My Love," and others. Some songs from Yoko's *Fly Album* are performed.

Outfits: Lennon creates his own type of style. So does Yoko. Often they were seen around New York in opposites. If he wore black, she wore white, and vice versa. Floppy berets, sunglasses, jeans.

Social Significance: A what-ever-happened-to curiosity. Lennon was, with Yoko, going beyond the public imagination at this point. His records, except for "Imagine," didn't sell well compared to the Lennon-McCartney stuff. It was a time of reappraisal, doing new things. The songs hold water better than McCartney's productions.

Trivia: Lennon was on his way to super-hit status again when he was gunned down. Three years after his death, "Nobody Told Me" became a hit. Imagine.

Jesus Christ Superstar

Company: Universal, 1973
Color, 108 minutes
Category: Musical

Screenplay by: Norman Jewison and
Robert Stigwood
Directed by: Norman Jewison
Produced by: Norman Jewison
Starring: Ted Neeley, Carl Anderson,
Yvonne Elliman, and Barry
Dennen
Group/Singer: Cast

Plot: Based on the popular rock opera based on the Christ story, this all-music, no-dialogue movie opens with an approaching bus. The actors and actresses pile out and begin donning their costumes. A play within a play.

Judas (Carl Anderson) laments that Christ's followers are fools. Jesus (Ted Neeley), being comforted with a wet cloth by Mary Magdalene (Yvonne Elliman), warns Judas and the others to confine their anger. High priests, led by Caiaphas (Bob

Jesus (Ted Neeley) looks on as Simon Zealotes (Lawrence Marshall) leads the Apostles and their debs in a wild dance of devotion.

163

Bingham), assemble and decide Jesus is a heretic who must die. Jesus enters Jerusalem with his flock, greeted by the song "Hosanna." Followers flock about saying "J.C., J.C. won't You die for me?" Pontius Pilate (Barry Dennen) is troubled because he will have to deal with all-too-popular Jesus.

Jesus is angered by the temple filled with money lenders and other vice peddlers. He is besieged by inhabitants of a leper colony. The burden of His work and the knowledge of His imminent death weigh heavily on Him.

The Last Supper is an outdoor picnic. Judas betrays Christ in a desert shattered by the sound and appearances of modern jets and tanks. A montage of crucifixion art is presented as Jesus laments having to die. Brought before a Herod wearing Bermuda shorts, Jesus is remanded to Pilate, condemned and crucified. Judas hangs himself but reappears as a ghost in a white fringed costume for the finale "Jesus Christ Superstar." Then the many subdued players reboard the bus.

Music: Composed by Andrew Lloyd Weber, lyrics by Tim Rice, and conducted by Andre Previn. Songs include "Heaven on their Mind," "What's the Buzz?," "Strange Things Mystifying," "Hosanna," "Simon Zealotes," "Poor Jerusalem," "I Don't Know How to Love Him," "Last Supper," and "Superstar."

Moves: The followers do several stunning numbers, particularly the frenzied dance of celebration led by Simon Zealotes (Larry T. Marshall) as Jesus enters Jerusalem.

Outfits: Hippie adaptations of Biblical costumes. Notable are Herod's Bermuda shorts.

Social Significance: Condemned by a national Jewish body as anti-semitic. Jesus-freaks generally liked it. Churches had mixed reactions, some thinking it brought the message to the rock generation, others considering it pap. Released as a record in 1970, the rock opera became a stage

production in 16 nations, and a concert tour attraction in the States.

Trivia: The film was made in Israel. Jewison directed *Fiddler on the Roof,* and it was while doing that 1971 film he heard of this property and pursued it.

Jimi Plays Berkeley

Company: Dor Jamm, 1971
Color, 45 minutes
Category: Rockumentary
Screenplay by: Peter Pilafian
Produced by: Michael Jeffrey
Starring: Jimi Hendrix, Mitch Mitchell, and Billy Cox
Group/Singer: Jimi Hendrix

Plot: This is a great rockumentary of the 1970 California concert by Jimi Hendrix, who some say was the greatest rock guitarist ever, certainly the one with the most symbiosis with his guitar. There are ten minutes or so of newsreels on the horror in Vietnam and all the social issues that turned on the bring-the-war-home generation. But then the remainder of this great, too-short film is given over to Jimi doing the incredible numbers he was famous for. Interspersed are interviews with "street-people" and hippies. Interesting and well photographed for a film of this nature; you can get into it.

Music: Jimi Hendrix plays "Pass It On," "Johnny B. Goode," "Voodoo Chile," "Purple Haze," and the truly wonderful version of the national anthem—Jimi's way.

Outfits: Hendrix-cool. Tassels galore, fuzzy looks, singing guitar.

164

Jimi Hendrix rocks
non-stop on his guitar.

Keep On Rockin'

Company: Pennebaker Films, 1973
Color, 102 minutes
Category: Rockumentary

Directed by: D.A. Pennebaker
Produced by: David McMullin, Peter
Hansen, Mark Woodcock,
and Chris Darymple
Starring: Chuck Berry, Little Richard,
Jerry Lee Lewis, and others

Plot: A concert documentary which is
actually a mix of two other films—Toronto

Pop (1970) with performances by John Lennon and Yoko Ono edited out for legal reasons and replaced with acts of Jimi Hendrix, Joplin, and others from film of the Monterey Pop Festival. Still, a chance to catch sound of the greatest rockers of all time.

Music: Bands and singers in flick include: Chuck Berry, Little Richard, Jerry Lee Lewis, Bo Diddley, Jimi Hendrix, Janis Joplin, Big Brother and the Holding Company. Songs include "I'm a Man," "Bo Diddley," "Great Balls of Fire," "Whole Lotta Shakin Goin On," "Sweet Little 16," "Johnny B. Goode," "Long Tall Sally," "Tutti Frutti."

Moves: People go wild in crowd, as audience gyrates nonstop to the throbbing sounds of the best rockers of all time.
Outfits: Designer hippie.
Social Significance: A great compilation of some of the best performers of early and middle rock and roll. Should be required viewing for all current music fans to see where it all began.

The Kids Are Alright

A concert goer exhibits stoned-out bliss in *Keep on Rockin'.*

166

Company: New World, 1979
Color and black and white,
108 minutes
Category: Rockumentary
Directed by: Jeff Stein
Produced by: Bill Curbishley and Tony Klinger
Starring: The Who
Group/Singer: The Who, Ringo Starr, Steve Martin, the Smothers Brothers, and Ken Russell

Plot: This documents the long career of the great British rock group the Who. There are bits and pieces from old promo flicks, concert material, some ancient and badly lighted, and TV interviews with the band. Keith Moon disintegrates on the air; guitars are rended in half, then in pieces; the Who perform energetically in hundreds of halls; the Who do their biggest smashes, in a blast of a film that seems to be put together

randomly and narrated on and off by Ringo.

Music: The Who do "My Generation," "A Quick One," "Who Are You?," "Roadrunner," "Anyway, Anyhow, Anywhere," "I Can't Explain," "Happy Jack," "Won't Get Fooled Again," and a half dozen others. An excellent soundtrack.

Outfits: The Who seem to prefer black, but they dress in different styles over the years. Dress not being their main thing, it's not the most spectacular part of this film.

Social Significance: Like *Quadrophenia*, establishes the Who as big movie box office attractions in their own right.

Ladies and Gentlemen, The Rolling Stones

Company: Dragon Aire, 1974
Color, 83 minutes
Category: Rockumentary
Screenplay by: Rollin Binzer

167

The Who during their mod era pose in one of the clips in *The Kids are Alright*.

Produced by: Marshall Chess, Rollin Binzer, Bob Fries, and Steve Gebhardt
Starring: The Rolling Stones, Nicky Hopkins, Bobby Keyes, Jim Price, and Ian Stewart
Group/Singer: The Rolling Stones, Nicky Hopkins, Bobby Keyes, Jim Price, and Ian Stewart

Mick Jagger performs.

Plot: This is the musical rockumentary of the Rolling Stones 1972 tour of the United States. Unlike most films about rock tours, this one doesn't attempt meaningless interviews, behind the scenes poking around, no fans extolling the virtues of the performers. Instead it's virtually all music and great stuff. Presented for "big bucks" ticket prices in quadrophonically equipped theaters, it records their onstage triumphs and is an interesting counter point to the unofficial film about this tour, *Cocksucker Blues*. The band—some say the greatest rock and roll band in the world ever—goes through 14 hot numbers.
Music: The Rolling Stones do "Bitch," "Gimme Shelter," "Tumblin' Dice," "Brown Sugar," "Jumpin' Jack Flash," "Street Fightin' Man," "Love in Vain," "Midnight Rambler," and others.
Moves: Mick's unmistakable gyrations.
Outfits: Mick does some changes, all snug in the crotch.
Social Significance: Counteracted bad publicity about their personal affairs in this tour.

Lady Sings the Blues

Company: Paramount, 1972
Color, 144 minutes
Category: Drama/musical
Screenplay by: Terence McCoy, Chris Clarke, and Suzanne De Passe
Directed by: Sidney J. Furie
Produced by: Berry Gordy, Jay Weston, and James S. White
Starring: Diana Ross, Billy Dee Williams, and Richard Pryor

Plot: It is the early 1930s and 14-year old Eleanor Fagan (Diana Ross) is raped by a drunken derelict. Her well intentioned mother sends her to a friend in Harlem, not knowing that the woman runs a brothel. Taken in as a maid, Eleanor finds pleasure only in listening to blues recordings. Anxious to earn money she becomes one of the house girls. A friendly jazz player, Piano Man (Richard Pryor), encourages her to sing and in time she gets her first job. Changing her name to Billie Holiday, she gets the attention of handsome gambler Louis McKay (Billy Dee Williams) and becomes his mistress. After being dubbed Lady Day because of her refusal to sing in the bawdy style of most black vocalists, she joins two white musicians, Reg Hanley and Harry, as a vocalist. Touring the South, she sees a black man hanged by the Ku Klux Klan and undergoes personal indignities because of her color. Disturbed by the violence and prejudice she succumbs to Harry's suggestions to use narcotics to keep out the

169

Louis McKay (Billy Dee Williams) berates Billy Holiday (Diana Ross) for her drug habit in *Lady Sings the Blues*.

ugly realities. Billie becomes an addict and Louis, unable to deal with her changed personality, throws her out. Billie's dependence on drugs grows when her mother dies. She seeks help by entering a sanitarium, but Billie is arrested while under treatment, convicted on a drug felony, and sent to prison. She is told that her New York cabaret license has been revoked. Upon her release, Louis and Billie's agent set up a national tour to rebuild her reputation to such an extent that she will get a one-woman concert at Carnegie Hall. Free of the drug habit, Billie is enormously successful, winning critical and popular acclaim around the country. They reach L.A. and when Louis leaves to set up the Carnegie Hall date, Billie becomes depressed and gets high with Piano Man. Several dope dealers break in and beat Piano Man to death. Racing to Billie's side, Louis brings her back to New York. Although her appearance is a triumph, her appeal for permission to perform in the city's clubs is rejected by the License Commission. She is again jailed for drug offences. From then on, the road is downhill and Billie dies in 1959, at the age of forty-four, lost and broken.

Music: Songs include "Lover Man (Oh Where Can You Be?)," "Don't Explain," "I Cried For You," "All of Me," "Strange Fruit," "My Man," "God Bless the Child," "You've Changed," "Them There Eyes," "The Man I Love," "Mean to Me," "Fine and Mellow," "What a Little Moonlight Can Do," "Lady Sings the Blues," "'T' Ain't Nobody's Biz-ness If I Do," "Our Love is Here to Stay," and "Good Morning Heartache."

Moves: Billie does some mild hoofing when she sings. Wild black dancing in some of the clubs.

Outfits: By Bob Mackie and Ray Aghayan. Handsome, expensive dresses and gowns, full breasted suits, ritzy hats for men.

Social Significance: One of the few tributes to America's great black entertainers and justly deserved. Gave Billie Holiday her

170

place, immortalized in cinema, though reviewers found many problems with movie.

Trivia: Cost over $5,000,000. Doesn't actually follow the life of Holiday, leaving out two of her husbands, Lester Young, Jimmy Monroe, and other facts.

Awards: Several Academy Award nominations.

The Last Waltz

Company: United Artists, 1978
Color, 117 minutes
Category: Rockumentary
Directed by: Martin Scorsese
Produced by: Robbie Robertson
Starring: The Band, Bob Dylan, Joni Mitchell, Emmylou Harris, Neil Young, Van Morrison, Ron Wood, Muddy Waters, Eric Clapton, the Staple Singers, Ringo Starr, Dr. John, Ronnie Hawkins, and Paul Butterfield

Plot: A film of the Thanksgiving farewell concert of the Band (Robbie Robertson, Levon Helm, Garth Hudson, Rick Danko, Richard Manuel) in 1978. Mostly shot at Winterland, except for the Band, the Staple Singers, and Emmylou Harris who performed on a sound stage. The Band was the back-up group for Bob Dylan. Emmylou and other country and blues stars are symptomatic of Dylan's multiple-exposure musicianship. This film is one of the best crafted concert films to come around. It makes you wish they were still playing.

Music: The Band performs "Cripple Creek," "The Night They Drove Old Dixie

Down," "The Weight" (one of the best ever), and "Stagefright." "Mannish Boy" is sung by Muddy Waters; "I Shall Be Released," and "Baby Let Me Follow You Down" are sung by Dylan, Ringo Starr, Ron Wood, and the Band; "Mystery Train" is done by Paul Butterfield, and "Helpless" is done by Neil Young. Emmylou does look good singing and strummin'! Joni Mitchell (who looks good swimming) sings "Coyote."
Outfits: Dylan in leather and hat, others in standard, simple fare. They're the greats, they don't have to zap us with clothes and sets.
Social Significance: Sighs.
Trivia: Features poet Lawrence Ferlinghetti ("Coney Island of the Mind") and Doug McClure.

Let It Be

Company: United Artists, 1970
      Color, 80 minutes
Category: Rockumentary
Directed by: Michael Lindsay-Hogg
Produced by: Neil Aspinall
Starring: The Beatles
Composer: The Beatles

Neil Young, Joni Mitchell, and Robbie Robertson sing in the great final performance of the Band in *The Last Waltz*.

171

Plot: The film follows the Fab Four through several rehearsals and recording sessions. We get to see them up close, as opposed to their giant concert flicks, their interactions, their slow moments. The film gives an intimate look at them including Yoko on the sidelines looking on, silent, mysterious, a truly haunting presence. A fascinating film, the viewer almost feels that they are right there, just feet away watching the Beatles work out new material. The film concludes with a spontaneous performance/rehearsal on the roof of their recording building, Abbey Road Studios. This is the most powerful moment, as they whip out their guitars, obviously thrilled themselves, and, smiling broadly, play some of their hits. On the streets below, the public goes wild as they hear the music and realize what's going on. Traffic comes to a stop, people begin climbing on top of lampposts, over rooftops to see the great ones.

Music: The Beatles perform "Don't Let Me Down," "Maxwell's Silver Hammer," "I've Got a Feeling," "Across the Universe," "I Me Mine," "Long and Winding Road," "Shake, Rattle, and Roll," "Kansas City," "Get Back," and "Let It Be." Billy Preston makes an appearance on the organ.

Moves: The boys do a few moves while they play. John dances with Yoko at one point, sweeping her around in waltz-like steps.

Outfits: Low key outfits, shirts, sweaters, as the Beatles were relaxing.

Social Significance: This was the last of the Beatles films and one can sense the tensions and frictions that the band was going through. Yet, although feuding (and soon to split up), the Beatles, even in intimate close-up, were still larger than life and ultimately fascinating in this last cinematic gift to their fans.

Trivia: The Beatles did split up soon after *Let It Be* was made and the other members of the band placed a lot of the blame on Yoko. Even in the film, one can sense the antipathy of the others toward her as John was pulled away from them and toward her in a romance that was to last until his death.

172

The Beatles put on an impromptu performance on the rooftop of Apple Studios while the crowds go wild below in *Let It Be*.

Mad Dogs and Englishmen

Company: MGM Releasing, 1971
Color, 119 minutes
Category: Rockumentary
Screenplay by: Pierre Adidge
Directed by: Pierre Adidge
Produced by: Pierre Adidge, Harry
Marks, and Robert Abel
Starring: Joe Cocker, Leon Russell, and
others
Group/Singer: Joe Cocker, the Grease
Band, and Leon Russell

Plot: Recounts the 1970 Joe Cocker tour
with 40-plus musicians, singers, wives,
girlfriends, hangers-on. They perform in
Minneapolis, San Francisco, Plattsburgh,
Dallas, and New York. They are beseiged by
fans; philosophy pours forth from Cocker
about ego, performing, everything. Mostly,
though, it's the music and performing of
Crazy Joe Cocker. The best scene is the
bucolic Oklahoma picnic. Shades of Willie
Nelson down home! Finally, there's the
Fillmore West. That's the grand finale. At
the end Lennon's "Give Peace a Chance" is
sung, fading into the credits. A good concert
film.
Music: Joe Cocker blasts out "Delta Lady,"
"Feelin' Alright," "The Letter," "Space
Captain," "Honky Tonk Women,"
"Something," "With a Little Help From My
Friends," "Lawdy Miss Clawdy," "She
Came in Through the Bathroom Window,"
"Change in Louise," and "Darlin' Be Home
Soon." All of these are done in his own style.
Seldom have we seen and heard this
material done as well. Also, Claudia Linnear

sings "Let It Be" and "Bird on A Wire."
The theme "Mad Dogs and Englishmen" is
done by Leon Russell.
Moves: Joe Cocker's stylized spasms, his
unearthly rhythms.
Outfits: Joe's shirt is wet, Leon's hair is
without a net, but the thing is not the
outfits, it's the songs that you all get.
Social Significance: Inspiring to fans.
Trivia: Vincent Canby raved that it was a
"cinema verité" concert film at its best.

Joe Cocker performs in his own distinctive style in
Mad Dogs and Englishmen.

The Magic Christian

Company: Grand Films-Commonwealth
United, 1970
Color, 93 minutes
Category: Comedy
Screenplay by: Terry Southern, Joseph
McGrath, and Peter
Sellers
Directed by: Joseph McGrath
Produced by: Dennis O'Dell
Starring: Peter Sellers, Ringo Starr,
Leonard Frey, Laurence
Harvey, Christopher Lee, and
Raquel Welch
Group/Singer: Paul McCartney, Yul
Brynner, Thúnderclap
Newman, and Tom, Pete,
and Mike
Choreographer: Lionel Blair
Additional Material: Graham Chapman
and John Cleese

174

Plot: Sir Guy Grand (Peter Sellers) is a
jokester, a nut in the extreme. He adopts a
tramp and names him Youngman (Ringo
Starr). The fun begins. Misanthropic Sir Guy
is out to convince Youngman that people are
money mad and will stop at nothing to get
it. They go on a grouse hunt with machine
guns, bribe a Shakespearean actor to strip
onstage during Hamlet (to an aghast
audience), make a scene at an exclusive
club, and fix a bout so the boxers kiss
instead of fight. After further nonsense and
bad behavior, they plan a dastardly deal for
the social event of the season, the cruise of
the giant liner *Magic Christian*. Men under
Sir Guy's direction are paid to dress as
monsters to frighten the passengers, and the
ship appears to be sinking (it is still docked.
It's all expensive effects prepared by Sir
Guy). Then Sir Guy mixes a pile of money
with urine and other nasties and they watch
as people dive into it.

Music: Badfinger wrote the soundtrack
score, performing most of it. Paul
McCartney sang "Come and Get It," and
also wrote "Carry On to Tomorrow" for
Tom and Pete. "Something in the Air"
performed by Thunderclap Newman and
"Mad About the Boys" sung by Yul
Brynner (to Roman Polanski, yet!).

Youngman (Ringo Starr)
accompanies his mad
mentor Sir Guy (Peter
Sellers) on the flute in
Magic Christian.

Moves: Rock-fright mish mash.
Outfits: Dracula and King Kong suits, tuxedos, casual seawear, social register stuffed shirts; Costumes designed by Vangie Harrison.
Social Significance: Provided further evidence of the breakdown of society and morality, a further statement about the idle rich disdaining the idle rich. Ringo was working hard to be a movie star and succeeding (slowly).
Trivia: Noel Coward wrote the song Yul Brynner sings. Why? Why are the characters involved with this film involved? Because they all feel satire is their vehicle—at least sometimes. See John Cleese as the director in Sotheby's auction. See Spike Milligan as a traffic warden. See money poured down the drain. Get drunk and see it.

The Man Who Fell to Earth

Company: Cinema V, 1976
Color, 2 versions: 145 and 118 minutes
Category: Drama
Screenplay by: Paul Mayersberg
Directed by: Nicholas Roeg
Produced by: Michael Deeley and Barry Spikings
Starring: David Bowie and Rip Torn
Group/Singer: Roy Orbison, Louis Armstrong, and others

175

David Bowie, playing an extraterrestrial, becomes the center of media attention for his odd appearance and behavior in *The Man Who Fell to Earth*.

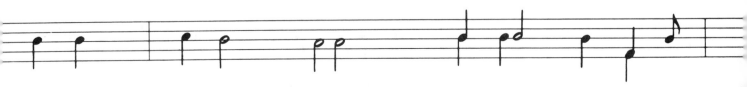

Plot: David Bowie plays a man who has come to earth from a parched-dry planet in search of water. He establishes an electronics company to aid him in his plans to assist his dying family back on the home world. He must invent new technology to do this. He does. He's a mysterious sensation to the press. He's not quite human, as we see when he is begged by a lover to show his real self; he's rather weird looking. The fragmented, abstract way this is put together does much to add to the sci-fi mood, as the haunting songs and the use of odd camera styles.

Music: The soundtrack songs are by Stomu Yamashta and Papa John Phillips, and they do much to add to the film's weird qualities. Also heard are Roy Orbison, Artie Shaw, Louis Armstrong, and others.

Outfits: Bowie's definitely a strange dresser. His space outfit is not your usual astrogarb. It's soft and silky and shiny. I think that it's reminiscent of *The Day the Earth Stood Still*. Bowie bears some resemblance to Michael Rennie in that classic.

Social Significance: Made Bowie a film star as well as rock star.

Trivia: Critics raved. The movie was based on a Walter Tevis novel. Audiences were so perplexed that the theater I went to issued a summary for people to read before they saw the movie.

176

Medicine Ball Caravan

Company: Warner Bros., 1971
Color, 90 minutes
Category: Rockumentary
Screenplay by: Suggested by Christian Haren

Directed by: Francoise Reichenbach
Produced by: Francoise Reichenbach and Tom Donahue
Starring: B.B. King, Doug Kershaw, Sal Valentino, the Youngbloods, Alice Cooper, Stone Ground, and Delaney and Bonnie

Plot: In the summer of 1970, a hot year in rock, 150 young musicians set out across the U.S. on a concert-tour adventure. There were 28 vehicles plus seven buses, and lots of camping out in psychedelically tie-dyed tents and partying. This is the documentary of that trip. There are interviews with the various stars and hangers-on, and the various concerts are excerpted. Alongside these images, middle America is seen in all

Musicians rock non-stop in *Medicine Ball Caravan.*

its placidity. Placitas, New Mexico, is the first stop where we see B.B. King, the great blues star, do his thing. Then it's on to bus accidents, hoboes, and another concert where Doug Kershaw (The Cajun Fiddler) is presented. Next Boulder, Colorado, home of the STP family, an odd group of cavemen/ex-green berets living in the mountains, who eat lots of hallucinogenic drugs and act threatening. Alice Cooper plays his weird stuff, then, at Antioch College, student radicals accuse the caravaners of "capitalism and exploitation." David Peel is in a knife fight, but the concert goes on. Washington, D.C., is the end of the road with a spectacular finale concert featuring the rest of the stars. While lots of the "story" is staged in seemingly impromptu fashion, this film has good music and some crazy atmospherics that make it okay.

Music: Songs include "Act Naturally" (the Youngbloods), and "Free The People" (Delaney and Bonnie).

Moves: The whole thing is sort of a dance to roadie-movies.

Outfits: Dregs of streetwear and "high" fashion levis. B.B. is suave in his sweaty togs, and everyone is dusty and worn in spots. Most interesting are the cavemen in their strange duds.

Social Significance: Just another roadie movie that gives a chance to lots of rock hangers on to appear in a film along with superstars. It might have shown Hollywood that concert films of the nature of *Woodstock* would have to wait for another Woodstock concert, which really never happened again.

Trivia: Coming too late after the great *Woodstock* film, this film rapidly disappeared off the screen and into obscurity. There are lots of camera tricks and split-screen stuff to hide the fact that some of the performers weren't so hot. The whole thing was put together so the caravan could become a movie, and it didn't work. But, what the heck . . . B.B. King is good. Martin Scorsese was associate producer and supervising editor.

Awards: The 1979 award for best feature documentary from the Academy Award committee. French filmmaker Francoise Reichenbach was joined by American disc-jockey Tom Donahue to make this thing.

Alice Cooper appears in *Medicine Ball Caravan.*

177

Nashville

Company: Paramount, 1975
Color, 159 minutes
Category: Drama
Screenplay by: Joan Tewkesbury
Directed by: Robert Altman
Produced by: Robert Altman
Starring: David Arkin, Barbara Baxley, Ned Beatty, and Karen Black
Group/Singer: Ronee Blakley, Keith Carradine, others
Composer: Keith Carradine for "I'm Easy"

Plot: Media hype opens the film, to be replaced by visions of urban lust and confusion, to be replaced by aerial shots, club shots, a cameraman's nightmare-fantasy vision of the world. Mostly this film deals with the people and scenes around the country music business, and I do mean *business*. The narrative has a dozen main characters so it's hard to say what's central to the issue here, but it's easy to say this is a great film. A beloved country music star, Barbara Jean (Ronee Blakley) is slain. She is unstable, frail, and destined for doom. But this doesn't happen before a panoply of characters parade their vices and virtues across the screen.

Haven Hamilton (Henry Gibson) is the scene's top male star and Bud (Dave Peel) is his lackey son. Lady Pearl (Barbara Baxley), is Haven's buddy, and she wants to reach the top. Tommy Brown (Timothy Brown) is a black star. Delbert Reese (Ned Beatty) is an upwardly mobile lawyer, and Linnea (Lily Tomlin), one of the more interesting characters, is in ambiguous love with Tom Frank (Keith Carradine), who sings the award winning "I'm Easy." Also seen are

178

Nashville swings—the film that most "country folk" disowned.

Geraldine Chaplin as Opal, a pushy BBC reporter determined to do a documentary critical of America, filled with car crack-ups and violence. Altman regular Shelley Duvall does her bit as L.A. Joan, and Michael Murphy is an avaricious campaign manager for a "Replacement Party" candidate for the presidency.

The climax is a political rally/concert where the candidate gets an endorsement from Haven. Barbara Jean, who's popular but at the end of her rope mentally and physically, is pressured into appearing to sing, and therefore improve the candidate's chances. Barnett (Allen Garfield), her manager-husband, also wants to assure the public she is okay. She isn't, but he wants the money to keep coming so she's up on stage, albeit unfit.

To the tune of "We must be Doing Something Right, to Last 200 Years...," the rally goes on, waiting for the candidate to arrive by limo. Barbara Jean is shot in a scene reminiscent of Kennedy's assassination, and Alberquerque (Barbara Harris), a desperate-to-succeed singer, grabs the mike, sings, and calms the people. The End. Whew. Something else. A tour-de-force by Altman.

This is what the magazines called "an epic." It is a vision of America that reflects the assassinations, ambiguous sex roles, social upheavals, and so on that make America what it is—some sort of wonderful mess. This movie was none too popular with the country-music folk in general, nor with Nashville residents in particular. Its length, its tragi-comic poise and its multi-dimensional denouement make it unique.

Music: Henry Gibson sings "200 Years" and "Keep A' Goin" Lily Tomlin wrote "Yes I Do," and Ronee Blakley wrote "Down to the River," "Bluebird," "Tapedeck in His Tractor," "Dues," and "My Idaho Home." Dave Peel wrote "The Heart of a Gentleman." Keith Carradine wrote "Honey" and "I'm Easy." Allan Nichols wrote "Rose's Cafe" and Karen Black wrote "Memphis," "Rolling Stone," and "I Don't Know If I Found It in You." Altman himself wrote the stirring "Day I Looked Jesus in the Eye." Keith Carradine's song, "It Don't Worry Me," closes the film.

Outfits: Country-western, business, average clothes.

Social Significance: This film made Nashville angry. It used "country stars" that really weren't along with a few that were. In any case, unlike the later *Coal Miner's Daughter*, it didn't *feel* country, it felt American.

Trivia: Altman's virtual repertory company of actors and actresses are incorporated throughout and do a good job! Even Elliot Gould and Julie Cristie make cameo appearances, and Howard K. Smith, the TV newsman, appears as himself.

Awards: Academy Award for Best Song ("I'm Easy"). Although it didn't cop top honors in general, it was said by some critics that this was the best film since *Citizen Kane*.

179

O Lucky Man

Company: Warner Bros., 1973
Color, 148 minutes
Category: Drama
Screenplay by: David Sherwin
Directed by: Lindsay Anderson
Produced by: Michael Medwin and
Lindsay Anderson
Starring: Malcolm McDowell, Rachel Roberts, and Ralph Richardson
Group/Singer: Alan Price

Plot: This film was shortened for its American release and is still a bit like *War*

and Peace. Lindsay Anderson made If, and this is a kind of sequel. Mick Travis (Malcolm McDowell), in this one, is a trainee salesman who gets sent from the home office to the Northeastern region of Britain to merchandise coffee. There, he stumbles on a secret installation of the government. That's after some odd happenings. For one, he witnesses a spectacular car wreck, and the subsequent looting of the car by the police. For another, the staid town has a pornographic show where he's invited to by the venal hotel manager. The manager's wife seduces the guileless youth and later an eccentric man presents him with a gold suit and the admonition, "Don't die like a dog." Far out. A nuclear explosion decimates the base

where he is held captive by the military and then escapes only to be experimented upon at a crazy doctor's clinic. Lot's more happens too, but the best is when, in the end, the director comes over and smacks Mick on the cheek with the script when he refuses to smile on cue. Weird, man, weird.
Music: Alan Price does "O Lucky Man," "Poor People," "Sell Sell," "Look Over Your Shoulder," "Justice," "My Home Town," and "Changes." With Alan on piano, Dave Markee on bass, Colin Green on guitar, Clive Thatcher on drums.
Outfits: Gold suit. Plus lots of uglies and really nice dress-up. Turtle necks, of course, for the Scottish moors.
Social Significance: Further paranoia for the masses.
Trivia: Special (and horrible) effects by John Stears (ugh,—the pigman).

Mick Travis (Malcolm McDowell) gets fitted for a gold suit in O Lucky Man.

180

Pat Garrett and Billy the Kid

Company: MGM, 1973
Color, 106 minutes
Category: Drama
Screenplay by: Rudolph Wurlitzer
Directed by: Sam Peckinpah
Produced by: Gordon Carroll
Starring: James Coburn, Kris Kristofferson, Bob Dylan, and Jason Robards
Singer: Bob Dylan
Score by: Bob Dylan

Plot: The familiar "Pat Garrett Kills Billy the Kid" theme. This time Dylan (who

disowned it) plays Alias, a sidekick of Billy's. The time is 1881. Two outlaws, Billy and Garrett, come to arguing. They split up, and Garrett goes on to support the establishment of cattle barons. He confronts Billy in Ft. Sumner, New Mexico Territory, and he arrests him. A hanging is scheduled but the Kid breaks out and kills two deputies. Dylan is his new sidekick, a taciturn ex-printer. The new gang is shot to pieces by Garrett's posse, though. Billy, despondent, takes for the border. After some sex and more gore, Garrett guns down the Kid. Dylan? It's a bit part.

Music: Dylan sings "Knockin' On Heaven's Door" which became a hit. The soundtrack is by Dylan, but don't rush out to buy it.

Moves: Fandango of death. Like in the Samurai epics, Peckinpah seems to get into a rhythm, a beauty of killing. Frankly, it works in the Japanese cinema, but here it's just disgusting.

Outfits: Western, spattered with ketchup.

Social Significance: None, though it further sickened Peckinpah audiences.

Trivia: Dylan, denied cutting privileges, disowned it, and this film soured him on dramatic roles. The next time we see Dylan on film for more than one minute is in the video of "What's a Sweetheart like You Doin' In a Place Like This" from his great *Infidels* album (1983).

Dylan is a natural before the camera, as you can see in *Don't Look Back* (1967). In Peckinpah's disaster, he looks shy. Perhaps he had an idea how bad the film was going to turn out. But don't blame Dylan. I rushed to see this western because I love Dylan. What a letdown. It's like an Elvis picture without Elvis singing.

Bob Dylan plays the new sidekick of Billy the Kid in the unmemorable *Pat Garrett and Billy the Kid*.

181

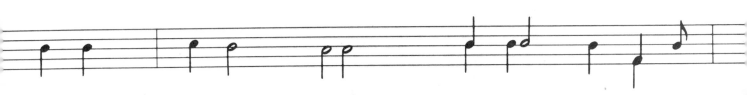

Performance

Company: Warner Bros., 1970
Color, 105 minutes
Category: Drama

Screenplay by: Donald Cammell
Directed by: Donald Cammell and
Nicholas Roeg
Produced by: Sanford Lieberson
Starring: Mick Jagger, James Fox,
Johnny Shannon, and Anita
Pallenberg
Group/Singer: Mick Jagger
Music Direction: Randy Newman
Composer: Mick Jagger and Jack
Nitzsche

Chas (James Fox) begins to look like reclusive rock star Turner (Mick Jagger) in *Performance*.

Plot: Set in the underground world of rock and drugs and crime, two unusual performers encounter one another, a reclusive rock star, Turner (Mick Jagger), and a sadistic mobster called Chas (James Fox). Chas likes to torture people for the mob. He views each act of depravity as a sort of performance art. He works for hoodlum Harry Flowers (Johnny Shannon) but he has to flee his association when he kills one of the organization's men. Now Chas, on his own, rents a room from Turner, pretending to be an out-of-work juggler to get the room. He falls for one of Turner's two bisexual girls, Pherber (Anita Pallenberg—actually Mick's girl then), and she psychologically tortures him with her sexuality and mocking words. The rock star, in a sort of drag, returns the money for the room, and Chas deflates him by asking what he would be like at fifty years of age. He gets to keep the room somehow. To impress Chas, Turner does a great rock number, then he finds out that Chas is a gangster. Now he's really intrigued, considering himself and Chas brothers-in-performance.

Turner is really too screwed up to perform anymore, and he thinks Chas is still capable of being "weird." Weirdness and performance are synonymous, it seems, to Turner. Pherber now asks Chas about the woman part of him and he replies with macho protestations, though there is a dreamlike sequence of Chas and Turner making love. This film, apparently, is about identity, and that means mostly sex. Clearly

now the persona of Chas and Turner are ambiguously identical. Chas makes love to Lucy (Michele Breton), Turner's other weird girl, a decidedly boyish woman. They all dress the same, act the same, and so on. Turner wants to be Chas and vice versa.

Now the weirdest part: To convert Turner into himself, Chas shoots him in the head. We see the bullet enter the brain and we enter with it, then Chas exits with Harry's white Rolls and the face in the limo next to Harry is Turner's, not Chas. Get it? We don't. But it's a trip, man. Besides, the music is really something, especially Mick strumming the acoustic guitar unaccompanied, singing his songs.

Music: Songs include "Gone Dead Train" (Randy Newman) and "Poor White Hound Dog" (Merry Clayton). Mick sings "Memo From Turner," co-written with Keith Richard.

Moves: Mick struts and does his bisexual macho/non macho stuff which, with him, is a dance.

183

Turner (Mick Jagger) begins to look like mobster, Chas in *Performance.*

Outfits: Multiple-sex costumes of gender-ambiguity.
Social Significance: Interestingly enough, this film, made before a slew of rock performers' deaths (Jimi Hendrix, Janis Joplin, Jim Morrison, Elvis and so on), is prophetic. Some time later, the Stones concert at Altamont was the scene of violence.
Trivia: Fox left acting after this to do religious work. Figures. This film is of appeal to anyone who might have imbibed an illicit substance in the micro-dot on a cube form, and others are advised to stay away.
Awards: We'll give it "Weirdest Film of 1970."

Quadrophenia

184

Company: World-Northall, 1979
Color, 115 minutes
Category: Drama
Screenplay: Dave Humphreys, Martin Stellman, and Franc Roddam
Directed by: Franc Roddam
Produced by: Roy Baird and Bill Curbishley
Starring: Phil Daniels, Leslie Ash, and Garry Cooper
Group/Singer: The Who

Plot: It's back to the 1960s and the Mods and Rockers of England. There's lot of violence, of course. As the U.S. gangs were dispersing, it seems the English cities were, more than ever, under seige by gangs. Here we see razor blades galore, drugs, and self destruction. A mod (Phil Daniels), the leader of a rock group called the Cross, is alienated, stoned out of his mind, sick, self-abnegating, hostile. He's on his way to death. The enmeshed plot and rock score do much to carry this film off. A must-see for Anglophiles.
Music: The film is really based on a 1973 album of the same name by the Who. There are songs by Booker T. and the MG's, a seminal Rock group, the Crystals, the Crusaders, the Ronettes, the Cascades, James Brown, the Kingsmen ("Louis, Louis"—remember?), and the Who. The Who do "Cut My Hair," "Quadrophenia," "I Am the Sea," "The Real Me," "The Punk Meets the Godfather," "Bell Boy," "Sea and Sand," "Doctor Jimmy," "Helpless Dancer," "5:15," "Love, Reigns O'er Me," and "I'm One."
Outfits: Mod and Rocker duds. Tough-guy leathers; lots of sneers.
Social Significance: The Who were getting into movies big. Always a main attraction in the rock world, they jumped into film with great impact. Good box office on this one.
Trivia: Who's playing? That's right. Corny, but better than The The.

Radio On

Company: British Film Institute, 1979
Black and white, 101 minutes
Category: Drama
Screenplay by: Chris Petit
Directed by: Chris Petit
Produced by: Keith Griffiths
Starring: David Beames and Lisa Kreutzer

Group/Singer: Sting (of the Police), Ian Drury and the Blockheads, Robert Fripp, David Bowie, and Kraftwerk

Plot: This is the somewhat left-hanging tale of a London DJ (David Beames) who travels way up north to investigate his brother's sudden death. Sting (of the Police) plays a gas station attendant and his obsession with the great American guitarist/singer Eddie Cochran is explored briefly. Kraftwerk, the electronic group from Germany, is prominent on the soundtrack as is the attendant alienation of the venture. Bowie has some cuts on the track. Devo and Lene Lovich round out the vibes. This is a haunting, black-mooded film with overtones of hopelessness abounding.
Music: "Trans-Europe Express" (Kraftwerk).

Social Significance: A haunting *noir* film of the endless road—a theme constant in western film.
Outfits: Lots of black.
Trivia: Documents England's teen alienation that led to punk.

Rock 'n' Roll High School

Company: New World, 1979
Color, 93 minutes
Category: Drama with music

David Beams plays a London DJ investigating his brother's sudden death in *Radio On*.

185

Screenplay by: Richard Whitley, Russ Dvonch, and Joseph McBride
Directed by: Allan Arkush
Produced by: Michael Finnell
Starring: P.J. Soles, Vincent Van Patten, Clint Howard, and Dey Young
Group/Singer: The Ramones
Story by: Allan Arkush

Plot: Lombardi High School is the school with the worst standing in all the state of California. New principal Togar (Mary Woronov) is determined to get the student's minds off rock and roll. Two monitors are sent to spy on the music-crazed student body. Cheerleader Riff Randall (P.J. Soles) is the ringleader of the students, and skips school to buy Ramones' tickets. She's even written a song ("Rock and Roll High School") for the group. Tom (Vincent Van Patten) has a thing for her, while brainy (and, therefore, unsexy) Kate (Dey Young) has a thing for him. Typical teenage problems of love. Tom goes to Eaglebauer (Clint Howard), a student with an uncanny ability to "fix" things. He will get Tom a date with his heartthrob. Kate also goes to Eaglebauer and he says he will get her a date with Tom. It's like this: Tom will "practice" a date with Riff by going out with Kate. Riff and Kate see the Ramones performance somehow, after shenanigans by Togar and others make the plot largely unfollowable. In short, the Ramones agree to use Riff's song on their next platter. Parents and the principal try to burn Ramones' albums, and the student body arises and takes over school, renaming it Rock and Roll High. Faced with a siege by the police, the teens blow up the school and continue their party elsewhere. Togar is off to the funny-farm.

Music: "Rock 'n' Roll High School," "Blitzkrieg Bop," "I Just Wanna Have Something to Do," "I Wanna Be Sedated," "I Wanna be Your Boyfriend," and "Pinhead." Also heard on soundtrack are such oldies as "Do You Wanna Dance," "Did We Meet Somewhere Before," "School Days," "Come Back Jonee," and "Rock and Roll."

Moves: The girls cavort in the gym in a sexy way as Riff's "Rock 'n' Roll High School" plays.

Outfits: Black-leather jacketed Ramones wiggle and look punk. Jeans are ripped at the knees, other kids wear gym shorts and tops or typical teen wear. The teachers,

186

The Ramones drive the students wild while they burn their school down during a police siege in *Rock 'n' Roll High School.*

including Coach Steroid, all are caricatures of teachers' pictures in yearbooks—stiffs!

Social Significance: Essentially, this film takes advantage of a revival of truly good rock and roll films of the fifties. The music and ambiance here is somehow not the same.

Trivia: Clint Howard is the brother of Ron Howard. Dey Young is the sister of Leigh Taylor-Young. P.J. Soles was in *Carrie* and *Halloween*, two much better films. She's great as an object of desire and as a teen teaser. Van Patten is son of actor Dick Van Patten. Warhol's glamorous Mary Woronov is the mean principal, and does the role justice. Real Ramones' fans were in the concert scene and created a near-riot that threatened safety, or so some cast members thought. It's a riotous affair.

Rockers

Company: Rockers Films, 1978
Color, 100 minutes
Category: Drama
Screenplay by: Theodoros Bafaloukos
Directed by: Theodoros Bafaloukos
Produced by: Patrick Hulsey
Starring: Leroy Wallace and Richard Hall
Group/Singer: Justin Hines and the Dominoes, Peter Tosh, Junior Byles, the Heptones, and Gregory Isaacs

Plot: Like the great, (though unapproachable,) *The Harder They Come,* this film tries to show a struggling reggae musician facing the criminal conspiracy known as the music industry. The promoters exploit and steal the genuine-roots music of the down-home people. Many musicians do their thing in the film, and the music is really rocking indeed. In fact, since the plot is so familiar and done so much better in *The Harder They Come,* just sit back and watch the colorful sequences, try to decipher the interesting Jamaican-English accent, and listen to the sweet, sweet sounds of the reggae singers as they enchant you with their island music.

Music: We hear "Slave Master" (Gregory Isaacs); "Jah No Dead" (Burning Spear); "Natty Take Over"(Justin Hines and the Dominoes); "Stepping Razor" (Peter Tosh); "Book of Rules" (The Heptones); "Fade Away" (Junior Byles); "Rockers" (Bunny Wailer). Other groups are Big Youth, Mighty Diamonds, Jacob Miller, Dillinger, Jack Ruby, Erroll Brown, and Prince Hammer.

Outfits: Colorful, big caps to be filled with dreadlocks, lots of open shirts, lots of frayed garments of the real Jamaicans, lots of island straw hats, sun wear.

187

Social Significance: *The Harder They Come* said it all, but this film highlights a lot of the other great reggae stars. There's nothing like true reggae to enliven a party; buy some (thank you, signed, Jamaica Chamber of Commerce).

The Rocky Horror Picture Show

Company: 20th Century Fox, 1975
Color, 100 minutes
Category: Musical/drama

Screenplay by: Jim Sharman and
Richard O'Brien, from a
play of the same name
Directed by: Jim Sharman
Produced by: Lou Adler and Michael
White
Starring: Tim Curry, Susan Sarandon,
Barry Bostwick, and Richard
O'Brien
Group/Singer: Cast
Composer: Richard O'Brien

Plot: A criminologist (Charles Gray) is
narrating his sad story. Brad (Barry
Bostwick) proposes to Janet (Susan

Sarandon). They go off together, get caught
in the rain, and find shelter in a spooky
castle. Riff Raff (Richard O'Brien), the weird
butler, leads them to maid Magenta
(Patricia Quinn). At this castle tonight, the
space people from the planet Transsexual
are holding a convention. Brad and Janet
are stripped to their scanties and Dr. Frank-
n-Furter (Tim Curry), in drag, comes to
them. He shows the couple his experiment—
Rocky Horror (Peter Hinwood), a monster

**Dr. Frank N. Furter, with Magenta and Columbia by
his side, announces the creation of his monster
Rocky Horror in *The Rocky Horror Picture Show*.**

188

he is bringing to life. Rocky Horror awakens, is scared, and flees. On a motorcycle arrives Eddie (Meatloaf) and Columbia (Little Nell) who swoons every time he's near. Doc kills Eddie with an ice pick. He seduces Janet and later Brad. Janet sings to Rocky Horror to have him make love to her.

Dr. Scott (Jonathan Adams) Brad's science teacher from high school in Denton, Ohio, arrives. He's looking for his nephew Eddie. Doc serves Eddie (literally) for dinner, then tells his guests. He turns Brad, Janet, Scott, and Columbia into statues. Magenta, Riff Raff, Scott (in a wheelchair), Rocky, and the Doc dance in front of the RKO tower to praise horror movies and please the conventioneers. Now Doc is off to Transylvania, the galaxy where Transsexual can be found. Riff Raff kills him with a raygun, and Rocky climbs the tower with the body. Magenta is blown up while Riff Raff prepares to space-transport the castle. Brad, Janet, and Scott escape as it explodes into non-time and space.

Music: Often accompanied by theater audiences, the songs include "Science-Fiction Double Feature," "Toucha, Toucha, Touch Me," "Sweet Transvestite," and "The Time Warp."

Moves: The dance in front of the tower, an homage to horror-films. Lots of prancing and over-acting.

Outfits: Mondo-wierdo Transsexual garb, licentious under-wear, space gear, laser-fare.

Social Significance: A phenomenon. A rite-of-passage for teen pubescents and older, *the* midnight movie in over 200 theaters nationwide to this day, *the* cult film of the century, perhaps. The de-inhibitor, and a campy, raunchy ode to everything parents are afraid of.

Trivia: A giant fan club, the National Rocky Horror Fan Club, participate along with thousands—dare I say millions—of teens and hipsters in the theaters, lip-syncing the performances doing the dance routines on stage dressing up to beat the band like the movie folk.

Saturday Night Fever

Company: Paramount, 1977
Color, 119 minutes
Screenplay by: Norman Wexler
Directed by: John Badham
Produced by: Robert Stigwood
Starring: John Travolta and Karen Lynn Gorney
Choreographer: Lester Wilson

Plot: Tony Manero (John Travolta) is a paint store clerk in Brooklyn. But he has dreams. On Saturday nights, he gets dressed up in his white vested suit and heads to "2001," a flashy disco where he is king of the dance floor with his wild moves and sensuality. He meets Stephanie one night and the two become dance partners, deciding to enter an upcoming dance contest. She is a public relations secretary and wants to leave Brooklyn behind and enter the more sophisticated world of Manhattan. Various subplots unravel including Tony dumping his girl Annette. On the night of the contest, Tony and Stephanie perform but are bested by a Puerto Rican couple who lose because of prejudice. Tony realizes this and gives the trophy to the couple. He makes a crude pass at Stephanie who runs off. Later, Tony's friend Billy, who has gotten a girl pregnant, falls (jumps) from the Verazzano Bridge. Terrified and shaken, Tony goes to Stephanie's apartment and apologizes for his actions. He dreams that someday perhaps he too can become someone, like Stephanie, and move to Manhattan.

Music: Although no bands appear in the film, several had their songs on the

189

soundtrack, including the Trammps ("Disco Inferno"), Kool and the Gang ("Open Sesame"), and K.C. and the Sunshine Band ("Boogie Shoes"). The Bee Gees were the mainstay of the film, though, and virtually everything they sang became a huge hit—

"How Deep is Your Love," "Night Fever," "More Than a Woman," and "Staying Alive."

Moves: Travolta performs, swirling, kicking, gyrating disco dances in his hottest performance ever. His most famous number is a solo to "You Should Be Dancing."

Outfits: Travolta wears a skintight, white disco suit, slicked back hair.

Social Significance: Millions of American male teens began dressing in Travolta suits and trying to do the moves he did. He created a symbol of masculinity for the young working class that is still emulated today.

Trivia: The soundtrack for *Saturday Night Fever* sold over 27,000,000 records. Made Travolta a superstar in the role that was perfectly suited for him. Made the Bee Gees the hottest group in the world.

190

Sgt. Pepper's Lonely Hearts Club Band

Company: Universal, 1978
        Color, 111 minutes
Category: Musical
Screenplay by: Robin Wagner and Tom O'Horgan
Directed by: Michael Schultz
Produced by: Robert Stigwood

Tony Manero (John Travolta) struts his stuff on the dance floor in *Saturday Night Fever*.

Starring: The Bee Gees, Peter Frampton, Aerosmith, Alice Cooper, Billy Preston, Earth, Wind, & Fire, Stargard, George Burns, and Steve Martin

Based on: The Beatles album of the same name

Plot: Probably overawed by the task of making a Beatle classic into a musical, the moguls called upon the best talent. How did they do it? Well, who's best if you can't get the Beatles? Why, the Bee Gees! (But wait, there's a problem. It takes four to be Beatle-ish so it's the Bee Gees three plus Peter Frampton, here as Billy Shears.) Many notables, including Wilson Pickett, even, appear in this flop. You know it's going to be bad when Strawberry Fields, an English girls school, becomes a person. Anyway, it contains valiant and not-half-bad tries at singing the tunes as well as the Beatles did.

Music: Earth, Wind, & Fire do "Got to Get You Into My Life;" Bee Gees do "Getting Better" with Peter Frampton; and we hear "Fixing a Hole" by George Burns; "Long and Winding Road" done by Barry Gibb; "Get Back" by Billy Preston; "Maxwell's Silver Hammer" by Steve Martin. There are 22, count 'em, other numbers, including ones by Wilson Pickett, Helen Reddy, Monte Rock III, Dr. John, Frankie Valli, Donovan, Minnie Ripperton, and Tina Turner.

Outfits: Now here's where the film excels. I liked those band outfits a lot. Of course, they mimic the cover of the Beatles album. Lots of color.

Social Significance: Made people that didn't have the *Sgt. Pepper* album (by the Beatles) go out and get it.

Trivia: George Martin, the genius of Beatle recordings, was brought in to help. He did, but not enough.

Riding on Mr. Mustard's bus, which they've captured, the Lonely Hearts Club lead a joyous parade in *Sgt. Peppers Lonely Hearts Club Band.*

191

Shaft

Company: MGM, 1971
Color, 100 minutes
Category: Drama
Screenplay by: John D.F. Black
Directed by: Gordon Parks
Produced by: Joel Freeman
Starring: Richard Roundtree, Moses Gunn, and Gwen Mitchell
Group/Singer: Isaac Hayes

Plot: John Shaft (Richard Roundtree) is a private eye who lives in Greenwich Village and works in Times Square. His contacts are in Harlem, where underworld czar Bumpy Jonas (Moses Gunn) rules. He orders Shaft dragged to his premises. Shaft gets an assignment: find Jonas's missing daughter Marcy (Sherri Brewer). Black Militant Ben Buford (Christopher St. John) has kidnapped her, it seems. However, the Mafia are really behind the abduction. Shaft rescues her by swinging on a rope through a hail of bullets and through an unopened hotel window.

Music: Isaac Hayes won an Academy Award for Best Song for his throbbing rock/soul theme from *Shaft*.

Moves: Harlem hustle.

Outfits: Super-fly cool.

Social Significance: A tremendous box office hit. Two more Shaft films followed; *Shaft's Big Score* and *Shaft in Africa*. The latter took a loss.

Trivia: Roundtree's first film role and a hit.

192

Richard Roundtree made it big as the "man" in this slick flick, *Shaft*.

Shampoo

Company: Columbia, 1975
Color, 109 minutes
Category: Drama with music

Screenplay by: Robert Towne and
Warren Beatty
Directed by: Hal Ashby
Produced by: Warren Beatty
Starring: Warren Beatty, Julie Christie,
Jack Warden, Goldie Hawn,
and Lee Grant
Group/Singer: The Beach Boys, the
Beatles
Musical Score: Paul Simon

Plot: This is twenty-four sexy hours in the life of a Beverly Hills, California, hairdresser. Exhausted from high paying

Jackie (Julie Christie) is one of the many lovers of George (Warren Beatty), a California hairdresser, in *Shampoo.*

193

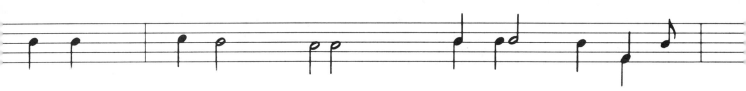

work and sexual favors, George (Warren Beatty) wants to settle down. However, all these gorgeous, rich women are mad about him. He has made it with nearly all his sexy women customers, the three main ones being Jackie (Julie Christie), ex-fiancee Jill (Goldie Hawn), and Felicia (Lee Grant). Jackie is also the mistress of Felicia's husband. This wonderful, scandalous movie doesn't take itself too seriously, and Warren Beatty has the right touch and looks to carry the difficult part off. This is a devastating satire of sexual mores, not a sexploitation movie.

Music: Musical score by Paul Simon. We hear the Beachboys sing "Wouldn't it Be Nice" and the Beatles "Strawberry Fields Forever" at just the right satirical moments.

Outfits: Warren Beatty in beat-up leather jackets, women in suburban wealthy togs and sexy underwear.

Social Significance: Aside from making enormous box-office, this film fascinated millions dealing with the mixed up sex lives of the rich and famous.

Trivia: Co-Screenwriter Towne also wrote *The Last Detail* and *Chinatown*, both Jack Nicholson vehicles. Grossed $60 million in its first round in the U.S.A. Beatty, a daring, multi-talented entrepreneur of the old style, went on to do *Reds*, a great film with apparently little box-office success because its heroes were—get this—communists!

194

Slumber Party '57

Company: Cannon-Happy, 1977
　　　　　　Color, 89 minutes
Category: Drama
Screenplay by: Frank Farmer
Directed by: William A. Levey

Produced by: John A. Ireland Jr.
Starring: Deborah Winger, Bridget Hollman, and Noelle North
Group/Singer: The Platters, Jerry Lee Lewis, Big Bopper, the Danleers, and others

Plot: Weren't the fifties the greatest? "Why not do one of those fifties pics again, J.B.?" "Sounds good, boy. You get on it right now." (That's what must have gone on at the office before they made this.) The guys on the set must have gotten a call to have some of the girls take off their clothes if the picture didn't look too good. Softcore rock and roll. Lines like "Hey, give me back my hula hoop" recall the era (vaguely). Anyway, the performers are great. It starts out at Beverly High School. Someone suggests a slumber party. Six cheerleaders take over one house while parents are away and run around in scanties as they recall how they "did it" the first time. Angie's (Noelle North's) hot story makes them hungry. They get burgers at a great fifties drive in, then tell more sexy stories to one another. Sherry (Rainbeaux Smith), who has the best story, invites the losing boys' basketball team over for snacks. Then she takes them upstairs for activities because she's the only girl among them still a virgin. The girls fret downstairs. All their stories were fictitious. They rush upstairs and find an exhausted basketball team lying around a bed with Sherry on it.

Music: Jerry Lee Lewis does "Whole Lotta Shakin' Going On." Big Bopper sings "Chantilly Lace." Other songs are by the Platters, the Danleers, Paul and Paula, Dinah Washington, and Patti Page.

Outfits: Evocative of the era, but did I see a digital something?

Social Significance: Man, it wasn't that way. You could hardly find this sort of permissiveness in the Eisenhower era. Unrealistic.

Trivia: Sure is.

The Platters songs liven
up a slumbering
Slumber Party '57.

195

Soul to Soul

Company: Cinerama Releasing, 1971
Color, 95 minutes
Category: Concert film
Screenplay by: Denis Sanders
Directed by: Denis Sanders
Produced by: Denis Sanders

Starring: Ike and Tina Turner, Wilson
Pickett, Santana, Roberta
Flack, the Isley Brothers, and
others

Plot: Here's a unique idea for a concert
film: Black western performers touring black
Africa. It works. The capital of Ghana was,
in 1971, celebrating independence day. The
nation was fourteen years old. That's not
much compared to 200, but it meant a lot to
those there. The celebration lasted eight

days and nights and there was a fifteen hour concert. This is the concert on film. There are interviews of the troup before and after, and native groups do their thing, entertaining them too. It's all in the spirit of real soul.

Music: Wilson Pickett does "Midnight Hour," "Funky Broadway," and "Land of 1,000 dances;" Ike and Tina Turner romp through "Soul to Soul," "I Smell Trouble," plus "You are Gone;" "Freedom Song" is notable by Roberta Flack. Other songs include: "Are you Sure" by the Staple Singers and "Soul to Soul" by the Voices of East Harlem.

Outfits: Tina has the shortest, most tattered skirt around; Wilson is natty in his neats until he strips off his jacket then he's pure soul. Lot's of bright eyes.

Social Significance: Camaraderie

Trivia: Not enough soul stuff on film. Have you noticed? This helps remedy that.

The Strawberry Statement

Company: MGM, 1970
        Color, 103 minutes
Category: Comedy/drama
Screenplay by: Isaac Horovitz
Directed by: Stuart Hagmann
Produced by: Irwin Winkler
Starring: Bruce Davison, Kim Darby, Bud Cort, Murray McCloud, and Tom Foral
Group/Singer: Buffy Sainte-Marie, Neil Young, John Lennon, Thunderclap Newman, and Crosby, Stills, Nash, and Young
Musical Score: Ian Freebairn-Smith

196

Tina Turner turns it on in *Soul to Soul.*

Plot: Obviously based on the Columbia University student takeover, the film moves to a "western" university (probably for legal reasons) and glorifies the protesters. Simon (Bruce Davison) is enamored of a student-protester female. He joins a sit-in to be with her, and is called a communist by a cop. This leads him into a life of "mobilized youth" and he unwittingly gets into hot water by hanging around with Linda (Kim Darby). He's swept into a bloody confrontation in which students sing "Give Peace a Chance."

Music: "Helpless," "Our House," "Suite Judy Blue Eyes," "Long Time Gone,"
(Crosby, Stills, Nash, and Young); "Thus Spake Zarathustra," a classical piece composed by Richard Strauss; "Circle Game," by Joni Mitchell, performed by Buffy Sainte-Marie.

Moves: Violent confrontation by Flower-children.

Outfits: Student casual.

Social Significance: This film was one of the few (the Kent State films were years later) to document a unique time in college life, when it was fun to go to college. The music and the period have never been equalled.

Trivia: Scenes were filmed in San Francisco. Worthy of a look now after all these years. Remember when youth was ready to breech the barricades and establish peace?

197

Simon (Bruce Davidson) and Linda (Kim Darby) relax between confrontations with authority in _The Strawberry Statement_.

Superfly

Company: Warner Bros., 1972
Color, 96 minutes
Category: Drama (labeled a black
exploitation movie)
Screenplay by: Phillip Fanty
Directed by: Gordon Parks, Jr.
Produced by: Sig Shore
Starring: Ron O'Neal, Carl Lee, Sheila
Frazier, and Julius W. Harris
Group/Singer: Curtis Mayfield

Plot: This allegedly first "Black" film financed and done by blacks, is hardly different from exploitative films done by non-blacks. It shows a world of pimps, killers, and drugged-up, violent maniacs. Not exactly role-models for the kids who flocked to see this one for the music, which is good.

It is an action filled movie, with a cocaine pusher as a hero. A black organization, BANG ("Black against Narcotics and Genocide"), called this film destructive to black youth, because it "glorifies dope pushers with its portrayal of a super-cool cocaine pusher who gets away." This glorified dope pusher is none other than Youngblood Priest (Ron O'Neal). He wears a crucifix that has cocaine in it. He wants to

198

**Curtis Mayfield performs
the theme from *Superfly*.**

retire rich with his girl Georgia (Sheila Frazier) and talks his partner Eddie (Carl Lee) in to investing their combined $300,000 in a 30-kilo shipment of high-grade "superfly" (cocaine). Scatter (Julius W. Harris), an old friend and semi-dealer who owns a restaurant, gets the dope for them. The money pours in so well that Eddie decides to keep doing these deals and to get Youngblood in hot water with the cops. When a "client," Fat Freddie (Charles McGregor), does a stickup to pay Youngblood for some dope, the cops are there to get the "dope" on Youngblood before he dies "in an escape." Since the biggest coke dealer is the deputy commissioner of the police, Youngblood, realizing he is next when Scatter is given a fatal overdose, sets up a hit on the deputy commissioner and his family, to be carried out if he himself is "hit." Youngblood gets the money from Fat Freddie and gives it to Georgia for safekeeping, then he is adbucted by the cops and taken for a ride. He escapes, using super-karate. The deputy commissioner has the drop on him after this, however. Youngblood tells the commissioner that he and his whole family will die if he pulls that trigger, and Youngblood is able to leave with Georgia with all the money.

Music: Curtis Mayfield sings the title song and others in a movie that became a classic of the genre. The album at last check, however, is out of print.

Moves: The coolest struts this side of the barnyard rooster roost.

Outfits: Super-cool suits, "Fly" clothing. The kind of stuff you'd buy at a subway arcade clothing store, flamboyant all-polyester pimp suits of outrageous colors, together with tasteless, gross jewelry.

Social Significance: Lambasted by blacks and whites as derogatory to blacks, women, and whites. However, a good money maker like this had lots of impact on Hollywood, which poured out more lethal doses of sky-high black thrill killers acting cool and getting rich.

Trivia: *Superfly*, featuring Curtis Mayfield, *Shaft*, with Isaac Hayes's music, and *The Harder They Come* with Jimmy Cliff and Desmond Dekker, were part of a whole series of black movies that made their early profits from black audiences, and were, surprisingly to their promoters, also supported by whites.

To Russia . . . With Elton

Category: Rockumentary
Screenplay by: Dick Clement and Ian La Frenais
Directed by: Dick Clement and Ian La Frenais
Produced by: Allan McKeown and Ian La Frenais
Starring: Elton John
Singer: Elton John

199

Plot: Rockumentary about Elton's 1979 concert tour of the Soviet Union. Yes, the Soviet Union. Lots of shots of staid Soviet audiences—you had to know an apparachik to get tix —and lots of pictures of Elton in various zany costumes, which doesn't seem to turn the audience on any more than the music. Oh well, it's good to hear Elton do some of his best songs. They are some of his best songs. They are, really.

Music: Elton sings "Back in the U.S.S.R." The Red answer to California girls paeans by the Beach Boys, this Lennon-McCartney hit wasn't sung in any other film. He also sings "Rocketman" and "Crocodile Rock."

Moves: Elton dances at and with the piano. Moscow and Leningrad will survive, however.

Outfits: Now we're talking. Elton is famous for strange-rimmed glasses and the really quite ordinary rock star proves that it's charisma not looks, style not . . . er.

Social Significance: Further broke down the barriers between east and west. Now if we could just do the same with that wall. . . .

Trivia: When the Nitty Gritty Dirt Band went to Russia years before, there was a great series of mob scenes and hysteria wherever they went; they were literally thrown out by the authorities. ABBA toured and, though popular, things were more under control as they were here. It's a sign of the times that Soviet audiences don't think it's such a momentous event anymore to see touring Western rock stars.

Elton John, in one of his characteristically weird glasses, enjoys himself performing for a Russian audience in _To Russia . . . With Elton._

200

Tommy

Group/Singer: Tina Turner, Keith Moon, Eric Clapton, Paul Nicholas, Elton John, John Entwistle, Arthur Brown, and Pete Townshend

Company: Columbia, 1975
Color, 111 minutes
Category: Rock opera
Screenplay by: Ken Russell, based on a rock opera by Pete Townshend and the Who
Directed by: Ken Russell
Produced by: Robert Stigwood and Ken Russell
Starring: Ann-Margret, Roger Daltrey, Oliver Reed, Robert Powell, and Jack Nicholson

Plot: This rock opera started as a Who recording session. The Who played it at the Met. The film was next. Ken Russell (*The Music Lovers, The Devils, Listomania*) was the natural choice for a director. The frenetic, surreal, intriguing director gets to do his thing again here. A triple-handicapped, deaf, dumb, and blind, pinball wizard, Tommy (Roger Daltrey), becomes the head of a religion. He had become handicapped by seeing his father killed. Ann-Margret, famed

201

Keith Moon of the Who can play more than his drums in *Tommy.*

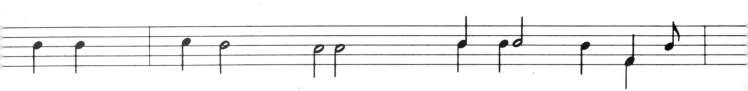

rock and roller and film star (remember her flicks with Presley?) is Tommy's mother. She's practically buried by baked beans out of a TV set. Surreal. Tina Turner is in a terrifying scene as the Acid Queen. All in all, a spectacular vehicle for the Who compositions, one of which, Ann-Margret's number "The Day it Rained Champagne" was specially penned for the film. Happily, Tommy, cured, becomes a rock superstar.

Music: The Who do "See Me, Feel Me," "I'm Free," "We're Not Gonna Take It," and "Eyesight for the Blind." Elton John does "Pinball Wizard" in giant platform shoes. Tina Turner sings "Acid Queen."

Outfits: Extremely bizarre, from Elton's super, giant platform shoes, to the brightly colored flash-duds of the rocksters. All captured with weird camera angles and highlighted by unusual lighting effects.

Social Significance: The Who, long a premier rock group, move into the mystical realm of Olympian rocksters, as the Beatles had.

202

Awards: Ann-Margret was nominated by the Academy Awards for best actress.

Two Hundred Motels

Company: United Artists, 1971
Color, 98 minutes
Category: Fable
Screenplay by: Frank Zappa. Additional material by M. Volman and H. Kaylan
Directed by: Frank Zappa and Tony Palmer
Produced by: Jerry Good and Herb Cohen

Starring: Frank Zappa and the Mothers of Invention, Mark Volman, Howard Kaylan, Keith Moon, and Ringo Starr
Musical Score: Frank Zappa. Played by the Royal Philharmonic Orchestra and chorus, and the Mothers of Invention

Plot: A fable of the musician (Frank Zappa) on the road. Frantic running from place-to-place a la rabbit in *Alice in Wonderland*. Cartoons, computer graphics, and so on, to "zappa" the mind. How does it feel to be a

Frank Zappa smiles on a brief rest during his hectic tour in *Two Hundred Motels*.

traveling performer, sleeping in 200 different motels? The answer is here, in this movie. It freaks you out, man.

Music: Frank Zappa and the Mothers of Invention do "Mystery Rock," "Dance of Rock and Roll Interviewers," "This Town Is a Sealed Tuna Sandwich," "Centerville," "Redneck Eats," "Touring Can Make You Crazy," "I'm Stealing This Car," "Penis Dimension," "Shove It Right In," and other fabulous Zappa tracks.

Outfits: Zappa is always wild looking. His hair interferes with his guitar strums at times. It's that long. Outfits looked either new wave or picked out of the garbage.

Social Significance: None. Zappa made this film too late. Big box office success never materialized.

Trivia: Originally made as a video tape in England.

What's Happening?

Company: Maysles Films, 1970
Black and white, 60 minutes
Category: Rockumentary
Directed by: Albert Maysles and David Maysles
Produced by: Albert Maysles and David Maysles
Starring: The Beatles, Ed Sullivan, and Murray the K
Group: The Beatles
Photographer: Albert Maysles

203

The Beatles pose together in this documentary of their trips and tours to the U.S.A.

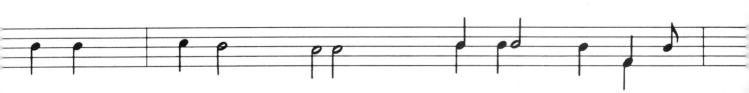

Plot: None. Facetious answers by Beatles to press; hysteria by fans; TV appearance on Ed Sullivan; interview with DJ Murray the K are shown. Documents the Beatles' trip to U.S.A.

Outfits: Beatles wear Beatle garb, squares wear square duds.

Social Significance: Everyone with a scrap of film of them, or a piece of the sheet they slept on (seriously), or a shred of the original cross . . . er, I mean hair, was in line to make a buck off the Beatles.

Trivia: Why were they so revered? When Lennon said the Beatles were more popular than Jesus, that set off a storm of controversy in the Bible Belt of America. Nobody asked if he thought that popularity was a good thing (He thought it wasn't). In any case, more believers in the Beatles existed in the sixties than had ever heard of Christ. But aren't the Beatles the bearers of the message "All You Need is Love?" Beatle songs have a strong spiritual significance. There are whole towns in the deserts of Southwest U.S.A. that worship the Beatles as prophets.

Quiz: Two of the four Beatles went spiritual to an extreme, in a totally different way. Which? How?

Answer: Harrison went for "Krishna consciousness" and John Lennon seemed to have his own religion with Yoko, somewhere along the lines of his song "Imagine." The Fab Four were each searching for different things. All have done work for charity and for peace at one time or another.

John, a familiar sight on New York City streets in the 1970s, having won his right to remain in the USA (a right hard to obtain for certain powers felt he might lead some sort of entertainers-for-revolution movement), was always searching. His death, and the following worldwide silent tribute, signified many know they are also on that journey, understood his quest, and participated in it in some way.

The Wiz

Company: Universal International, 1978
           Color, 133 minutes
Category: Musical
Screenplay by: Joel Schumaker
Directed by: Sidney Lumet
Produced by: Rob Cohen

204

Lavish and extravagant numbers fill *The Wiz.*

Starring: Diana Ross, Richard Pryor, Michael Jackson, Lena Horne, and Nipsey Russell
Choreographer: Louis Johnson
Composer: Charles Smalls and Quincy Jones

Plot: A remake of the original *Wizard of Oz,* the film takes place in New York in the 1980s. Dorothy is now Diana Ross in the lead, as a shy schoolteacher in Harlem. She encounters a wild snowstorm while chasing her little dog Toto, and is lifted in a whirlwind into a fantasy world of Manhattan. From then on, the film more or less duplicates Dorothy's adventures in Oz, only everyone is played by black actors. Fervently wet-eyed, Diana sings songs of happy hopefulness in relentlessly dragging arrangements. Nipsey Russell is great as the Tinman, likewise, Michael Jackson as the Scarecrow. Richard Pryor is the Wiz and Mabel King the Wicked Witch.
Music: "Believe In Yourself," "Brand New Day," "Home," "He's the Wizard," "The Feeling That We Have," "Soon as I Get Home," "You Can't Win," "What Would I Do If I Could Feel," "Slide Some Oil to Me," "I'm a Mean Old Lion," "Be a Lion," "Ease on Down the Road," "Emerald City," "March of the Munchkins," and "End of the Yellow Brick Road."
Moves: Large scale, forties-feeling, gargantuan, flashy dance numbers staged by the Louis Johnson Dance Theater. Best Dance and show stopper—Mabel King as evil witch Evilene and the Flying Monkeys from her sweat shop as they perform "Don't Bring Me No Bad News."
Outfits: Wild black city clothes, pimp outfits, glistening shoes, and jewels too shiny to look at, feather hats, lots of makeup and lipstick.
Social Significance: Tried to resurrect the almost mystical charm of *Wizard of Oz* for a modern black audience but lost something in the translation.

Trivia: One of the most expensive film flops ever.
Awards: The song "Ease on Down the Road" was a hit on the radio.

Woodstock

Company: Warner Bros., 1970
Color, 184 minutes
Category: Rockumentary
Directed by: Michael Wadleigh
Produced by: Bob Maurice
Starring: Joan Baez, Crosby, Stills, Nash, and Young, Arlo Guthrie, Richie Havens, the Who, and many others

205

Plot: A filmed concert at Woodstock, N.Y., featuring a half (or more) million extras, the concert goers. This biggest-ever affair was billed as a music and art outdoor fair. The Woodstock Nation, the youth of America that was into rock, came out in droves for this giant concert that lasted 3 days. Law enforcement, sanitation, and food problems (mostly the latter two; the concert goers were mostly peaceful types) didn't spoil the mood. The biggest rally since the Nazis put on their shows, only this one was more to proclaim peaceful attitudes and loosening up, not war and tightening up. The blissed-out campers, lovers, rock fans, beer guzzlers, dogs, cats, kids (there were births), knew they were at a phenomena, and so did the performers who gave it their all.
Music: Especially memorable performances: the Who doing a "Tommy" medley; Jimi Hendrix doing "The Star-Spangled Banner" (since this kind of portrayed the birth of a

new nation, the new America has a rock version of the S.S.B.); Joe Cocker sings "With a Little Help from My Friends"; and "Higher" is done by Sly and the Family Stone; Crosby, Stills, Nash and Young do a great "Woodstock." Also featured were

Country Joe and the Fish, Santana, John Sebastian, Sha-na-na, Ten Years After, and others.

Musicians jam furiously to please the enormous crowd at *Woodstock*.

206

Outfits: Camping gear, nudity, superfluidity, practicality,T-shirts, jeans, beads, blankets, bandannas, hair, hair, hair. The performers in their hip, sometimes down-home country outfits.

Social Significance: Tremendous. A mind-boggle to the media. No one ever expected this. Proved the power of the new rock, the new youth, the new consciousness (ecology). Sure there was a lot of garbage left behind, but there should have been more. The place was spiffy in a few days.

Trivia: A shorter version appeared on TV.

WUSA

Company: Paramount, 1970
Color, 115 minutes
Category: Drama with music
Screenplay by: Robert Stone

Rainey (Anthony Perkins) hears some disquieting facts about how he's being used as a dupe by Fascist radio owner Bingamon in *WUSA*.

207

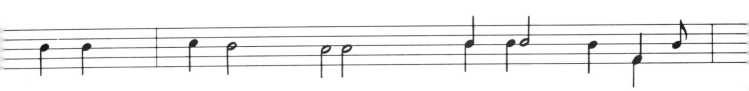

Directed by: Stuart Rosenberg
Produced by: Paul Newman and John Foreman

Starring: Paul Newman, Joanne Woodward, Anthony Perkins, and Laurence Harvey
Composer: Lalo Schifrin

Rainey (Anthony Perkins) looks up at the right wing mob about to kick his brains out after he's killed one of them in *WUSA*.

208

Plot: A drunken drifter, Rheinhardt (Paul Newman), collects a favor from his old pal Farley (Laurence Harvey), a con artist currently playing the role of a revivalist preacher in New Orleans. He learns from him that right-wing radio station WUSA needs an announcer. That night, in a dock bar, he meets Geraldine (Joanne Woodward), who is hustling a sailor. After Rheinhardt buys her some food, she brings him to her room where they make love. The next day, he meets Bingamon, the station's boss, and is hired on the agreement that he read right-wing commentaries on the air. Soon he also meets the liberal and naive Rainey (Anthony Perkins), who has been unwittingly tricked into taking part in a phoney investigation of welfare actually designed to create backlash among whites. Because he, too, is being used, Rheinhardt gets depressed and drunk. He quarrels with Rainey and then leaves Geraldine. Later, after Rainey has also learned the truth of the whole thing from black newsman Roosevelt Berry, WUSA sponsors a giant political hate rally with gospel singers, an aging cowboy star, and a demonstration by black militants outside the stadium. Rainey, now totally disillusioned, tries to kill Bingamon in front of everyone but only gets one of the man's assistants. He tries to escape but the enraged crowd stomps him to death. Meanwhile, the gospel singers, made up of Geraldine's hippie friends, are afraid that the riot will lead to drug arrests and they give Geraldine their grass. When the cops discover the drugs and arrest her, Geraldine hangs herself in jail. Rheinhardt hears the news from her crippled friend Philomene. After visiting the grave, he takes his bags and leaves the city.

Music: Neil Diamond and backup musicians sing "Glory Road" and others.

Outfits: Business suits, dashikis, late 1960s hippie.

Social Significance: An attempt by Newman and company to create a liberal exposé of the right but it didn't catch on with audiences.

209

the Eighties

Rockin' Reels

The New Wave
(1980-1984)

Rock films of the 1980s have, without question, delved deeper into the dark, nihilistic side of the genre than those of any other period in their evolution. At the start of the decade, rock music began to feel the profound effects of a new rock form—punk—a style which blossomed in Britain in the mid and late 1970s with groups like the Sex Pistols and the Clash. Punk was first cultivated by working-class youths who sincerely felt, in the words of the Sex Pistols' song "God Save the Queen," that "there is no future in England's dream."

The truth of the matter was, and is, that to be born into Britain's working class most likely is to be condemned to a life at the bottom of the heap, with very little opportunity to advance. With the decline of the British economy, the working class seemed to suffer more than anyone. While saved from outright starvation by the dole, the working classes traditionally have been prevented from moving upward by the powerful class system, and life, especially for the numerous unemployed, appears to offer little future beyond sitting around the pubs throwing darts and getting drunk.

Locked into a bleak and gritty existence by a society that cannot accommodate them gracefully and yet does not totally abandon them, and lacking a political awareness that would bring them to the point of outright class revolution, the punk generation turns upon itself, ripping its clothes, shaving its heads, sticking safety pins into its flesh. Look

at me, it says; pity me if you dare, hate me if you like, but look at me. Look, it snarls; look at what you have done to me.

"God Save the Queen," the first big punk hit, was banned from British radio as being "insulting to royalty," but it became an underground national hit as young musicians everywhere played it to each other. When Johnny Rotten and the Sex Pistols brought the song with them to the U.S., it generated the same kind of excitement among the youth and the same kind of negative hysteria among the older generation. Influenced by the British groups, American punk musicians began to spring up, primarily in New York's Lower East Side and in Los Angeles. Performers like Blondie, Patti Smith, Richard Hell and the Voidoids, Black Flag, and the Ramones all created their own style of hard music, concerned with the realities of modern life. A particular bone of contention was the way rock music itself had been taken over by big business and superstars; music was so drastically overproduced (48-track recordings, truckloads of studio musicians) that only those with incredible financial backing could get airplay. The punkers felt that rock had lost touch with the real people who made it in the first place. Their own, new music was raw, underproduced, often recorded live without thousands of over-dubbings—but it possessed an energy and an urgency that the radio hits couldn't touch.

Again, the filmmakers picked up on this latest trend in the evolution of rock, although generally with low-budget productions. *The Decline of Western Civilization* (1980), *D.O.A.* (1981), and a number of other raw, punk-influenced films gave new infusions of blook into the cinematic scene. *Rock 'n' Roll High School* (1979), featuring the Ramones, who had made a tremendous splash in the U.S. with their spirited two-minute singles, was the biggest budgeted punker of the time. The larger studios finally got the message, and soon more highly financed films depicting the punk world emerged, among them *Quadrophenia* (1979), *Breaking Glass*, and *The Blank Generation*.

With the explosion of independent films came a new phenomenon in distribution—the underground theater. As many of these films appeared to be too raw, obscene, sexy to show to "normal" audiences, a number of smaller, more arty theaters began showing them, often at midnight, to what quickly developed into cult followings. The 1980s have seen a tremendous growth of this countercinema, with larger and larger audiences appearing as word of mouth spreads.

Reggae, the musical sound from Jamaica, has entered rock music and film as well. The creation (in large part) of the late Bob Marley and the Wailers, with Jimmy Cliff and Peter Tosh, reggae was initially slow in coming to the U.S., although it has become increasingly popular, with groups like the Police and other stars using its rhythms in their own music. With such films as *The Harder They Come* and *Reggae Sunsplash*, the form has actually entered popular music more than many people realize.

The newest of rock's many mutations is New Wave. The term is somewhat difficult to define, as many different styles from dance music to avant garde are lumped under the same label. An offshoot of punk and disco, new wave has a multi-layered, polyrhythmic, often synthesized sound with often surrealisitic lyrics and loosely structured song forms. At best, new wave creates an eerie texture and has a definite rhythm that is often irresistible. Such performers as Laurie Anderson, Brian Eno, the Eurythmics, Talking Heads, Nina Hagen, Madness, and Culture Club are the best-known proponents of this new sound. To accommodate this rich sound, a new visual medium, music video, has been created. With its wildly imaginative scripts and sets, hypnotically pulsing and suggestive music, and short (three- to five-minute) format, rock video borrows as much from TV commercials as from traditional film.

What the future will bring only time, and the songwriter-performers of the future, will tell. Surely, rock and roll seems to have a unique ability to regenerate itself just when it seems to have lost steam. And, in the prophetic words of Neil Young, "Hey, hey, my, my, rock and roll will never die."

213

American Pop

Company: Columbia, 1981
  Color, 97 minutes
Category: Animated drama
Screenplay by: Ronni Kern
Directed by: Ralph Bakshi
Produced by: Martin Ransohoff and
  Ralph Bakshi
Group/Singer: Pat Benatar, Fabian, the
  Doors, Big Brother, and
  Bob Seger
Animator: Ralph Bakshi

Plot: The animated story (using the dubious process of rotoscope) of four generations of an American family, the film documents the music of each generation. From the Vaudeville days of tap dancers and cane twirlers, to the modern punk and post-punk periods, it's all here. Ralph Bakshi's other films, *Fritz the Cat, Heavy Traffic,* all cartoons, were better than this one. Still, he's a unique talent, even trying to do this adult-theme cartoon stuff. He certainly picked out representative music, and good music at that.

Music: The Doors sing "People are Strange;" Fabian does his famous "Turn Me Loose" (to generate the fifties feeling); Pat Benatar sings "Hell is For Children;" Big Brother sings "Summertime;" Bob Seger rounds the film out with the impressive "Night Moves."

Moves: Animated dancing and wiggling, from the first hesitant vaudeville hoofer numbers to the crazy punk slam-dancers. If you are a kid at heart, dig the crazy jitterbug number.

Outfits: Cartoon re-creations of a cool piano player, cigarette dangling from his mouth; vaudevillians in straw hats; the works from all eras. Bakshi's impressions of people are insulting-amusing.

Social Significance: Again Ralph Bakshi proves himself the premier cartoonist since the death of Walt Disney.

Trivia: Too adult for kids. Too kiddie for adults. Your move.

A cool pianist at work in Ralph Bakshi's *American Pop*.

Atomic Cafe

Company: New Yorker Films, 1982
Color and black and white,
100 minutes
Category: Documentary with music
Directed by: Kevin Rafferty, Jayne
Loader, and Pierce Rafferty
Produced by: Kevin Rafferty, Jayne
Loader, and Pierce
Rafferty
Group/Singer: The Commodores and
many others
Featured: Harry Truman, the pilot of
Enola Gay, and common folks
in air-raid garb

Plot: This almost entirely musical documentary delivers a hysterical (that's the word indeed) look at atomic war preparations and defense attempts (shelters, gasmasks) of the 1950s and 1960s. It makes it all look so stupid and quaint, sad and insane, that it's a sick laugh riot much like *Dr. Strangelove.* The songs are great, or at least mind-boggling, and the choosing of material must have taken a decade, so well is this put together. It's definitely anti-powers-that-be. It is a paranoid, panoramic montage of military training films, newsreels, U.S. propaganda, TV shows, and more—interviews with the President, Nixon-noses, Tricky Dickie stuff, and, need we say it, Hiroshima. All original material, nothing added, it makes its case. Man, we are crazy to blow the hell out of ourselves unless sanity somehow creeps into the cracks in our little heads! The end, of course, is a future holocaust of the type portrayed in the popular book *Doomsday Warrior.* The best parts are the kids taking shelter, the bomb

masks, and plans to "survive." What's to survive? That's the point of the film.
Music: The film is filled with, as it advertises, "Radioactive Rock and Roll, Blues, Country, and Gospel." The songs are often camp, mocking, or, worst, sincerely pro-atomic. They include "The Day They Dropped the Atomic Bomb" (Jackie Doll and the Pickled Peppers), "Uranium" (the Commodores), "Fifty Megaton" (Sonny Russell), "Atomic Cocktail" (Slim Gaillard Quartette), "Satellite Baby" (Skip Stanley), "Atomic Love" (Little Caesar and the Red Callendar Sextet), "Atomic Telephone" (Spirit of Memphis Quartet), "Red Dreams" (Louisiana Red), "Atom and Evil" (Golden Gate Quartet).

A "prepared" family live in their fallout shelter in *The Atomic Cafe*.

215

Outfits: Fifties, but you should see the clothes that we were supposed to wear in the bomb shelter—daddy squeezing a gamma-gas mask on junior who wears a pathetically open rad-suit, and all the military men in uniform.

Social Significance: This film is having an impact comparable to *The Day After*, the ABC TV dramatization of a nuclear war. It makes one see the insanity of the whole thing. Still, are the right people seeing this, both here in the good old USA and abroad, behind the sinister Red curtain?

Trivia: A cult movie on underground movie circuit. See it at midnight in a cult movie house. Warning: Most of the soundtrack isn't melodic, just campy. You can't get these songs anymore, folks—why even Roy Rogers's famous backup, the Sons of the Pioneers, do a ditty. That's camp!

The Big Chill

Company: Columbia, 1983
Color, 97 minutes
Category: Drama
Screenplay by: Lawrence Kasdan and Barbara Benedek
Directed by: Lawrence Kasdan
Produced by: Michael Shamberg
Starring: Tom Berenguer, JoBeth Williams, Kevin Kline, William Hurt, Glenn Close, Jeff Goldblum, Mary Kay Place, and Meg Tilly

216

The friends that were reunited under less happier circumstances renew their friendships in the *Big Chill.*

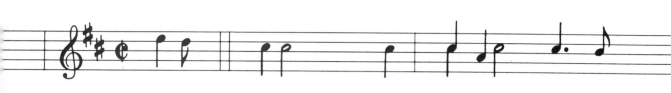

Group/Singer: Marvin Gaye, the Exciters, Three Dog Night, the Rascals, the Temptations, the Miracles, Aretha Franklin, and Procol Harum

The Blues Brothers

Plot: Someone is being dressed by female hands. We find out he is dead—a suicide. This is an excuse for all the old college buddies to come to the funeral. They are a bunch from the 1960s and they spend a long weekend in an enormous house, where the suicide occurred reliving and reevaluating their relationships with one another. Good editing and a terrific soundtrack carry this one to heights it might otherwise not reach. In many theaters the audience cheered and clapped at the end. Nostalgia for the good old college-in-the-sixties rides high. There is lots of bedhopping and soul-searching, lots of what-the-hell-has-happened-to-us, and can't-we-do-it-over-againism.

Music: "I Heard It Through the Grapevine" (Marvin Gaye); "Joy to the World" (Three Dog Night); "Good Lovin'" (the Rascals); "You Make Me Feel (Like a Natural Woman)" (Aretha Franklin); "I Second that Emotion" and "The Tracks of My Tears" (Smokey Robinson and the Miracles); "Ain't Too Proud to Beg" and "My Girl" (the Temptations); "Tell Him" (the Exciters).

Moves: A few turns around the kitchen for old times sake.

Outfits: Eighties' fashion.

Social Significance: Recollections of the good old days. Sigh. Remember hanging around the Harpur campus being bored? Sigh.

Trivia: Really, go see *Return of the Secaucus Seven* if you want nostalgia for that era and its events. It's more gripping and less hype. However, isn't this a neat soundtrack, and aren't the production values super?

Company: Universal, 1980
Color, 130 minutes
Category: Musical/comedy
Screenplay by: John Landis and Dan Ackroyd
Directed by: John Landis
Produced by: Robert K. Weiss
Starring: John Belushi and Dan Ackroyd
Group/Singer: The Blues Brothers, Aretha Franklin, and others
Musical Direction: Ira Newborn

Plot: The Blues Brothers (John Belushi and Dan Ackroyd) are sprung from the hoosegow and in short order are in the music business once more. They are putting on a show, it seems, for charity. Lots of evil, pro-Nazi forces are determined to stop them. All of this of course, is merely a vehicle. Vehicle? Thousands of cars, trucks, busses, and police cars are demolished in an endless and often meaningless car chase-and-wreck sequence that must have cost millions. Anyway, the real film here is the great music. The Blues Brothers like to harken back to rhythm and blues and other early rock and soul. So here we have the likes of Aretha Franklin, Cab Calloway (yet!), James Brown, and Ray Charles. Man, what a show. The Blues Brothers themselves, hip whitesters, er, white hipsters, do their harmonica and beat, their spinning and posturing in wraparound sunglasses and mafioso suits, and it all comes off well. The Nazis, as they should be, are defeated and the charity makes a bundle. So did Ackroyd

217

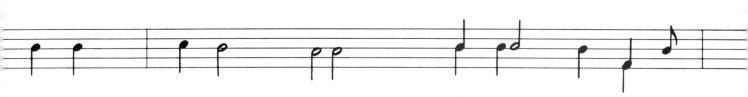

and Belushi, in this spinoff of their TV triumph on *Saturday Night Live* which probably can still be seen in reruns in your area.

Music: Aretha Franklin sings "Think," probably the best number. Also the Blues Brothers do their thing and sing, Ray Charles belts out "Shake a Tail Feather," Cab Calloway re-creates his "Minnie the Moocher," and James Brown sings "The Old Landmark." Booker T. Jones, Steve Cropper, and John Lee Hooker also appear and sing.

Moves: Blues Brothers freneticism.

Reverend Cleophis James (James Brown) injects a little soul in his sermon in *The Blues Brothers*.

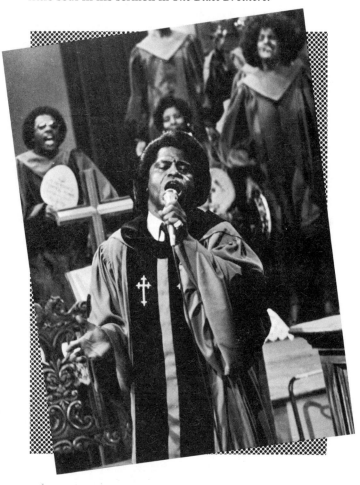

Outfits: Tight dark suits and alpine hats a la mafia-hipster-cool on the Blues Brothers, others come as they are. Nice to see Booker T., one of the pioneers recognized here.

Social Significance: Continued the adoration of these musical comedians, sure to be a team to rival Jerry and Dean, Donald and the Mule, Bob and Bing, Laurel and Hardy, Abbott and Costello. But that, of course, was cut short by Belushi's untimely death.

Trivia: Could the Blues Brothers act be based in part on Sam and Dave?

Cat People

Company: RKO-Universal, 1982
　　　　　　Color, 118 minutes
Category: Drama
Screenplay by: Alan Ormsby, based on a
　　　　　　story by Dewitt Bodeen
Directed by: Paul Schrader
Produced by: Charles Fries
Starring: Nastassia Kinski and Malcolm
　　　　　　McDowell
Group/Singer: David Bowie

Plot: There is an opening title scene with David Bowie playing on the soundtrack as the desert winds clear away some skulls. Then there is an erotic animal-worship, sex-with-black-leopard scene. Then we are transported to New Orleans. Irena (Nastassia Kinski) is getting off a plane to meet her long lost brother Paul (Malcolm McDowell). He shows her around and puts her up. She gets a job in the zoo. The fun begins. Seems that they are a pair of cats

really, of a race born long ago. If they have sex with anyone except one another, they each turn into a giant, ferocious leopard. This causes a lot of blood to flow in this evocative, stunning, scary, sensuous, and subtle horror-fantasy movie.

Music: David Bowie sings and wrote the lyrics for "Cat People (Putting Out the Fire)." The music is by Giorgio Moroder. Also on the track are "Autopsy," "Irena's Theme," "Leopard Tree Dream," "Paul's Theme," "The Myth," "The Bridge," "Transformation," and "Bring the Prod."

Outfits: ASPCA-type uniforms at zoo, torn tops on Kinski, lots of nudity, lots of black leopard.

Social Significance: Furthered Kinski's career. Best of all, it proved that it is still possible to make a great horror film nowadays.

Trivia: Bondage turn-on.

Caveman

Company: United Artists, 1981
Color, 92 minutes
Category: Comedy with music
Screenplay by: Rudy DeLuca and Carl Gottlieb
Directed by: Carl Gottlieb
Produced by: Lawrence Turman and David Foster
Starring: Ringo Starr, Barbara Bach, Dennis Quaid, and John Matuszak
Group/Singer: Ringo Starr and his cavemen
Music by: Lalo Schifrin

219

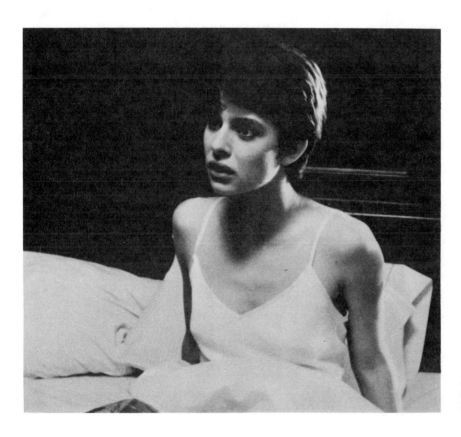

A black leopard's cry awakens Irena (Nastassia Kinski) in *Cat People*.

Plot: It's millions of years B.C. Caveman Atouk (Ringo Starr) has got problems, the least of which is a world full of dangerous animals and plants. For one thing, and we do mean Thing, there's bully Tonga (John Matuszak), who's vying for the hair of lovely cavewoman Lana (Barbara Bach). Atouk is a wee-sized caveman in a world of muscle. In order to win Lana he must learn to stand erect, cook (which means discover fire), and, as the cavepeople sit about the first campfire, he discovers musical instruments. Atouk soon becomes a rock drummer, literally. Dinosaurs cause a scare or two, all for comedy effect, and Atouk gets the girl, at least for a while. There is a 15-word language that is pretty funny, and the whole thing looks more Mexican rural than prehistoric. Still, Ringo and the satiric score make it worthwhile, as do the scantily clad cavegirls.

Music: A stone age jam session is a highlight. The music won't remind you too much of the Fab Four, but is tolerable and amusing.

Moves: Strictly dinosaur-prehistoric.

Outfits: Fur, bones, rocks.

Social Significance: Only for Ringo; he married Barbara.

Trivia: Carl Gottleib wrote, in part, *Jaws*, *Jaws II*, and *The Jerk*—a far funnier movie with Steve Martin playing the title role. The dinosaurs are state-of-the-art, and the language has a smidgeon of Yiddish, does it not?

Class of '84

Company: Mark Lester-United Film-Guerilla High, 1982
Color, 93 minutes
Category: Drama
Screenplay by: John Saxon, Tom Holland
Directed by: Mark Lester
Starring: Perry King, Roddy McDowell, Timothy Van Patten, and Merrie Lynn Ross

220

A giant bug startles Atouk (Ringo Starr) and more than startles his friend in *Caveman*.

Plot: Didn't Dick Clark do this one back in the sixties? Gee, it sure sounds like it. A teacher tries to stop violent students from taking over the school. At least they're not gonna blow it up like they did in Rock n' Roll High School. The predictable plot is graced by the old-timer expertise of Roddy McDowell.

Moves: Yeah.

Outfits: Rubber and leather, shorts on girls, gloves without fingers. Guys could slide down a wall without burning themselves. Graffiti-ish influence in jewelry and grooming.

Graffitied walls and black leather enhance an image of toughness in *Class of '84*.

Coal Miner's Daughter

Company: Universal, 1980
Color, 125 minutes
Category: Drama/biography
Screenplay by: Tom Richman
Directed by: Michael Apted
Produced by: Bernard Schwartz
Starring: Sissy Spacek and Tommy Lee Jones
Group/Singer: Sissy (as Loretta Lynn), Ernest Tubb, Beverly D'Angelo (as Patsy Cline), and other Grand Ole Opry stars

Plot: Superstar of country music Loretta Lynn had a hard climb to the top, born a coal miner's daughter, raised in abject poverty, and rocketed to riches on the basis of her songs. In Kentucky, Loretta Lynn (Sissy Spacek) is a thirteen-year old living with father Ted Webb (Levon Helm—the Band drummer in a stupendous film debut) and mother (Phyllis Boyens). A brash soldier just back from the army is wildly driving his jeep outside the company store when Mr. Webb goes to get supplies with Loretta. Loretta is taken by the charming wild guy, whose name is Mooney (Tommy Lee Jones). At a church social bake sale, Mooney outbids all others for Loretta's questionable cake (she used salt instead of sugar). She goes on dates, against her father's wishes, with Mooney in his war-surplus jeep. Mooney wins her, promises never to hit her or take her far away, and marries her at a tender age. On her wedding night, knowing nothing whatsoever about sex, Loretta and the twice as old Mooney have some trouble.

221

In the morning she won't eat in a nearby restaurant because of the scandal of what they had done. Mooney goes to work in the mines, unhappy and comes home to a wife who can't cook or clean right, and worst she won't read the sex-manual he has provided. She returns to her family but misses Mooney. He starts flirting with another woman. She catches the girl and hits her with a stick. They get back together and she becomes pregnant. He migrates without her to Washington state for work as a logger. He sends for her when she's seven months pregnant and there they start their family.

She is encouraged in her singing and guitar playing by her husband. She gets gigs at local roadstops, is a hit, and cuts a record. They run around like mad in their car promoting it and it finally hits the charts. Loretta now makes it to the stage of the legendary Grand Ole Opry. Patsy Cline (Beverly D'Angelo) and she become great friends. Mooney is feeling unimportant and jealous. They quarrel but eventually straighten it out. The stress of touring, family life, and the death of Patsy in a plane crash take their toll. Battered by life and the music grind, she nearly collapses on stage, but soon makes a recovery. The fans go wild at her comeback, for she is more than a singer to them now.

Music: Sissy Spacek, Ernest Tubb, Beverly D'Angelo are sensational. "I Fall to Pieces" and "Honky Tonk Girl" are big songs in this movie. Other Grand Ole Opry stars make appearances.

Outfits: Show-biz country and down-home country. Country, both in songs and mood.

Social Significance: A sensation when it opened, especially in Britain, and considered an early contender for the Oscars. The effect of this film was the opposite of that of *Nashville*. Altman's film was (rightly, in part) seen as a putdown of "country," a distortion of the Nashville scene and sound. This movie lauds country music and country ways.

Awards: Hollywood-made biographies always could draw audiences, and this film is the prime example of drawing power. Many awards, including Best Actress for Sissy Spacek, and rightly so.

Cruising

Company: United Artists, 1980
Color, 106 minutes
Category: Drama
Screenplay by: William Friedkin
Directed by: William Friedkin
Produced by: Jerry Weintraub
Starring: Al Pacino
Group/Singer: John Hiatt, Willie De Ville, Rough Trade, and others

Plot: Gays protested this film that is about life in the gay community (purportedly) and the killing spree of a gay murderer. Pacino is such a good actor here that it's a shame the film was crippled at the box office. He is a New York detective who disguises himself as a gay and infiltrates the gay community looking for the killer. We see men dancing with men (true enough) at gay bars, lots of dimly lit rendezvous (true enough) but gays protested the association of murdering types with gays. *Boys in the Band* was also protested years earlier because in that film gays were portrayed as sad.

Music: The sound track is largely punk-rock. The Cripples, John Hiatt, Madelyn Von Ritz, Egberto Gismonti, Willie De Ville, Rough Trade, the Germs, Mutiny, Barre Phillips, Ralph Towner, and Tom Brown all contribute the music.

Moves: Lots of rough-trade dancing man-to-man in gay bars.
Outfits: Tank tops, black denims, captain's hats, leathers, boots, short haircuts, chains.
Social Significance: Howls of protest from gay community.
Trivia: Location shooting in the Village was interrupted by protests. Remember the hassles *Fort Apache, the Bronx* had in shooting in the South Bronx?

Steve Burns (Al Pacino) is an undercover cop trying to penetrate the gay community in *Cruising*.

Diner

Company: MGM, 1982
             Color, 110 minutes
Category: Drama/comedy with music
Screenplay by: Barry Levinson
Directed by: Barry Levinson
Produced by: Jerry Weintraub
Starring: Steve Guttenberg, Paul Reiser, Kevin Bacon, Mickey Rourke, Timothy Daly, Ellen Barkin, and Daniel Stern

223

Plot: It's 1957, Baltimore, Maryland, and a mixed bunch of Catholics and Jewish young men are having french fries in a diner and thinking about girls. They are in their early twenties and long on talk and short on experience, sexually. They stay up late, run about in the car, and do errands. Infantile existential pranks and jokes are performed, friendships explored. We get to see they are knowledgeable about pop culture and sports, and full of a certain embarrassing sexual panic. This film tries to show why they would opt for early marriage without experience of love and sex. The really fine cast and the excellent screenplay plus soundtrack make this one a winner.

Music: "Honey Don't" (Carl Perkins); "A Thousand Miles Away" (Heartbeats); "Whole Lotta Shakin' Going On" (Jerry Lee Lewis); "I Wonder Why," "A Teenager in Love" (Dion and the Belmonts); "Don't be Cruel" (Elvis Presley); "Come Go With Me" (Del Vikings).

Moves: Well, for one, Steve Guttenberg does an onstage number with a stripper. He's pretty stiff, he's inexperienced, but willing.

Outfits: Strictly teen fifties. Square guys with plastic holders filled with ballpoint pens and pencils in their knit shirt pockets.

Eddie (Steve Guttenberg) dances onstage with a stripper in *Diner*.

224

Eddie and the Cruisers

Company: Embassy, 1983
Color, 92 minutes
Category: Drama
Directed by: Martin Davidson
Produced by: Joseph Brooks and Robert Lifton
Starring: Tom Berenger and Michael Paré
Group/Singer: Beaver Brown, Kenny Vance, and Ben E. King
Original Music by: John Cafferty

Plot: The story of Eddie (Michael Paré) and his band and their unrelenting drive to the rock and roll top of the charts. They encounter stiff resistance from the fiercely corrupt promoters, they wade through girls

like seashells at high tide, and yet they try not to compromise their sound and their vision.

Music: Kenny Vance sings "Those Oldies But Goodies" and "Betty Lou's Got a New Pair of Shoes"; Beaver Brown performs "On the Dark Side," "Wild Summer Nights," "Tender Years," and "Season In Hell."

Moves: Trying to recall the teen delinquent era and eeking by with a lindy-like step or two.

Outfits: Leather jackets, shirt collars up.

Social Significance: Trying to relive the fifties and iffy. See the great *American Hot Wax* and *The Buddy Holly Story* for better reference to the times.

Trivia: This film *is* trivia.

Volatile Eddie (Michael Pare) is held back by other members of the band when he lunges at a record company executive in *Eddie and the Cruisers*.

Fame

Company: MGM, 1980
Color, 134 minutes
Category: Musical drama
Screenplay by: Christopher Gore
Directed by: Alan Parker
Produced by: David DaSilva and Alan Marshall
Starring: Irene Cara, Barry Miller, Paul McCrane, Linda Gifford, and Laura Dean
Group/Singer: Cast
Choreographer: Louis Falco

225

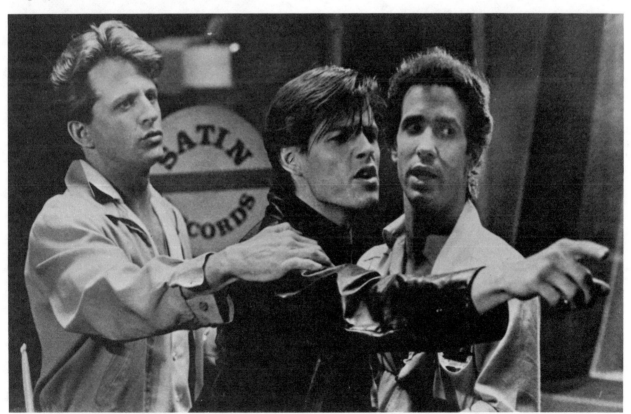

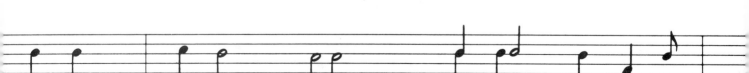

Plot: The story is set in New York City's High School for Performing Arts, on the west side of Manhattan. A group of talented, sometimes troubled, kids are seen growing up, taking the good with the bad, falling in love, out of love, disillusioned, and so on. Actually, it is carried off wonderfully and the music is dynamite. A truly memorable graduation concert-dance performance contains some semi-classical numbers. Truly inspiring performances that made Irene Cara, for one, a superstar. Speaks to a whole generation, as much as *Rock Around the Clock* did to the first rock generation. A must see. Oh, they manage to graduate, some go on to be performers, some face unemployment and uncertainty, or get lucky.

Music: "Fame (We're Gonna Live Forever)," "Red Light," "I Sing the Body Electric."

Moves: Frenetic dancing in the streets, on top of cabs, in the halls, all modern. Some classical ballet during class time.

Outfits: Lots of leg warmers and leotards, sweat shirts and jogging pants. Lots of color.

Social Significance: Spoke to a whole generation and sparked an interest in modern dance.

Trivia: Some scenes in this movie actually happened.

The entire school performs at its graduation ceremonies in *Fame*.

226

Flashdance

Social Significance: Like *Fame*, *Flashdance* again makes creative modern-type dance more accessible to the young audience.

Trivia: The usual stand-in for the dances by Beals was Marin Jahan.

Company: Paramount, 1983
Color, 100 minutes
Category: Drama/dance musical
Screenplay by: Tom Hedley and Joe Eszterhas
Directed by: Adrian Lyne
Produced by: Don Simpson and Jerry Bruckheimer
Starring: Jennifer Beals and Michael Nouri
Group/Singer: Donna Summer, Cycle V, Irene Cara, Shandi, Michael Sembello, Laura Branigan, Kim Carnes, and others
Musical Supervisor: Phil Ramone
Score by: Giorgio Moroder

Plot: An insecure, but talented young performer climbs to the top. The dancer is aided or hindered in her Rise by other people. The real plot here is the physicality of the dances and the great soundtrack. A lot of people view this as one long music video, and not a movie in the old sense at all.

Music: "I'll Be Here Where the Heart Is" (Kim Carnes); "Romeo" (Donna Summer); "Seduce Me Tonight" (Cycle V); "Imagination" (Laura Branigan); "Maniac" (Michael Sembello); "Manhunt" (Karen Kamon); "Lady L" (Joe Esposito); "He's a Dream" (Shandi); "Love Theme" (Helen St. John); "Flashdance (What a Feeling)" (Irene Cara).

Moves: The dances *are* the thing here, performed by a stand-in usually. They are sexy, stimulating, incredible, wet, wild, and well-done.

Outfits: Wet leotards and cut-off sweatshirts. Standard teen togs.

Jennifer Beals poses in the whole new style that swept the nation—the cut-off sweatshirt—in *Flashdance*.

227

Footloose

Company: Paramount, 1984
Color, 99 minutes
Category: Drama/musical

Kevin Bacon plays the new boy in a town where all music and dancing has been banned in *Footloose*.

228

Screenplay by: Dean Pitchford
Directed by: Herbert Ross
Produced by: Louis J. Rachmil and Craig Zadan
Starring: Kevin Bacon, Dianne West, John Lithgow, and Lori Singer
Group/Singer: Kenny Loggins, Shalamar, Deniece Williams, Mike Reno, Ann Wilson, Bonnie Tyler, and Karla Bonoff
Musical Supervisor: Becky Shargo

Plot: The American musical film definitely has new look. A young Chicagoan named Ren (Kevin Bacon) settles in a small town. There he fights a never-ending battle for holding a senior prom. You see, popular, that is, rock music has been banned, and dancing is strictly out. This is because a few years back the son of the local church's pastor was killed in an automobile mishap after coming from a dance where liquor and who knows what else was served. The pastor (John Lithgow) states that kids dancing together become sexual. The film proves it.
Music: "Never" (Moving Pictures); "The Girl Gets Around" (Sammy Hagar); "Somebody's Eyes" (Karla Bonoff); "Holding Out for a Hero" (Bonnie Tyler); "Almost Paradise" (Mike Reno and Ann Wilson); belts out "Lets Hear It for the Boy" (Deniece Williams); "Dancin' in the Streets" (Shalamar); "Footloose" and "I'm Free" (Kenny Loggins).
Moves: Lot's of rhythmic stepping. In the big Kevin Bacon number, he goes to an abandoned warehouse and dances away his bad feelings. (Actually double Peter Tramm does most of the great dancing.)
Outfits: Truly Levis, with rivets and all. Lots of colored T-shirts and farm dungarees. Teen girls in tank tops and did I say boots abundant?
Social Significance: Made more money for Paramount. They have a good thing going

here, what with *Flashdance* and this. They'll keep em coming too, as long as box office is bursting.

Trivia: So this is the real 1984! A far cry from Orwell, or . . . .

Get Crazy

Company: Rosebud Films, 1983
     Color, 98 minutes
Category: Rock drama
Screenplay by: David Opatoshu, Henry Rosenbaum, and David Taylor
Directed by: Alan Arkush
Produced by: Hunt Lowry
Starring: Malcolm McDowell, Allen Goorwitz, Gail Edwards, Daniel Stern, and Miles Chapin
Group/Singer: Lou Reed, the Ramones, Marshall Crenshaw, Lori Eastside and Nana, Sparks, and Malcolm McDowell

Plot: This loosely put together plot concerns a theatre owner, Max Wolfe (Allen Goorwitz), and his ambitious, obnoxious nephew Sammy (Miles Chapin). There are lots of run-arounds and complications as the music goes on, but they are not memorable. The rival concert promoter Colin Beverly (Ed Begley Jr.) and his henchmen, Marv (Fabian Forte) and Mark (Bobby Sherman), are out to make mischief. King Blues (Bill Henderson) just wants to sing, and gives an inspired performance at Max's fifteenth anniversary party for his Saturn theatre. Ah, the trials and tribulations of rock performers and promoters—will they never end?

Music: The Sparks do "Get Crazy;" Lou Reed sings "Little Sister;" The Ramones do "Chop Suey;" Marshall Crenshaw belts out "It's Only a Movie." Lori Eastwood and Nana do "I'm Not Gonna Take It," and Malcolm McDowell is redoubtable doing "Hot Hot."

Moves: Performers wiggle, girls giggle, spotlights sizzle.

Outfits: King Blues is in shiny suit, with an open shirt and a suede hat. Sammy dresses like you would expect, tasteless gaudy suits and ties. Max is typically dressed for a promoter, hip casual. The bad guys sometimes wear monogrammed jackets.

Trivia: Marshall Crenshaw bound for the top.

229

Rival concert promoter Colin Beverly (Ed Begley Jr.) and his henchmen Marv (Fabian Forte, left) and Mark (Bobby Sherman) are out to make mischief for Max Wolfe in *Get Crazy*.

Grease II

Produced by: Robert Stigwood and Alan Carr
Starring: Maxwell Caulfield, Didi Conn, Michelle Pfeiffer, Adrian Zmed, and Lorna Luft
Group/Singer: Cast
Choreographer: Patricia Birch
Musical Production: Louis St. Louis

Company: Paramount, 1982
Color, 114 minutes
Category: Musical
Screenplay by: Ken Finkelman
Directed by: Patricia Birch

The students at Rydell High exhibit enthusiasm for more than academics in *Grease II*.

230

Plot: Filled with special appearances to heighten the period mood, this film takes off where *Grease* left off sort of. We see Sid Caesar, Connie Stevens, Dody Goodman, Tab Hunter, and others in brief cameos. Patricia Birch lends her considerable choreographic talents, as she did in the first film. Maxwell Caulfield and Michelle Pfeiffer try awfully hard. The spectacular dance numbers, if anything, outdo the original. We see leaps and slides, bumps and grinds, in a frenetic effort to outdo the first smash, but alas its just not there. This one is even further removed from the spirit of the fifties than the original. Still, its rock/disco beat is alluring, and if you get into it . . . .

Music: "Back to School Again" (Four Tops). "Cool Rider," "Love Will Turn Back the Hands of Time," and "We'll Be Together" (Louis St. Louis, who also arranged the numbers and provided the musical production).

Moves: Hands thrown in the air, the cast leaps together outside the (Bobby?) Rydell High School. Lots of acting cool, posing, combing hair type numbers evoking the era.

Outfits: Check and plaid shirts on the guys, chinos and jeans; the girls wear bare midriffs. There are lots of hush puppies and old-type sneakers with all that lace showing. Toreador pants or pedal pushers complete the female outfits. D.A.s on guys.

Social Significance: There will probably be a Grease 3.

Trivia: Sid Caesar seemed to be the inspiration for a comedian named King in *My Favorite Year*, a truly great look back to 1954. Nostalgia fans should see that one, although there's not much music in it, for an accurate look-see at the fifties.

Honeysuckle Rose

Company: Warner Bros., 1980
Color, 119 minutes
Category: Drama with music

231

Willie Nelson and the rest of his road-weary crew perform one more for the road in *Honeysuckle Rose*.

Screenplay by: Carol Sobieski, William Whittliff, and John Binder
Directed by: Jerry Schatberg
Produced by: Sidney Pollack and Gene Taft
Starring: Willie Nelson, Dyan Cannon, Amy Irving, and Slim Pickens
Group/Singer: Willie Nelson, Emmylou Harris, Hank Cochran, John Gimble, and Jody Pyne

Plot: The ultimate road movie. Willie Nelson travels around the U.S.A. doing his musical thing, and being unfaithful to his wife, played by sexy Dyan Cannon. Amy Irving plays the other romance interest. There is a reconciliation, and Dyan joins the recalcitrant Willie on stage to sing one of the numbers. There is some unnecessary gunplay between a "wronged" daughter's father and Nelson that ends inconclusively in another reconciliation.

Willie gives us all a good taste of the down-home country-rock concert fare. It's such a good pile of music (if you like crossover and country) that it's almost a shame that they put any plot in it at all.
Music: "On the Road Again," "Blue Eyes Cryin' in the Rain," "Whiskey River," and others are sung by Willie Nelson. Hank Cochran warbles out "I Don't Do Windows." Jody Payne sings "Working Man Blues;" John Gimble sings "Cotton Eyed Joe" and "Jumpin'." Emmylou Harris sings "Angel Eyes" with Willie, and "So You Think You're a Cowboy" solo.
Moves: Country good-time stompin.
Outfits: Country-western, ragged roadie, tired folky.
Social Significance: None, except you wish you were at his big picnics in the old days. Furthered the adoration of Willie as a true grass-roots type performer who did his thing long before it was so immensely popular— even when the record company people kept saying no.

232

Trivia: The plot is borrowed from *Intermezzo*. This film further proved, if needed, that Dyan can fill a pair of jeans and a checkered shirt. What does she eat?

No Nukes

Company: Warner Bros., 1980 Color, 103 minutes
Category: Rockumentary
Directed by: Julian Schlossberg and Danny Goldberg
Produced by: Julian Schlossberg and Danny Goldberg
Starring: Bruce Springsteen, James Taylor, Carly Simon, Chaka Khan, others

Graham Nash, Jackson Browne, and John Hall relax backstage at the *No Nukes* concert.

Crosby, Stills and Nash harmonizing effortlessly at the *No Nukes* Concert.

233

Plot: A film of the famous No-Nukes benefit concert held at Madison Square Garden in 1980. It was to raise money (and public consciousness) of the anti-nuke, pro-solar movement. Got the old-timers, folk singers, and modern big names like Springsteen together for a night of unusually friendly and talented performing. Shades of the 1960s with its social consciousness and sense of family. Some money even made it to the anti-nuclear movement. Bands and singers came on and did a few numbers together, but one of the unique things was the teaming up of different groups and singers to share singing on a number of the songs, creating spontaneous and memorable sounds.

Music: Songs include "Times They Are A Changing," "Mocking Bird" (James Taylor and Carly Simon), "Runaway" (Bonnie Raitt), "Teach Your Children Well," "Long Time Gone" (Crosby, Stills, Nash, and Young), "Lotta Love" (Nicolette Larson), "Before the Deluge" (Jackson Browne), "Get Together" (Neil Young), "Stay," "Devil

with the Blue Dress On" (Bruce Springsteen). Other groups include Gil-Scott Heron, Jessie Colin Young, John Hall, Chaka Khan, Ry Cooder, Raydio, Sweet Honey in the Rock, and the Doobie Brothers.

Moves: Did somewhat laid-back moves on stage. Occasional fast footwork by some of the rockers, including Chaka Khan and Springsteen.

Outfits: Hippie, gospel, rocker, funk . . . .

Social Significance: The concert was held to raise public awareness and some money for the no nukes movement. That it did and more. Performers have a unique ability to affect the mass consciousness. Sometimes for good, as when they promote positive political motions, sometimes not, as when they sing the praises of heroin. This one was a labor of love and people felt it.

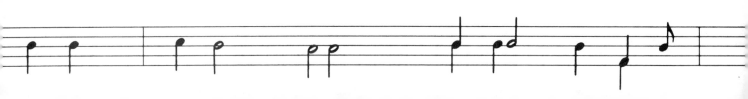

Pink Floyd The Wall

Company: MGM, 1980
Color, 102 minutes
Category: Rock musical
Screenplay by: Roger Waters
Directed by: Alan Parker
Produced by: Alan Marshall
Starring: Bob Geldof and Kevin McKeon
Group/Singer: Pink Floyd
Animation Director: Gerald Scarfe

Plot: Alan Parker says it's a shuffle of time and place, reality and nightmare. For rock star, Pink, painful memories are each a brick in the wall that he built around his feelings. Burned-out Pink (Bob Geldof) sits in a hotel room in L.A., watching the boob tube, feeling sick. He's played as a child in flashbacks by Kevin McKeon, and it's all very abstract. Outside, the apocalyptic winds blow worse and worse; it's the end, man, the end. Gerald Scarfe's looming animation, such as a cannibal-fornicating plant, scares and disgusts. Pink smashes the furniture and the TV. It's really not a movie, it's the violent cover of a late seventies rock album, that's what it is. Flashes of war and death, bodies and blood abounding. Wakes the kids out of their sleep, perhaps . . . .

Music: Pink Floyd does "Another Brick in the Wall," "In the Flesh," "Comfortably Numb," "Run Like Hell," "One of My Turns," "Young Lust," and others, accompanied by the howling winds, special effects, and all the things we have come to expect from videos.

234

Burned-out rock star Pink (Bob Geldof) is confronted by one of his painful memories in *Pink Floyd The Wall.*

Outfits: As a child, a sweater with winter pattern, long overcoat; as an adult wears sweaty T-shirts, jeans. Lots of tatters too.
Social Significance: Pink Floyd building a following.
Trivia: Pink Floyd played to an empty stadium in *"Pink Floyd a Pompeii"* (1971). They did seven looooonnnnnggggg songs in that one.

Porky's

Company: 20th Century Fox, 1981
Color, 99 minutes
Category: Comedy
Screenplay by: Bob Clark
Directed by: Bob Clark
Produced by: Don Carmody and Bob Clark
Starring: Kaki Hunter, Kim Cattrall, and Scott Colomby

Plot: This film concerns the guys and girls at a South Florida high school who are the sickest, most sadistic, and stupid since the gang in *Carrie*. Guys watch girls take showers, girls talk about the guys' things . . . you get the picture. It's worse than that. There are guys lined up for a gang bang who wind up making it with the alligators in the swamp instead. Older people are stereotyped as losers and pathetic jerks who hang out in the bar at the edge of the Everglades known as Porky's.
Moves: Lots of wigglin' lewdness.
Outfits: Nudity, towels, sweat shirts, unzipped flies. Teen togs.
Social Significance: Big hit, of course.
Trivia: Set and filmed in Florida, but it's a Canadian film.

235

Kaki Hunter and her friends have discovered the much-used peephole in their shower in *Porky's*.

Private Lessons

Company: Universal, 1981
Color, 87 minutes
Category: Drama
Screenplay by: Dan Greenburg
Directed by: Alan Myerson
Produced by: R. Ben Efraim
Starring: Sylvia Kristel, Eric Brown, and Howard Hesseman
Group/Singer: Rod Stewart, Air Supply, Earl Klugh, John Cougar, Willie Nile, and Earth, Wind, & Fire

Plot: Eric Brown plays a recently pubescent teenager who is left alone at his semi-palatial suburban home by his dad. Dad, it seems, has hired the sexiest older woman around to be housekeeper, and maybe to show the kid the ropes. The chauffeur, rather sinisterly played by Howard Hesseman, is cooking up a deal. Sylvia Kristel, (who normally had played in soft-core porn films like *Emmanuelle* and *Emmanuelle II*) is the housekeeper. She pretends to die at the precise moment the kid does it to her in a scheme to get the kid to steal his dad's money for her and the chauffeur. But she kind of likes the kid and comes back from the "dead" to re-do the dirty deeds under the sheets.

Amorous housekeeper (Sylvia Kristel) gives her charge some *Private Lessons* to get him to steal his father's money.

236

Music: "Lost in Love" (Air Supply); "Hot Legs" and "Tonight's the Night" (Rod Stewart); "Spanish Night" (Earl Klugh); "Fantasy" (Earth, Wind, & Fire); "That's the Reason" (Willie Nile); "I Need a Lover Tonight" (John Cougar).

Outfits: She takes it all off, the kid too. Otherwise, when dressed, the kid has suburban rich kid shirts with those little crocodiles on them, and she is in short skirts and revealing tops.

Social Significance: By integrating the rock soundtrack with porn for the nubile set, the movie makers have a big winner, a harbinger of more outrageous and usually worse films to come. Blasted by parents and anti-porn groups, this film is so good it's an argument against censorship.

Reggae Sunsplash

Company: International Harmony, 1980
Color, 107 minutes
Category: Rockumentary
Directed by: Stefan Paul
Produced by: Kino Arsenal Tubigen
Starring: Bob Marley and the Wailers, Peter Tosh, Third World, and Burning Spear

Plot: This German made documentary-concert film is centered around the famous

237

Bob Marley—the charismatic singer, and Jamaican hero is all too briefly heard in *Reggae Sunsplash*.

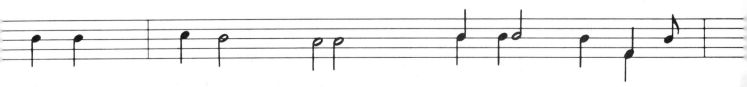

1979 Sunsplash Festival Two at Montego Bay in Jamaica. It alternates between being a concert film, a cinema verité interview film, and a mess. But who cares, with such super stars of reggae as Bob Marley and Peter Tosh on the bill? There are shots of the backs of empty chairs, people walking away from the camera, lots of useless footage, or perhaps a stoned view of the world? Rasta prophets speak on and on about their philosophy. Hard to follow. We're supposed to be learning about the Rasta lifestyle but it comes off like Lou Ferrigno in *Hercules*—not at all. Bob Marley and the Wailers and reggae music are the attraction here. When Marley died, the anguish of the Jamaican people was overwhelming. He was a prophet to them, a peacemaker between factions, a folk hero. He will be missed, and don't you miss any of his performances that survive on film.

Music: Marley and the Wailers do their thing. Also appearing are Peter Tosh, Burning Spear, and Third World.

Outfits: Reggae. Lots of giant caps to hold dreadlocks, lots of bright colored shirts and pants.

Social Significance: Reggae influence is seen in the Police, the Clash, many other groups. Is reggae rock? It rocks.

Trivia: Pot is illegal in Jamaica, though it is a sacrament in Rastafarian religious order. The nation's leading export, it has an ambiguous status. Not so the music.

Directed by: Alan Rudolph
Produced by: Carolyn Pfeiffer
Starring: Meatloaf, Art Carney, and Kaki Hunter
Group/Singer: Meatloaf, Debbie Harry, Alice Cooper, Roy Orbison, Pat Benatar, Cheap Trick, and Jerry Lee Lewis

238

Roadie

Company: United Artists, 1980
Color, 105 minutes
Category: Musical/comedy
Screenplay by: Michael Venture and Big Boy Medlin

Plot: Essentially a vehicle for the big stars of rock, it is the tale of one called Meatloaf, the portly, cowboyhatted Texas car mechanic that gets all caught up with a group of traveling musicians. He tours around with them, listens to Debbie Harry make music by banging on beer bottles, watches some rasslin around, does some gesticulating and it's all for comedy's sake. Except it isn't terribly funny. Oh well, the groups are very good. Orbison is always a treat to see and hear, the stiffest man in rock loosens up a teensy weensy bit here, and Alice Cooper, who is all loose, performs. What is best about this film is those Jerry Lee Lewis cuts on the soundtrack.

Music: Meatloaf smiles; Cheap Trick sings "Everything Works if You Let It;" Debbie Harry does "Ring of Fire," not one of her best. Alice Cooper does "Road Rats;" Lewis pounds out "I'm a One Woman Man;" Asleep at the Wheel does "Texas" and "Me and You;" Roy Orbison and EmmyLou Harris team up for "That Lovin' You Feelin' Again;" Jay Ferguson does "A Man Needs a Woman;" Pat Benatar does "You Better Run;" Eddie Rabbitt does the hit "Drivin' My Life Away;" Styx does "Crystal Ball."

Outfits: Western and down-home, diner-casual, roadie wearable, cowboy and cowgirl hats, western shirts.

Social Significance: None, except furthers the mystique(???) of Meatloaf.

Trivia: Compare to Willie Nelson's *Honeysuckle Rose*. Now there's a roadie movie!

239

Cheap Trick (top left), Pat Benatar (lower left), and Teddy Pendergrass are among the performers on the original soundtrack album for *Roadie*.

Rude Boy

Company: American Cinema, 1980
Color, 133 minutes
Category: Rockumentary
Screenplay by: David Mingay, Ray Gange, and Jack Hazan.
Directed by: Jack Hazan and David Mingay
Produced by: Jack Hazan and David Mingay
Starring: The Clash and Ray Gange
Band: The Clash

Plot: This is a mixture of concert movie and stark realism on film. This film is largely about the class system as it exists and oppresses in the British Commonwealth, especially England. Here we see Ray Gange being economically repressed, we see the Clash lashing out at this oppression in their raw, rocking way. We see the bankruptcy of the establishment, the agony of youth, and mostly the Clash doing some great numbers. A must for Clash fans, of which there are more and more each day.

Music: The Clash sing and perform "White Riot," "The Prisoner," "Tommy Gun," "Complete Control," "All the Young Punks," and "London's Burning."

Moves: Shades of the Mods and Rockers, there's still action there in the streets.

Outfits: Tough, working class, real. Grimy.

Social Significance: The Clash brought back non-hyped up music more than any other group did. Started a trend to raw sounds, gut level playing and singing that got lost in the airy strings and orchestrations of the seventies super groups.

Trivia: They even sound good off key. For a while, the Clash promoters deigned to sell Clash records at about a dollar less per album in the States. This a blow to Capitalism? It stopped.

The Clash appear in DOA. One of the strongest New Wave acts.

240

Rumblefish

Dillon appears in white T-shirt and vest, jeans, and basketball sneakers.
Social Significance: Showed once again the iffy success possibilities of Coppola.

Company: Universal, 1983
Color, 102 minutes
Category: Drama
Screenplay by: S.E. Hinton and Francis Ford Coppola
Directed by: Francis Ford Coppola
Produced by: Francis Ford Coppola
Starring: Matt Dillon, Dennis Hopper, Vincent Spano, Diane Lane, and Diane Scarwid
Group/Singer: Stewart Copeland (of the Police)
Music by: Stewart Copeland

Plot: If it isn't bad enough to get chucked out of school, Rusty James (Matt Dillon) is going to get in trouble with the street gang that terrorizes the area. Coppola got mixed reviews for this violent and grim huge production. Some critics said it was incoherent and needlessly violent. In the film, Michael Rourke plays the Motorcycle Boy, a kid most unpopular with the local hoods. Supporting roles by Nicholas Cage, Diana Scarwid, and Diane Lane are particularly well carried out. The film is a gutwrenching nightmare.
Music: Songs include "Don't Box Me In," "Tulsa Tango," "Our Mother is Alive," "Motorboys Fate," "Brothers on Wheels." Highly electronic. Stewart Copeland of the infamous Police composed, arranged, and performed the stylized soundtrack for this Coppola budget buster.
Outfits: Leather, rubberized jackets, short skirts, motorcycle wear, gloves without fingers, jeans, sneakers. The meanest looking gang-wear this side of 42nd Street. Matt

Motorboy (Matt Dillon) is in trouble. He's been kicked out of school and now the gang is out to get him in *Rumblefish*.

241

Staying Alive

Company: Paramount, 1983
Color, 100 minutes
Category: Musical/dance
Screenplay by: Sylvester Stallone and
Norman Wexler

Directed by: Sylvester Stallone
Produced by: Robert Stigwood and
Sylvester Stallone
Starring: John Travolta, Cynthia Rhodes
Finola Hughes, and Steve
Inwood
Group/Singer: The Bee Gees, Frank
Stallone, and Tommy
Faragher

242

**John Travolta with the cast of
dancers of** *Staying Alive.*

John Travolta poses backstage.

Plot: A guy (John Travolta) wants to make it big in the dance world. He wants the ultimate performance. He will not stop until he wins. Sounds like Rocky? Well, look who directed it. Sylvester himself. It's always a winning story, the come from behind, the love entanglements, the last minute snags, the ultimate achievement. Too bad Stallone's relative got to do 2 songs on the track. It was supposed to be a follow up on the tremendously successful *Saturday Night Fever,* and the song "Stayin' Alive" is not enough to keep this one alive. Back to the drawing board for Stallone. Energetic dancing seems to be mostly bits and pieces, never a coherent, cohesive number.

Music: "The Woman in You," "I Love You Too Much," and "Life Goes On" (Bee Gees); "Far From Over" and "Moody Girls" (Frank Stallone); "Lookout for No. 1" (Tommy Faragher).

Moves: The dances are a series of stunts, sex twirls, and bits and fragments that no one would want credit for. Lots of sweat and exuberance signifying nothing. See *Fame* for good dancing.

Outfits: Leotards, tights. Remember when dancing like this was sissy stuff? No more. In the fifties a guy in tights was a guy in the river. Times change.

Social Significance: Set back Stallone's pocketbook again. The guy can't miss with his great, great *Rocky* hits, but this expensive flop adds to his bad luck in non-*Rocky* films.

Trivia: They appeared together on commercials for the film, at press conferences, talk shows, everywhere. But John Travolta appeared in the film without Stallone, and lots of people who got the impression it was a film team-up were disappointed. Stallone was in a cameo, bumping into Travolta on a sidewalk.

243

Xanadu

Company: Universal, 1980
Color, 96 minutes
Category: Musical
Screenplay by: Marc Reid Rubel and
Richard C. Danus

Directed by: Robert Greenwald
Produced by: Lawrence Gordon
Starring: Olivia Newton-John, Gene
Kelly, and Michael Beck
Group/Singer: Olivia, the Tubes,
Electric Light Orchestra,
and Cliff Richard

Michael Beck, Gene Kelly, and Olivia Newton-John celebrate the opening of a new boutique in *Xanadu*.

244

Plot: In Venice, California, there is a lovely mural. Her name is Olivia Newton-John. She comes to life (shades of *One Touch of Venus!*) to help a young artist (Michael Beck). She sings, she rollerskates, she muses, all for the young artist. She's inspiring. Gene Kelly (he came out of semi-retirement for this) plays a clarinetist who also once was inspired and energized by the sexy apparition. The film started, we're told, when the producers had the rights to Olivia's songs. From that they built the film. Slim. There are stunning visual effects, but where's the simple elegance and grace of the old *Singing in the Rain?* The glitz and flashes of light, the overbright colors are more shattering than stunning. There's the battle of the bands with the Tubes performing, there's the "Dancin' " number, there's the hit song "All Over the World," but moviegoers should avoid going to this one.

Music: "I'm Alive," "Magic," and "Suddenly" were sung by Olivia Newton-John; also appearing were the Tubes. Singing on the soundtrack are Cliff Richard and the Electric Light Orchestra.

Moves: Olivia steps about with Gene well enough.

Outfits: Olivia's best in her high on the calf boots and her short tiger-skin shirt. Ladies step about in scanties or tiger skin suits. Men wear their hot clothes—open shirts, jumping-pants; Gene Kelly is dapper in a pastel suit.

Social Significance: None. Except the puzzlement of producers—why didn't the audiences come? They came for *Grease*.

Trivia: Some say that this film is reminiscent of the old Hollywood classic *Down to Earth* (1947), starring Rita Hayworth, a whimsical, delightful follow-up to *Here Comes Mr. Jordan*. In that one, a muse called Terpsichore comes down from above to help a Broadway producer fix a show in which she is starring.

245

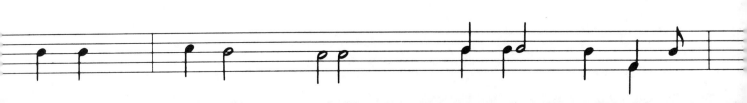

Index

Movie

Ski Party 108-109
Slumber Party '57 194-195
Soul to Soul 195-196
Spinout 109
State Fair 110
Staying Alive 242-243
Strawberry Statement, The 196-197
Superfly 198-199

T

T.A.M.I. Show, The 111-112
Tammy Tell Me True 113-114
Tammy and the Doctor 112-113
To Russia...With Elton 199-200
To Sir With Love 114-115
Tommy 201-202
Trip, The 116-117
Twist All Night 117
Twist Around the Clock 117-118
Two Hundred Motels 202-203

V

Valley of the Dolls 119-120
Village of the Giants 120-121

W

WUSA 207-209
What's Happening? 203-204
What's New, Pussycat? 121-122
What's Up, Tiger Lily? 122-123
When the Boys Meet the Girls 123-124
Where the Boys Are 124-125
Wild Angels, The 125-126
Wild Wild Winter 127-128
Wild in the Streets 126-127
Wiz, The 204-205
Woodstock 205-207

X

Xanadu 243-245

Y

Yellow Submarine 128-129
You Are What You Eat 131-132
You're a Big Boy Now 129-131
Young Animals 132-133

Actor

A

Ackroyd, Dan 217
Aerosmith 191
Albertson, Jack 55
Albright, Vicki 128
Allen, Woody 122
Alvina, Anicee 152
Anderson, Carl 163
Anka, Paul 20

Ann-Margret 54, 143, 201
Arkin, David 178
Armen, Kaye 88
Armstrong, Louis 123
Ash, Leslie 184
Ashley, John 23
Aulin, Ewa 54
Avalon, Frankie 38, 43, 45, 48, 60, 85, 96, 108
Aznavour, Charles 54

B

Bach, Barbara 219
Backus, Jim 33
Bacon, Kevin 223, 228
Baez, Joan 64, 144, 205
Bancroft, Anne 77
Band, The 170
Barkin, Ellen 223
Bates, Jeanne 151
Baxley, Barbara 178
Beach Boys, The 193-194
Beals, Jennifer 227
Beames, David 184
Beatles, The 38, 76, 79, 83, 91, 128, 136, 171, 203
Beatty, Ned 178
Beatty, Warren 193
Beck, Michael 244
Beckwith, Reginald 88
Bee Gees, The 191
Belushi, John 217
Berenguer, Tom 216, 224
Bergen, Candice 155
Berry, Chuck 21, 111, 165
Bikel, Theodore 64
Bill Haley and the Comets 34
Black, Karen 178
Blondie 140
Bloomfield, Mike 64
Bob Marley and the Wailers 237
Bondi, Beulah 113
Bono, Sonny 76
Boone, Pat 31, 110
Bostwick, Barry 188
Bowie, David 175
Bowles, Peter 50
Bradshaw, Carl 160
Brambell, Wilfred 79
Brando, Marlon 39, 54
Bridges, Beau 120
Bron, Eleanor 83
Brown, Eric 236
Brown, James 111
Brown, Les Jr. 128
Brown, Lowell 23
Burke, Paul 119
Burning Spear 237
Burns, George 191
Burton, Richard 54
Bury, Sean 152
Busey, Gary 141
Butera, Sam 117
Butterfield, Paul 170
Butterworth, Donna 100
Byrnes, Edd 41

C

Caen, Herb 105
Callan, Michael 46, 72

Cambridge, Godfrey 149
Cannon, Dyan 232
Capucine 122
Cara, Irene 225
Carere, Christine 33
Carey, MacDonald 113
Carey, Michele 55
Carney, Art 238
Carol, Cindy 75
Casey, Sue 44
Caster, Cynthia P. 158
Castle, John 50
Cattrall, Kim 235
Caulfield, Maxwell 230
Cavett, Dick 146
Chadwick, Les 63
Chamberlain, Richard 102
Chandler, Gene 57
Channing, Stockard 157
Chapin, Miles 229
Charles, Ray 52
Charlton, Bobby 160
Checker, Chubby 57, 118
Cher 76
Christie, Julie 102, 193
Clanton, Jimmy 21
Clapton, Eric 149, 170
Clark, Dick 46
Clarke, Gary 128
Clash, The 212, 239
Cliff, Jimmy 160
Close, Glenn 216
Coburn, James 54, 180
Cocker, Joe 173
Coe, Barry 33
Cole, Clay 118
Colomby, Scott 235
Conaway, Jeff 157
Conn, Didi 230
Cooper, Alice 176, 191
Cooper, Gary 184
Corey, Jeff 155
Corff, Robert 153
Cort, Bud 196
Cox, Billy 164
Crawford, Johnny 120
Crosby, Gary 31, 33
Crosby, Stills, Nash, and Young 205
Curry, Tim 188

D

Dale, Alan 34
Daltrey, Roger 201
Daly, Timothy 223
Dana, Vic 57
D'Angelo, Beverly 159
Daniels, Phil 184
Danova, Cesare 75
Darby, Kim 196
Darin, Bobby 110
Darren, James 18, 72, 75
Dave Clark 5, 80
Davidson, Lenny 80
Davis, Ronnie 105
Davison, Bruce 196
Day, Annette 60
De Coff, Linda 138
Dee, Joey 88
Dee, Sandra 18, 113

247

248

Director

Producer

Screenplay

Composer and Musical Performers

253

255

256

Choreographer and Dancers